THE MANAGERIAL GRID ®

The Managerial Grid®

Key Orientations for Achieving Production Through People

ROBERT R. BLAKE, PH.D
President, Scientific Methods, Inc., Austin, Texas

JANE SRYGLEY MOUTON, PH.D
Vice President, Scientific Methods, Inc., Austin, Texas

GULF PUBLISHING COMPANY
HOUSTON, TEXAS

THE MANAGERIAL GRID
Copyright© 1964 by Gulf Publishing Company,
Houston, Texas

Library of Congress Catalog Card Number 64-14724

First printing January, 1964
Second printing March, 1964
Third printing October, 1964
Fourth printing January, 1965
Fifth printing April, 1965
Sixth printing July, 1965
Seventh printing September, 1965
Eighth printing May, 1966
Ninth printing September, 1966
Tenth printing May, 1967
Eleventh printing January, 1968
Twelfth printing October, 1968
Thirteenth printing June, 1969
Fourteenth printing May, 1970
Fifteenth printing March, 1971
Sixteenth printing August, 1972
Seventeenth printing September, 1972

To

H. V., R. M., and H. M., three pioneering industrial
managers, and to B. F. W., an experimentalist in the
administration of government. Each of these men has
initiated unique projects of management education from
which much of what is presented here has been learned.

ISBN 0-87201-474-6

Preface

What is the route to organizational excellence? Students of management theory and management training have been searching out the answer for this question ever since they decided that management is a science rather than an art, and that it can be learned.

Invariably the focus of attention is: what type of leadership behavior produces organizational excellence? Admittedly an organization's structure, plan, and concept are basic to its effectiveness, yet beyond these the greatest single variable lies with the behavior of the management team. Its members must act as leaders. They must accomplish their objectives through their ability to guide, motivate, and integrate the efforts of others. How best to do this?

Early contributors to management theory stressed that there were specific methods needed to control and direct the work of others. The assumptions were that means must be found to delineate what people's tasks were, and then to maintain positive forces which would insure that people performed as ordained.

As students of behavior in the social sciences became more interested in the industrial arena, they began to demur with this. Their research began uncovering the beneficial effects when behavior in an organization was more highly self-controlling than a response to imposed controls. They discovered that less authoritarian methods of leadership produced gains in cooperation, effort, and effectiveness.

A dichotomy was created. Proponents of one side were identified as the "scientific management" school; the opposite as the "human relations" school. A search for proof of the benefits of one type of leadership vs. the other was started—and continues to this day. This book on the Managerial Grid is unique in that it avoids the argument of one extreme vs. the other, and shows the possibilities in various blends of leadership styles.

We have long needed a better system to examine styles

of leadership. The "either/or" styles have been characterized variously as: autocratic/democratic, or authoritarian/participative, or production-centered/people-centered, and even as Theory X/Theory Y. These labels have been admittedly inadequate and confusing. The stress on terms which represent extremes has placed many managers in a position where they felt they could not accept *either* alternative. It placed researchers in a position of trying to prove the benefits of one system over the other, when they rarely could locate behavior which was clearly either one of these extremes. It led many teachers of management theory to overemphasis of the human relations side of the dichotomy, and thus their efforts were seen by many managers as promoting "soft" leadership.

The Managerial Grid method of designating various styles of leadership avoids these semantic traps. Even more, it shows how a leader can simultaneously maximize both the methods which are production-oriented and those which are people-oriented. Thus instead of putting a manager in a dilemma of choosing one or the other alternative, it illustrates that there are ways he can gain the benefits of both. It puts various methods of managing problems into a framework where the leader can identify, study and change his own behavior. Thus he is in a position to understand it better, to evaluate the results it produces, and to encourage its use by others.

The ultimate purpose of studies of managerial style is to aid in the training and development of those who would become better leaders. Such theory becomes pertinent when choosing and training those individuals who show the greatest management potential. It also has utility for the majority of organizations who have to accept their people as they are and try to add to their capability of working effectively as individuals and as a team. In such efforts the Managerial Grid has demonstrated its utility as a philosophy.

Harry D. Kolb
Employee Relations Dept.
Humble Oil & Refining Company

Contents

Introduction

One of the challenges of modern times is that of developing greater managerial capability. The goal is to solve human problems of production where they originate—among those who work together—regardless of level. If it can be accomplished, it insures continuing "grass roots" vitality, because men remain in control of their fate. They have stakes in the outcome of their own efforts. It is likely to be the best way, long term, to preserve the right to autonomous action.

Every manager carries on his own shoulders responsibility for solving human problems associated with achieving maximum results *through the productive utilization of people*. The question is, "How can this be best accomplished?"

The idea that a qualified manager manages only the nuts and bolts of production, without regard for people, now can be seen as a limited definition of his task, regardless of his level in the organization hierarchy. The broader view, which maintains that production takes care of itself when the perceptive manager manages people by motivating and communicating with them, also is a limited picture of the supervisory requirements necessary for achieving organization problem-solving competence.

The sound description is the one that defines a manager's task as one of developing and maintaining a *culture* that promotes work. To do so requires far greater understanding than "thing-oriented" supervision centered on nuts and bolts or human management, concentrating as it does on motivating and communicating with the people. Mature management demands a keen awareness of and an uncommon capability in dealing with the total complex of forces which constitutes the work culture of an industrial organization. Yet in the final analysis, organization culture determines the degree of effectiveness actually achieved.

Thus a manager's job is to perfect a culture which (1) promotes and sustains efficient performance of highest quality and quantity, (2) fosters and utilizes creativity, (3) stimulates enthusiasm for effort, experimentation, innovation and change, (4) takes educational advantage from interaction situations and (5) looks for and finds new challenges. Such managerial competence can be taught and it can be learned.

Truly great strides have already been taken toward the ideal of genuine organization competence. However, further fundamental strides toward organization excellence are possible, and some companies already are taking them. They are based on currently available behavioral science knowledge.

The Managerial Grid provides a framework for learning some of this knowledge. It offers some guidelines for putting this learning to concrete use in managing production through people. In its various versions it has been tested through a series of experiments conducted in industry and government over several years. Through their studies and efforts to apply the theories to be described and the resulting criticisms of them, which have been taken into account as far as possible in this writing, approximately 5,000 managers have contributed in various way to the version presented here.

The Managerial Grid appears to be an *inclusive* statement for orienting managerial actions. This conclusion is suggested in different ways. First, it has been applied in widely different organizational settings in the United States, Canada, Europe and Asia. Included are industrial facilities of manufacturing, sales, R&D, and union organizations, as well as military, governmental, professional and welfare settings such as community agencies. The Grid has been employed as a basis for management improvement in nationalized industries and in other service-oriented institutions. Second, it seems to provide descriptions of managerial alternatives which are equally useful when applied to managerial dilemmas in the U.S., in countries of Europe which are somewhat similar to our own, and in cultures of Asia, which are far different. The schema, in other words, seems to be relatively culture-free and, therefore, of *general* relevance for understanding problems of management wherever men work in concert. A possible conclusion is that sound management of production through people transcends political and cultural boundaries.

Evaluated from an incompany point of view, the Grid is seen to be a useful framework for analyzing production-people problems and for suggesting effective solutions for them. Its application is not limited to any particular level in the organization hierarchy. It applies in solving problems at the bottom where concrete supervisory skills are required and at the top where executive decision-making involving far more subtle and complex judgments is demanded.

The book is a comparative treatment written to accomplish several results. First, it compares major alternatives available to a manager in achieving production through people. Such understanding increases the prospect of improvement in personal effectiveness. Second, it provides a way for aiding the reader to measure his own managerial style. Third, it defines the behavioral requirements of shifting from any one style toward any other. Finally, it pictures how, through educational effort, an entire system like a company can change its culture and raise itself by its bootstraps toward organization excellence.

As a university text, the Managerial Grid serves as one basis for preparing students who are about to take on managerial responsibilities by aiding them to become more effective in their initial job assignments.

Alvin C. Bidwell and John J. Farrell, both of Humble Oil & Refining Company, aided in investigations of the Grid during the earlier phases, and Freddie Little Groveton McCann and Richard L. Sloma, both of Scientific Methods, Inc., during the later phases of its development.

Robert R. Blake
Jane Srygley Mouton

Austin, Texas
January 15, 1964

CHAPTER ONE

Self Assessment of Key Managerial Orientations

As an aid to personal study during the reading of this book, it is suggested that a preliminary self assessment be made from the materials included in the rest of this chapter.[1]

Managerial Styles

Rank the paragraphs from *most* to *least* typical, as a description of yourself; 1 is most typical, 2 is next most typical, and so on to 5 which is least typical of you. When you have finished ranking, there should be only one of each number from 1 to 5. There can be no ties.

———a. I accept decisions of others. I go along with opinions, attitudes, and ideas of others or avoid taking sides. When conflict arises, I try to remain neutral or stay out of it. By remaining neutral, I rarely get stirred up. My humor is seen by others as rather pointless. I put out enough effort to get by.

———b. I place high value on maintaining good relations. I prefer to accept opinions, attitudes, and ideas of others rather than to push my own. I try to avoid generating conflict, but when it does appear, I try to soothe feelings and to keep people together. Because of the disturbance tensions can produce,

1

I react in a warm and friendly way. My humor aims at maintaining friendly relations or when strains do arise, it shifts attention away from the serious side. I rarely lead but extend help.

———c. I search for workable, even though not perfect, decisions. When ideas, opinions, or attitudes different from my own appear, I initiate middle ground positions. When conflict arises, I try to be fair but firm and to get an equitable solution. Under tension, I feel unsure which way to turn or shift to avoid further pressure. My humor sells myself or a position. I seek to maintain a good steady pace.

———d. I place high value on making decisions that stick. I stand up for my ideas, opinions, and attitudes, even though it sometimes results in stepping on toes. When conflict arises, I try to cut it off or to win my position. When things are not going right, I defend, resist or come back with counter arguments. My humor is hard hitting. I drive myself and others.

———e. I place high value on getting sound creative decisions that result in understanding and agreement. I listen for and seek out ideas, opinions, and attitudes different from my own. I have clear convictions but respond to sound ideas by changing my mind. When conflict arises, I try to identify reasons for it and to resolve underlying causes. When aroused, I contain myself, though my impatience is visible. My humor fits the situation and gives perspective; I retain a sense of humor even under pressure. I exert vigorous effort and others join in.

ELEMENTS

Consider all of the "1" statements (i.e., a1, b1, c1, d1, e1) and select from them the one which best describes you. Do the same for all "2" elements (a2, b2, c2, d2, e2) *circling* the one which typifies you. Follow the same procedure for the "3," "4," "5," and "6" elements.

Element 1: Decisions

a1. I accept decisions of others
b1. I place high value on maintaining good relations
c1. I search for workable, even though not perfect, decisions
d1. I place high value on making decisions that stick
e1. I place high value on getting sound creative decisions that result in understanding and agreement

Element 2: Convictions

a2. I go along with opinions, attitudes, and ideas of others or avoid taking sides
b2. I prefer to accept opinions, attitudes, and ideas of others rather than to push my own
c2. When ideas, opinions, or attitudes different from my own appear, I initiate middle ground positions
d2. I stand up for my ideas, opinions, and attitudes, even though it sometimes results in stepping on toes
e2. I listen for and seek out ideas, opinions, and attitudes different from my own. I have clear convictions but respond to sound ideas by changing my mind

Element 3: Conflict

a3. When conflict arises, I try to remain neutral or stay out of it
b3. I try to avoid generating conflict, but when it does appear, I try to soothe feelings and to keep people together
c3. When conflict arises, I try to be fair but firm and to get an equitable solution
d3. When conflict arises, I try to cut it off or to win my position
e3. When conflict arises, I try to identify reasons for it and to resolve underlying causes

Element 4: Emotions (Temper)

a4. By remaining neutral, I rarely get stirred up
b4. Because of the disturbance tensions can produce, I react

in a warm and friendly way

c4. Under tension, I feel unsure which way to turn or shift to avoid further pressure

d4. When things are not going right, I defend, resist or come back with counter arguments

e4. When aroused, I contain myself, though my impatience is visible

Element 5: Humor

a5. My humor is seen by others as rather pointless

b5. My humor aims at maintaining friendly relations or when strains do arise, it shifts attention away from the serious side

c5. My humor sells myself or a position

d5. My humor is hard hitting

e5. My humor fits the situation and gives perspective; I retain a sense of humor even under pressure

Element 6: Effort

a6. I put out enough effort to get by

b6. I rarely lead but extend help

c6. I seek to maintain a good steady pace

d6. I drive myself and others

e6. I exert vigorous effort and others join in

After reading the remainder of the book, it will be possible for you to interpret your rankings and to compare them with the norms presented in Chapter 10.

References

1. *The Managerial Grid: An Exploration of Key Managerial Orientations.* Austin, Tex.: Scientific Methods, Inc., 1962.

CHAPTER TWO

The Managerial Dilemma

To see the dilemma of management in full perspective, it is necessary to examine first *what* is being managed. Since management takes place within an organizational system, attention must be turned first to what organization *is*. Then it will be possible to concentrate on an examination of the problems and possibilities involved in improving competence in managing *it*.[1]

ORGANIZATION UNIVERSALS

Several characteristics of organizations seem to be *universal*. They are present, in some degree, regardless of the specific product or line of work of the organization.[2] Effective management of these universals is the condition of efficient production through sound organization.

Purpose(s)

The first universal is *purpose(s)*.[3] Try to imagine a purposeless organization. Can you picture to yourself an organization that lacks purpose?

Those who have attempted to do so have been unable to identify an organization that does not have a purpose. Admittedly, it is not always easy to identify *what* the purpose is. Furthermore, the purpose for which the organization exists may, or may not, be the same as the purpose people experience as the basis for joining or remaining in it. Too frequently, organization and individual purpose may seem to be unconnected with one another, or even to be contradictory.

Although more or less specific purposes can be stated for educational, governmental, hospital, military, political, religious and family organizations, it is somewhat easier to describe the purpose of industrial organizations. Here, organization purpose is spoken of in terms of profit. Even the purpose of government is *to supply* service(s), not at a profit, but at the minimum necessary expense. The possibility of direct P/(L) (profit-loss) evaluation of human effort, particularly in service organizations, is not too common. Though P/(L) statements frequently are unavailable in service institutions, the organization's intention is consistent with profit motivation. Therefore, for this discussion, the equivalent of profit, that is, the production of *things or services,* will be regarded as the production aim of industrial and governmental organization — that is, those activities in which people engage toward organization purpose.

For the moment then, production can be accepted as an indication of organization purpose(s). It is to be regarded as universal of organizations.

People

Another characteristic of organization is *people.*[4] No organization is without them. It might be said that it would be desirable to eliminate people. Indeed, in some instances it seems wiser to replace people with technological procedures and automated processes, so that human energy is not being wasted in doing work that machine systems can do as well, or even better. But, if a peopleless arrangement were possible to achieve, it is unlikely that the word *organization* would be used to describe it. Other language already has been developed to picture machine operations of production that can be manned by one acting alone. The phrase *automated factory* depicts peopleless operations where organization, as we know it, has been eliminated.

Organization purpose then, cannot be achieved without people, nor does it exist under circumstances where one person is acting alone. To achieve it, others need to be drawn in. Needing more than one person to achieve a result such as production is what leads to the condition of organization.

Hierarchy

Hierarchy is a third attribute. Some people are bosses. Others are bossed. Some are more responsible for solving problems than others. That is the dimension of hierarchy.[5]

The process of achieving organization purpose (the first universal) through the efforts of several people (the second universal) results in some people attaining authority to supervise others; that is, to exercise the responsibility for planning, controlling and directing the activities of others through a hierarchical arrangement (the third universal).

While every organization has hierarchy and while many organizations have job descriptions that depict an individual's responsibility under his hierarchical position, the problem of boss-subordinate relations is far more complex than can possibly be pictured by a job description. But the foundation for understanding management is in recognizing that a boss' actions are dictated by certain *assumptions* he makes regarding how supervision should be exercised.[6]

Sometimes supervision is applied dramatically, such as when a boss tells others what he expects of them in no uncertain terms. But it also is possible that a person may not act like a boss. For instance he may not hold tight rein on subordinates. In those situations, then, people may not feel like they are being bossed at all; they have little or no feeling that influence is being exerted by those in the hierarchy, one level or more up. Yet the fact is that organizations, by necessity, are hierarchical. No matter how it is utilized, hierarchy is seen to be an essential condition of organization.[7]

Other universals of organization play an additional part in understanding problems of managerial competence. They are not introduced at this time, but one of them, organizational culture and its significance on managerial behavior is discussed in Chapters 12 and 13.

This book is concerned with a fundamental inquiry regarding how these three organization properties are interrelated. The question is, "How are organization purposes achieved through people by bosses?"[8]

THE MANAGERIAL GRID

A variety of theories regarding managerial behavior can be identified. These theories—or sets of assumptions—are based on the way in which the three organization universals just discussed are connected to one another.[9]

One of the three is *concern for production;* the amount of emphasis supervision places on achieving production. A second is *concern for people;* the productive unit of organization. The third is *hierarchy;* the *boss* aspect. Whenever a man acts as a manager, he is in some way making assumptions about how to solve problems of achieving organization purposes of production through people.[10]

Dimensions of the Grid

Before going on let's define exactly what we mean by "concern for." This is not meant to indicate *how much* (such as, how much production, meaning quantity), nor is it intended to reflect the degree that the needs of people actually are met. Rather emphasis here is on the *degree* of "concern for" which is present in the *boss* because his *actions* are rooted in, and flow out of his own *basic attitudes.* What is significant is *how* a supervisor is concerned about production and *how* he concerns himself about people, and *how* these concerns intertwine.[11,12]

Concern for Production. The words *production* or *people* cover a range of considerations. Attitudes of concern toward production, for example, may be seen in the quality of policy decisions, the number of creative ideas that applied research turns into useful products, procedures or processes; number of accounts processed;

quality and thoroughness of staff services; workload and efficiency measurements; volume of sales or units of physical output. Production as used here, is not limited to *things*. Its proper meaning covers whatever it is that organizations engage people to accomplish.

At the lowest level, it is true, concern for production may take the form of the number of units of things that can be counted or of time required to attain a certain production schedule. But at the top of an organization, concern for production may be demonstrated in the kind of policies which are established and the character of direction given to major programs of organization effort. Indeed, the concern for production at the top may be expressed through finding new directions or new products to sustain organization growth and development.

Concern for People. In a similar fashion, concern for people can be expressed in a variety of different ways. Included are concern for degree of personal commitment to completing a job one is responsible for; accountability based on trust rather than obedience; self esteem or the personal worth of an individual; establishing and maintaining good working conditions; maintaining an equitable salary structure and fringe benefits; desire for security in work; social relations or friendships with associates; etc.

As will be seen, *concern for production* and *concern for people* are expressed in vastly different ways, depending on the specific manner in which these two concerns are joined.[13]

"Pure" Theories

The *Managerial Grid,* depicted in Figure 1, shows these two concerns and a range of possible interactions between them. The horizontal axis indicates concern for production while the vertical axis indicates concern for people. Each is expressed as a nine-point scale of concern. The number *1* in each instance represents minimum concern. The *9* stands for maximum concern.

At the lower left corner of the Grid is the 1,1 style. This has a minimum of both concerns; that is, of con-

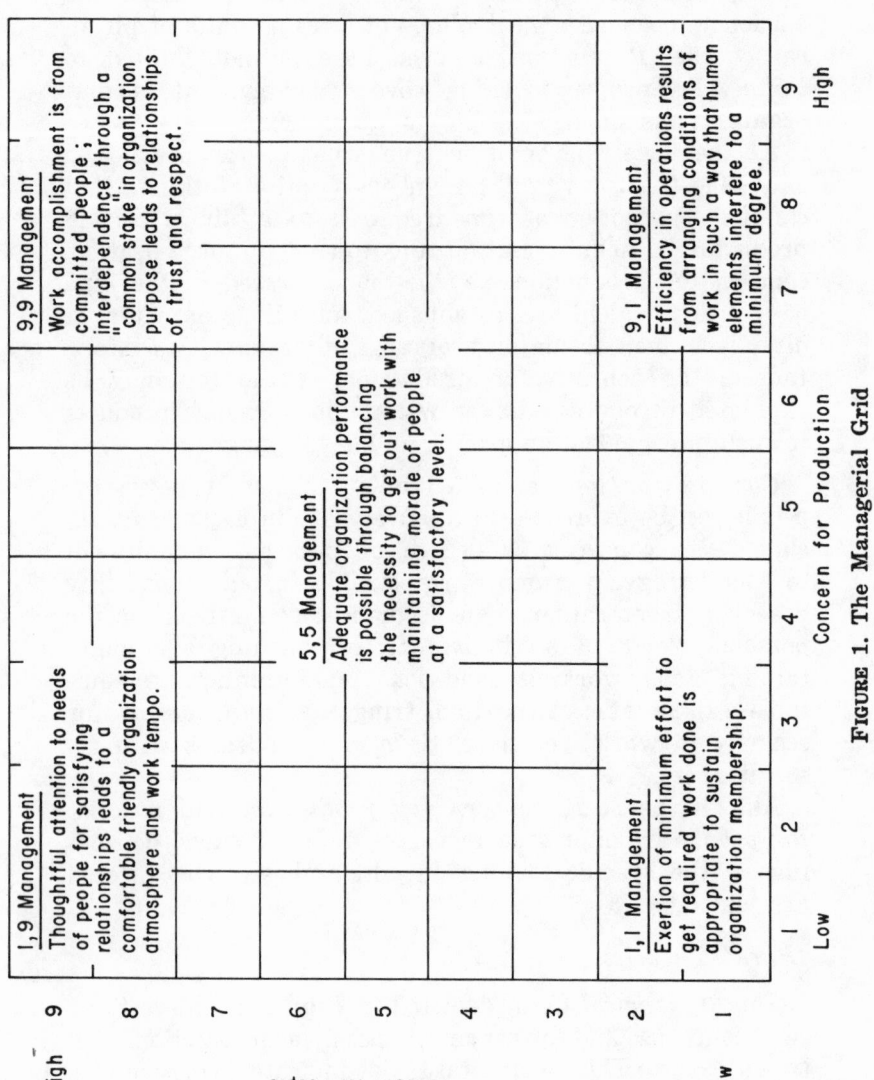

1,9 Management

Thoughtful attention to needs of people for satisfying relationships leads to a comfortable friendly organization atmosphere and work tempo.

9,9 Management

Work accomplishment is from committed people ; interdependence through a "common stake" in organization purpose leads to relationships of trust and respect.

5,5 Management

Adequate organization performance is possible through balancing the necessity to get out work with maintaining morale of people at a satisfactory level.

1,1 Management

Exertion of minimum effort to get required work done is appropriate to sustain organization membership.

9,1 Management

Efficiency in operations results from arranging conditions of work in such a way that human elements interfere to a minimum degree.

Concern for People

High 9 8 7 6 5 4 3 2 1 Low

Concern for Production

1 Low 2 3 4 5 6 7 8 9 High

FIGURE 1. The Managerial Grid

cern for production and concern for people. At the top left corner of the Grid is found the 1,9 style. Here there is a minimum of concern for production but maximum concern for people. In the lower right corner is 9,1. This style has a maximum concern for production and a minimum for human aspects. In the upper right corner is the 9,9 style, where concern for both people and production reaches maximum. Then, in the center is the 5,5 style, which is a "middle of the road" or an intermediate amount of both kinds of concerns.

It should be emphasized that the manner in which these two concerns are linked together by a manager defines how he uses hierarchy. In addition, the character of *concern for* at different grid positions differs, even though the *degree* may be the same. For example, when high concern for people is coupled with a low concern for production, the type of people concern expressed (*i.e.*, that people be "happy") is far different from the type of high concern for people shown when a high concern for production is also evident (*i.e.*, that people be involved in the work and strive to contribute to organization purpose).

A number of additional managerial theories may be shown on this grid. Indeed, in a 9-point system such as is employed here, 81 "mixtures" of these two concerns might be pictured. However, emphasis first will be placed on analyzing the assumptions at the corners and midpoint. Each of these five theories defines a definite but different set of assumptions regarding how individuals, in fact, do orient themselves for managing situations of production that involve people.

As such, each theory can be seen as a set of possible assumptions for using hierarchy to link people into production. Each constitutes an alternative way of thinking. Each can be applied for analyzing how a given situation is being or might be managed. Each of the theories in actual practice is found, to some degree, in concrete situations in industrial and government organizations. Equally, the kinds of assumptions to be described are universal and, in a certain sense, common throughout various cultures. But the important point here is that when a manager confronts a situation in which work is to be accomplished through people, there are, indeed, a *range* of alternative ways for him to go about supervising. To increase his managerial competence he needs to know them and to be able to select the best course of action for any given situation from among a number of possibilities.[14]

As in any field of applied endeavor, disagreement can arise between what is the best theory and what theory is most realistic for practical application in a "live" situation. However, as in any applied setting, the answer regarding what is best can only be given in the light of existing realities. There is no ideological way of saying what is best without reference to actual circumstances. But the choice is neither arbitrary nor random. The *results* a manager obtains will reflect, in predictable ways, the kinds of assumptions he applied in that situation.[15] If the assumptions do not "fit" the situation well, poorer results will be obtained than if they do. More will be said on this later.

Significance and Interpretation of Grid Positions

Should the five "pure" theories be viewed as defining a set of personality characteristics? If not, then in what manner should they be considered?

One answer is that these positions constitute anchorages for managerial attitudes and practices. Conceived of in this manner, aspects of the Grid are more accurately regarded as describing systems of pressures acting on an individual to manage in a certain fashion.[16] Such pressures arise:

1. From inside himself

2. From the immediate external situation, and/or

3. From characteristics of the organizational system including traditions, established practices and procedures.

Though most people seem to be predisposed to manage in one way or another, points on the Grid are *not* to be thought of as personality types that isolate a given individual's behavior. They do not slot him in a rigid and inflexible way into a certain place. Behavior is more changing and flexible than that.

In comparison with a mechanical explanation of managerial behavior, the Grid pictures a number of different sets of assumptions about how an individual *can* manage. Any set of assumptions is subject to change. Whenever a person changes his underlying managerial assumptions, his actual managerial practices shift accordingly, or else a gross discrepancy is present between the attitudes he expresses and the actions he takes. A given individual's style, then, may be viewed as a dominant set of assumptions.[17] These assumptions orient his thinking and his behavior in dealing with production/people relationships. Furthermore, he may or may not be aware of the assumptions that are guiding his actions.[18] The purpose of this book, and of much management training, is to aid an individual to become more knowledgeable regarding his own assumptions about how to manage.

Observe an individual's behavior in a variety of situations. It becomes clear that even the notion of one *dominant* style, a single set of managerial assumptions, is not sufficient to catch the full implication of a person's managerial approach. In addition to a dominant set of managerial assumptions, which are the most characteristic of the managerial style a person has adopted, the concept of a *backup* set of assumptions is a useful one. An individual's backup theory is the one he uses when his dominant theory fails to get the desired results. It is the style he falls back on. Any style may be a backup to any other theory as a dominant style.

Which managerial style is dominant for any given person in any particular situation can be determined by any one or several sets of conditions in combination.

Organization. Managerial behavior frequently is determined by situational factors, such as the organization in which a person operates. Thus, when organizational practices are so fixed or rigid as to permit only small variations in individual behavior, the managerial style exhibited may reflect little of a man's personal thinking and much of his organization beliefs about "the right way to manage." Therefore, one section within each of the anchor positions in the following chapters is concerned with organization or situational requirements which are likely to call forth various managerial styles.

Situation. The situation itself may be the determining or overriding factor dictating which set of managerial assumptions are employed to deal with it. Management of people in the crisis of an explosion situation is likely to be different than it would be under circumstances that are routine.

Values. Any individual's choice of managerial assumptions may be based on values or beliefs he holds concerning the "right" way to treat people, or the way to manage to achieve "best" results. Any given set of assumptions can have a personal value attached to them which represents an individual's private conviction concerning the desirability of any managerial style as a dominant one.

Personality. The dominant managerial style may, to an important degree, result from deep-rooted personality characteristics which predispose an individual to prefer one approach over another. Thus, in the sections concerned with the five anchor positions (Figure 1), the personality dispositions likely to be found in conjunction with a given managerial style are presented.

Chance. Finally, a set of managerial assumptions may guide a person's behavior because he has not been confronted with, nor has discovered in his own experience, that other sets of assumptions about how to manage are available. "Chance," so to speak, has not helped him learn. But many managers, upon learning the variety of managerial styles available to them, do shift, sometimes rather dramatically, from one style to another, as they seek to integrate people into production. Seeing alternatives, they embrace a different set of assumptions.

The point to be emphasized here is that managerial styles are *not* fixed. They are not unchanging. They are determined by a range of factors. Many are subject to modification through formal instruction or self-training of the kind possible from this book.

PLAN OF THE BOOK

Primary emphasis is to be placed on analyzing managerial assumptions. Five sets of key managerial orientations are described in the first part of the book.

In these chapters, managerial actions are divided into several segments. Each chapter has sections that are concerned with goal setting, direction and control; boss-subordinate relationships, i.e., those aspects of management traditionally connected with supervision, planning, execution and followup. Other topics include conflict; creativity; commitment; management development; and communications. Although the interconnections between each cluster are numerous, these aspects of managerial effort can be discussed separately with profit. Then, personality characteristics likely to predispose the selection of one dominant managerial style as against others are outlined. Finally, organization factors likely to prompt application of one style over another are discussed.

In the second section of the book, managerial *facades* are explored. These are deceptive ways of managing which are adopted to hide one's true motivation. Then, attention is turned to an examination of managerial practices where two or more theories are applied simultaneously or in succession within a given situation.

In the third section of the book, research which has been conducted to evaluate managerial styles of American managers of today is reported and interpreted. Also in this section, the scores you made on the instrument you completed, in Chapter 1, will be interpreted so that you can estimate the assumptions underlying your own managerial practices. This will give you a basis for thinking about any changes in your own approach you may wish to consider.

Finally, the significance of the organization culture itself as a critical ingredient influencing managerial behavior will be discussed. Strategies for increasing organization effectiveness, which include individual management development as well as organization development, will be outlined. An assessment is provided of one such development effort.

References

1. The line of thinking that leads to the generalized version of the Managerial Grid is consistent with work by C. Argyris, *Personality and organization*. New York: Harper, 1957; K. D. Benne and P. Sheats, Functional Roles of Group Members. *Journal of Social Issues*, 2, 1948, 42-47; E. A. Fleishman, E. F. Harris, & H. E. Burtt, *Leadership and Supervision in Industry*. Columbus, Ohio: Bureau of Educational Research, Ohio State University, 1955; R. Likert, *New Patterns of Management*. New York: McGraw-Hill, 1961; D. McGregor, *The Human Side of Enterprise*. New York: McGraw-Hill, 1960; D. Moment & A. Zaleznik, *Role Development and Interpersonal Competence*. Boston: Harvard University, 1963; and, T. Parsons, R. F. Bales & E. A. Shils, *Working Papers in the Theory of Action*. Glencoe, Ill.: Free Press, 1953.

2. Sherif, M. & Sherif, C. *An Outline of Social Psychology*. (Rev. Ed.). New York: Harper & Bros., 1956, 143-180.

3. Simon, H. A. Recent Advances in Organization Theory. *Research Frontiers in Politics and Government*. Washington, D. C.: Brookings, 1955.

4. Allen, L. A. *Management and Organization*. New York: McGraw-Hill, 1958, 58.

5. Bavelas, A. Communication Patterns in Task-Oriented Groups. *Journal of the Acoustical Society of America*. 22, 1950, 725-730. Also in D. Cartwright & A. Zander, (Eds.), *Group Dynamics: Research and Theory*. Evanston, Ill.: Row, Peterson, 1956, 493-506. Pfiffner, J. M. & Sherwood, F. P. *Administrative Organization*. Englewood Cliffs, N. J.: Prentice-Hall, 1960, 52-73. Kelley, H. H. Communication in Experimentally Created Hierarchies. *Human Relations*, 4, 1951, 39-56.

6. Appley, L. A. *Management in Action*. New York: American Management Association, 1956, 20-22.

7. Likert, R. A Motivational Approach to a Modified Theory of Organization and Management. In M. Haire (Ed.), *Modern Organization Theory*. New York: Wiley, 1959, 184-217. Stanton, E. S. Company Policies and Supervisors' Attitudes Toward Supervision. *Journal of Applied Psychology*, 44, 1960, 22-26.

8. In this book, attention is not focused on organization and managerial principles and functions *per se;* such as unity of direction, span of control, delegation of authority, etc. Rather, consideration is limited to the assumptions a manager operates under when, for example, he delegates authority, or plans a given work activity. Organization principles and management functions are treated as neutral or as givens, whereas the *ways* in which they are applied under different managerial styles *are* subject to examination.

9. Blake, R. R., Mouton, J. S. & Bidwell, A. C. "The Managerial Grid," *Advanced Management—Office Executive*, 1, 1962, 12-15, 36.

Blake, R. R., and Mouton, J. S. "The Developing Revolution in Management Practices, *ASTD Journal*, 16, 1962, 29-50.

10. McGregor, D. *The Human Side of Enterprise*. New York: McGraw-Hill, 1960, 6.

11. Bales, R. F. The Equilibrium Problem in Small Groups. In T. Parsons, R. F. Bales, & E. A. Shils, *Working Papers in the Theory of Action*. Glencoe, Ill.: Free Press, 1953, 111-161. Also, abridged in A. P. Hare, E. F. Borgatta, & R. F. Bales (Eds.), *Small Groups*. New York: Knopf, 1955, 425-456.

12. The two Grid dimensions, *concern for people and concern for purpose* (production in this particular context) toward which interaction is pointed appear to be basic variables. That is, essentially the same assumptions regarding the integration of people and purpose can be applied in a wide variety of settings; from the family situation to medical and educational institutions; from sales organizations to R&D facilities; from American to Asiatic cultures; etc.

13. It is possible to add a number of dimensions to the Grid; such as activity—passivity; unit of social action, from one to many; self *vs.* other or team orientation; degree of actual effectiveness (Reddin, W. *The Tri-Dimensional Grid*. University of New Brunswick: mimeograph). While these additional dimensions have research value, at this stage in development, they appear to add unduly to the complexity of the task of seeking a meaningful, systematic framework for managerial theories, which has direct application in concrete action situations. Thus, they will not be included further.

14. Shibutani, T. Reference Groups as Perspectives. *American Journal of Sociology*, 60, 1955, 562-570.

15. McGregor, D., *op. cit.*, 11.

16. Lewin, K. *A Dynamics Theory of Personality*. New York: McGraw-Hill, 1935. Lewin, K. *Field Theory in Social Science*. New York: Harper & Bros., 1951.

17. Mead, G. H. *Mind, Self, and Society*. Chicago: Univ. of Chicago 1934; Festinger, L. *A Theory of Cognitive Dissonance*. Evanston, Ill.: Row, Peterson, 1957.

18. Katz, D. The Functional Approach to the Study of Attitudes. *Public Opinion Quarterly*, 24, 1960, 163-204.

CHAPTER THREE

The 9,1 Managerial Style

In the lower right hand corner of the Grid is 9,1. At this position a high concern for production, *9*, is coupled with a low concern for people, *1*. In the 9,1 managerial style, the assumption is made that, somehow, there is an inevitable contradiction between organizational needs of production and personal needs of people.[1, 2] If one is met, the other must be sacrificed. Yet, people must be used to attain the production for which the manager feels responsible. If he acts from a 9,1 orientation, he seeks to resolve the dilemma by arranging conditions of work which minimize feelings and attitudes.[3] He does so in a way that prevents the "human elements from interfering with efficiency and output."

A manager operating at a 9,1 level, in the extreme, might be characterized as an exacting task master. He drives himself and his people alike. One thought monopolizes his concern and action—*production*. 9,1 personifies the entrepreneurial spirit.[4]

9,1 is one of the positions on the Grid where concern for people is low. Thus, it is not surprising that topics such as conflict, creativity, and commitment receive little attention. This does not indicate that topics such as conflict, creativity and commitment do not contain managerial assumptions under 9,1. Indeed, they do. The point is that they are weighted unevenly. Far more attention is given to how to organize work than to the conditions of organizing people in order to make it possible for them to work with maximum productivity.[5]

MANAGEMENT UNDER 9,1

Under a 9,1 theory, a manager has a position of authority in the hierarchy and he knows it. He feels his responsibilities are to plan, direct, and control the actions of his subordinates in whatever way is necessary to reach the production objectives of the enterprise. The boss plans, subordinates execute. They carry out the various plans, directions and schedules placed upon them. The aim under this approach is to get production! Schedules are to be met! People are expected to do what they are told to do—no more, no less![7]

A 9,1 managerial orientation is typified in the following quotations:[8]

> Planning. "I do planning by setting the production quotas and schedules to be followed by each subordinate. Then, I work out the procedures and operating ground rules and I make individual assignments. I also establish check points so I can ascertain that actions I have authorized are being taken as I intended them to be done."
>
> Work Execution. "I watch the work closely. I criticize as I see the necessity for it and authorize changes as needs for them arise."
>
> Follow-up. "I have plans laid for the next assignments and move people on to them as operations dictate. Recognition and corrective action are extended to individuals on a one-by-one basis."

These three statements contain a number of 9,1 assumptions concerning how to manage performance. Some major elements will be discussed in greater depth below. However, the above orientations to managerial responsibilities are, in themselves, keys to understanding the 9,1 style. The success of 9,1 management is measured solely in terms of production and profit.[9] Personal managerial success in this context, then, has its reward in achieving production goals. Achievement becomes the watchword of the 9,1 approach.[10] Here organization is like a competitive hurdle race. Victory goes to the swiftest, the one able to surmount each hurdle he confronts — without help. To the victor belong the spoils of organization.

9,1 DIRECTION AND CONTROL

Direction and control are key managerial concepts. They can lend a better understanding to the 9,1 managerial style. The question is, "What is the 9,1 approach for orienting and correlating individual effort toward organization purpose?" Only those aspects of direction and control concerned with the coordination and execution of work effort are described to place 9,1, task management, in perspective.

Under 9,1, the relationship of a supervisor to a subordinate is along lines of *authority* and *obedience*.[11] The manager may exercise authority, in the extreme, over the slightest motions of the subordinate. The person whose work is supervised is obligated to obedient performance. The condition of work is that he must do what he is told — no more or less. Authority of hierarchy is not to be questioned. Lines of accountability and responsibility are clearly drawn. They are to be adhered to.[12]

If a subordinate should question a 9,1 oriented supervisor about the advisability of the method by which work is to be performed, he might get an answer such as, "These are your instructions. Do them and don't give me any lip. If there's anything I don't like, it's insubordination."

The underlying assumption that guides 9,1 action in this aspect of management is that externally imposed direction and control, of necessity, must be applied down through the organization hierarchy. Why? First, people are believed to dislike work inherently.[13] Therefore, they must be pushed. Secondly, they are likely to be seen as less than fully capable of intelligently organizing their efforts effectively at their own levels of operation.[14] If capable, they would not be there. While supervisors at lower echelons are held responsible for work, the planning and organizing aspects of their jobs are thought to be done more effectively up the line where perspective, skill, and information are present. And third, to manage otherwise would seem to weaken the structure of established authority, assumed to be necessary if the efforts

of "unwilling" subordinates are to be directed toward
organization goals. As will be discussed when the personality aspects of individuals acting from a 9,1 background
are examined, it has been "learned," long ago, that the
actions of subordinates are very much like those of children. They must be strictly watched over by the supervisor who, in a sense, is a parent figure.[15]

This attitude also is apparent in middle and upper
management levels.[16] For example, the following advice was
given to managers just below the top level in a large
corporation. It is typical of 9,1 oriented management.
"For an executive to challenge orders, directions, policies
and procedures, rules and regulations, etc., smacks of insubordination, of lack of cooperation. It shows his failure to understand the need for decisions at highest level
and for firm direction and control of operations."[17]

The primary direction and control over production
then, is through the exercise of authority. However, in
exchange for compliance with resulting effort, a man is
"paid," sometimes extremely well.[18] As one subordinate
executive remarked, "You have to pay well to get a man
to take the ———— I take."

Mistakes and Violations

Mistakes by subordinates, under a 9,1 style, are most
likely to be viewed as due to human error. When something goes wrong on the job or an error is discovered,
the manager with a 9,1 style is likely to say, "My immediate reaction is to find out who is responsible for the
mistake and to mete out the appropriate disciplinary action in a swift and compelling manner. When people
know that errors are not tolerated, they straighten up.
If you don't nip such action in the bud, they will take
advantage of you." The assumption is that the source of
error is "in the person." It is the supervisor's responsibility
to find it. Subordinates should pay for it.

Under the "produce or perish" concept, guilt is sought
out so blame can be placed squarely and corrective action, with discipline to reinforce it, taken as indicated.[19] In
this way, the manager is able to control closely the actions of subordinates and is assured that a job will be

carried out as prescribed, even if he is not present to oversee its actual execution.

A 9,1 managerial attitude toward control can be illustrated in connection with policies and procedures. *Uniformity of action is the aim.*[20] Through uniformity, orderly behavior occurs. Thus, a manager with a 9,1 orientation might say, "Uniform policies are indispensible to orderly production. Formal policies and procedures should be well defined to cover even emergency situations. They also should be enforced continuously whenever deviations from them arise." In a sense, then, the rule is not upheld merely for the rule's sake, but because in this way predictability of behavior can be insured. Standard operating procedures, for example, are designed to leave little to thought or chance.[21] Failure to deal with them when violations do occur, is tantamount to abdication of responsibility. To take prompt action is to insure it will not happen twice.

THE CONCEPT OF GOALS UNDER 9,1

In the introduction, it was mentioned that a key managerial dilemma involved the relation between individual purpose and organizational purpose. The purpose (goal) of the organization, it was said, may or may not be the same as the goal(s) of people in the organization. Under 9,1, the manager's concern for organization goal (or purpose) is likely to be high, while goals of subordinates are, in fact, more or less ignored as a possible significant contributing factor.[22]

Goal-setting under 9,1 is, in many respects, a disregarded concept, if participation of those who work to achieve them is considered.[23] However, in another aspect the concept *goal* is very likely to be found in 9,1. In the concept of *quota*, as used here, is some performance objective which is set by one level in the hierarchy in line with organization goals to be accomplished by those at a lower level. Though the quota may be quite clear, subordinates take no part in setting it. Depending upon how realistic the quota is and how much control is imposed upon those responsible for accomplishing it, the quota may come to have a mechanical or arbitrary quality about it. The subordinates' goal is to achieve the quota by whatever means necessary.[24] Industrial literature describing the operation of the Russian economic system contains many examples of the price paid in quality, quantity and in the integrity of human action when management of production is by the quota method.[25]

Quotas, in a real sense, also can become restrictive of production. Consider the following situation. A quota is set, based on past performance, available manpower, machines and materials, market analyses, and other relevant variables. Once set in people's minds, unlike genuine goals, a quota can assume the quality of a "ceiling." Unanticipated changes in the factors that went into the setting of the quota often occur. The market may be better than anticipated. A shift downward in materials costs may occur. More can be produced at a lesser per unit cost than anticipated and thus a competitive advantage gained from exceeding it. But, quotas have been assigned and have become frozen. Under these circumstances, efforts to raise the quota are seen as a management strategy of exploitation. They usually meet stiff resistance. If quotas are raised and are met, quality may suffer. The expectations of subordinates have been violated. There are ways to retaliate.[26] As will be discussed under 9,9, goal-setting, on the other hand, imposes no ceiling on effort. The way is clear — the *goal* is to move as far in the established direction as possible. Changing circumstances present opportunities for innovation. They constitute a challenge toward exceeding the goal.

The quota as used in 9,1 has a close connection with deadlines, which are used for the same purpose: to put pressure on production. By setting a tight deadline, the 9,1 manager can exert force in the direction of results. As he might say to a subordinate, "The same job a month ago took two days to complete. Get it done this time in a day and a half."

Also used is the "squeeze" play, with a constant deadline. "The same job took four days for ten men the last time it was done. Get it done in four days with seven men on this trip."

Notwithstanding the restrictive and control qualities of a quota, or a deadline, the method of imposition under 9,1 conditions almost insures their attainment will in some degree be thwarted.

Resistance to quota setting is, perhaps, too well known to require further elaboration at this point.[27]

BOSS-SUBORDINATE RELATIONSHIPS IN 9,1

A basic assumption of the 9,1 approach is that the "people unit" to be managed in a work situation is the individual *man* (not the team, etc.). The supreme relationship is that of the supervisor over the subordinate.[28] Supervisors make decisions. Subordinates carry them out. Supervision is one to one. No provisions are made for interaction patterns between peers at an equal level and boss and subordinates in a one-to-all setting.

Acccording to a 9,1 managerial orientation, subordinates are likely to be viewed in the following way. "My subordinates are a means to the organization's success and to my own as well. As such, they are useful in getting the job done. Human relations are okay, but in the final analysis it is a produce-or-perish reality that people must learn to recognize."

Indeed, the managerial control strategy may be to keep subordinates separated.[29] According to 9,1, when people are isolated from one another, they are less likely to engage in the useless social interactions that are so detrimental to the performance on the job. Also, when informal work groups do form undercover, so to speak, the result frequently is a restriction of output. Under 9,1, this eventuality is closely guarded against. The concept of the "one-man gang" is an excellent example of isolation at the worker level.

A closer glance at any traditional organization chart will confirm how this concept of one to one is built into organizational working relationships.[30] Lines of accountability in the chain-of-command move vertically through the organization.[31] The mind's eye cannot miss how positions are structured one over the other. Job and position titles reinforce the concept. Functional lines are parallel and "wired" vertically. These lines are well insulated to insure that "sparks" do not jump the circuit, horizontally, and short-circuit the downward flow of communication, direction and control.

There is an actual office arrangement, which has been observed, that typifies the vertical structuring of working relations and that isolates those at peer levels. This large office accommodates the Accounts Payable and Accounts Receivable units within an accounting section. Six accountants are employed in each unit. One man supervises each unit. These two supervisors in turn report to the section manager.

The design of this office is such that each accountant works within a foggy-glass cubicle. The cubicles are closed on three sides and open to the front. A five-foot pathway separates the six cubicles of the one unit from the other. In front of each group of six cubicles is another cubicle. These two cubicles are for the unit supervisors. The unit supervisors' cubicles are closed on two sides. The front and the back are open. Splitting the pathway and at the opposite extreme of the office is the section manager's office. From here, the section manager can see into the cubicles of his two section supervisors. The section supervisors, in turn, can look "upward" toward their boss or "downward" toward their subordinates. The two supervisors cannot see each other. The subordinate accountants can see neither to the right nor to the left. They only can look upward to their supervisor.

The flow of communication and work direction is from the manager to each supervisor, separately. From here the two supervisors carry the work to their subordinates. From their vantage points in the office, the manager and each supervisor are able to visually "oversee" the work of those for whom each is responsible. The supervisors and the accountants do not, and are not expected to, know what is happening to the right or left. Decisions or judgments affecting both sections are made or interpreted at the manager's level. They are passed down the line, individually, to those below him.

As a final gesture of supreme verticality, the manager enters his place of work "from the top." The two supervisors enter through a side door, in the middle. The twelve accountants come and go through a door that opens into the center pathway—in the *rear*. The section manager, quite proudly, designed this arrangement. His style of management requires little probing for understanding. Subordinates know what is expected of them.

Meeting with Subordinates

At higher levels of management, interaction patterns between a boss and his subordinates may vary from lower levels. A reason is that the pooling of information often is required in order for complex decisions to be made. This results in various kinds of meetings. How meetings are used and the way in which interactions take place can be a signal of what managerial style is operating.

A manager with a 9,1 orientation is likely to utilize periodic meetings he initiates the following way:

"Accountability means that *I* am responsible for making decisions. Meetings are to communicate information or changes or to have progress reports to keep me abreast of work."

Thus, in the vast majority of instances, decision making is seen as the sole responsibility of the person who wears the highest cloak of authority.[32] Information is gathered from lower levels in order to permit the best possible one-alone decisions. Even one-to-one decisions, where a subordinate *participates* in the decision-making process, are likely to be relatively rare. This does *not* mean that a manager operating under a 9,1 orientation does not utilize meetings. He does, but the character of discussion gives a clue as to his assumption regarding the ways meetings are employed.

Interactions in such a meeting are predominantly one to one.[33] The boss speaks to each subordinate in turn. Little interaction between subordinates takes place.[34] A meeting of this sort can, in effect, be a time saver for the boss. He can make announcements simultaneously to several people rather than on a one-by-one basis. The pattern of interaction is essentially the same however. Each subordinate, when asked, speaks only from the standpoint of his own job description and about those areas for which he is responsible. The manager is the focal point of the interaction. Just as in the accounting office arrangement, they physically are a group; psychologically, they are isolated one from each other. Instructions flow down and reporting information flows up on a straight line-hierarchical basis.[35]

9,1 Attitudes Toward His Boss

The other side of the coin—the 9,1 attitude as a subordinate—is as follows:

"I want to prove myself via production figures and by being on top of details. I run my organization with minimum interference."

A manager with a 9,1 orientation, in other words, wants to be known by his works and evaluated according to results! The boss controls the performance rewards. As such, showing his boss what he can do is a major aim as a manager whose style is 9,1. Just as the subordinate manager rewards top performance (almost without regard for how it is obtained), so he expects his boss to recognize his achievement. The relation is a business one. It asks no leniency; it extends no sympathy. Performance, and only performance, counts.

The supervisor whose approach is 9,1 wants to "run his own show."[36] Any success, then, is a demonstration of his own performance and efforts. In keeping with this attitude a supervisor whose style is 9,1 is likely to report to his boss on results and any unusual problems or exceptions. But, "as long as things are on schedule," he (the boss) has no business worrying about routine details.

Creating and Maintaining Morale

A final aspect that is related to the boss-subordinate relationship is concern for morale. Morale wants watching after, for, out of hand, it can play havoc with production. But equally dangerous is an oversolicitous interest in employee welfare. It can corrode the moral fiber of men.[37]

The basic attitude then is: "Men are employed to work. Supervised well, there should be no morale problem. If morale problems arise, their causes are likely to be traceable to 'soft' leadership." As a supervisor with a 9,1 orientation remarked, "Seeing to it that subordinates have plenty to do, with clear, high-quality instructions, leaves neither time nor inclination to gripe."

Again, the focus for resolution of morale problems is through heightened emphasis on achieving production as a sound way of controlling griping. Failure to do so means that people problems can, in an insidious way, erode the efficiency of an organization.

Communication Activities Under 9,1

9,1 management communication is formal and is the media through which the authority-obedience system of direction and control is exercised. The hierarchy is for the purpose of dispensing orders downward and controlling the coordination of effort. Communication upward is limited to reporting on actions accomplished and deviations from expected results. The formal organization chart defines legitimate channels.[38]

In the 9,1 communication system, control is exercised by reducing to writing—in black and white—the information, orders, and procedures which are of major and minor significance. In this way, checks can be made, accountability for errors placed and corrective action administered.

It is possible that a manager in a 9,1 oriented organization might realize that things are not going well. Rather than use such mechanisms as opinion polls, surveys, etc., to find out what is going on, he is more likely to cut through organization lines of command and find out for himself, directly.[39] Touring the organization unannounced and asking probing questions to spot bottlenecks and trouble spots can "keep people on their toes." Such action is feared by managers at intermediate levels, because "swooping down" to catch irregularities or to get to the root of matters can expose a man without a defense. But this method of control through interruption in the communication system is likely to be a 9,1 characteristic.

While the downward jumping of levels occurs, sometimes to the extent of being an accepted organizational style, short-circuiting one's boss by "going over his head," to his boss is strictly frowned upon. To do so is to challenge established authority, an act which is abhorrent, viewed from a 9,1 orientation.

Office bulletin boards under 9,1 commonly resemble those associated with the military including duty rosters, performance results (high *and* low), etc. Communications are approved and dated before being posted. Trivia, such as cartoons, jokes, and the like, have no place. Here management's position with respect to the union, competitor products or sales and so forth are to be found, posted as official.

The 9,1 approach in using the company internal publication is to make known upper management's positions on a variety of issues and matters. The intention is to do so in such a manner as to insure that there is full understanding at lower levels of what management expects.

The reason such an approach is 9,1 is that thinking is concentrated on getting production results *directly*— by close supervision and tight control. Attention is not applied to the question of how individual and organization goals can be meshed so that achieving production results becomes of widely shared, spontaneous concern of all.

9,1 Approaches to Managing Conflict

Conflict comes to expression in its various forms—illogical disagreement, win-lose arguments, open fighting.[40] In one way or another, all constitute evidences of emotional tension and disturbance between individuals or groups. Excluded, of course, are differences in viewpoint based on factual information, on the need to exercise complex judgment, etc. The latter tend to disappear under analytical study and review, while the former tend to persist, or, if brought to resolution, to reappear in new issues and topics. It is as though the interpersonal conflict which is present can find an endless number of forms through which to express itself.

In what is being said here, reference is to disagreement and competitiveness between individuals and groups holding membership in the same organization.[41] This is *direct* interpersonal and intergroup competition of a psychological character. Excluded from consideration is interorganizational competitiveness, as between companies. Here the competition is *impersonal;* it is sociological and economic. While the latter is indispensible for industrial progress, the former is mostly—though not entirely—disruptive of progress and growth.[42]

As has already been discussed, production comes first. Any disruption that might prevent its attainment is looked upon as a barrier. As such, interpersonal conflict must be dealt with promptly. A second consideration is with respect to authority-obedience. Authority is the backbone of achieving production through people under 9,1; it is also employed to eliminate conflict. Beyond that, conflict, disagreements and dissension among those responsible for production can undermine the authority structure. Therefore, conflict cannot be allowed to permeate the work situation. It must be brought under control before it becomes unmanageable. Managing conflict under 9,1 can therefore be examined best in the context of 9,1 assumptions surrounding the production-people dimension.

From the Boss' Perspective

The approach to conflict management is to insure that conflict does not appear. When there is a difference in point of view as to how to do something, as between a boss and a subordinate, the fundamental rule of the game in 9,1 is *suppression.* This can be done by a boss, once disagreement arises, by simply "cutting it off."[43] A boss need not tolerate disagreement—he has the authority to deal with it in the way he likes. Operating from a 9,1 theory, a boss is likely to see disagreement as first cousin to insubordination.

When his decision is challenged by subordinates, for example, a boss operating under 9,1 assumptions is likely to feel that questioning by subordinates implies insubordination. His more usual reaction might be, "Look . . . that's the decision, and that's it. Anything that smacks ot resistance ought to be eliminated so that it will not occur again. Here is my answer for what will be done." So, the approach to resolving disagreement is that of enforcing subordinate action consistent with the boss' will.[44]

Most major organizations of today have suppression programs of one sort or another that are built in to formal practices. Such programs may extend from a warning letter in a file, to one day off without pay, to three days off without pay, to, in the extreme, summary dismissal. The underlying assumption of a warning letter is that a person should be forewarned that his actions, which are in disagreement with the system, are unacceptable. Thus, he is put on notice that a further act of disagreement will bring more severe punishment. No provision to evaluate the possibility the rules need changing to bring them in line is made. Furthermore, no basis is provided for examining the *why* of the infraction—whether it occurred from ignorance, misinterpretation, maliciousness, etc. Thus, the possibility of using disagreement as educational subject matter is not considered.[45] As a result, an assumption, perhaps unwittingly, is that if the disagreement is prevented from coming out into the open, this will correct or adequately handle the situation. At the very least, those consequences that can interfere with operations remain under the surface. The expression of conflict, in other words, is prevented by a supervisor applying the authority-obedience control formula and saying, "That's it! Here's the way it's going to be!"

When two or more subordinates get into open conflict with one another, again, the 9,1 approach is to suppress it by dealing firmly with those concerned. The appearance of interpersonal frictions as well as disagreements over how to get work done is interpreted under 9,1 to mean that people are not acting in a rational manner. Rather they are reacting emotionally. 9,1 has no tolerance for human emotional fraility.[46]

Though suppression by "chewing out," "reading the riot act," etc., many times is effective in ending open conflict, it often fails to get at the core of the problem. It does not correct the underlying causes of conflict. Sources of conflict remain. The result is that unresolved, but hidden, conflicts many times reappear in disguised ways (slowdowns, careless errors, misinterpretation of instructions, etc.) to lower the quality of cooperation and reduce production effectiveness.

If a manager with a 9,1 orientation runs into headon contradiction, as the man-in-the-middle, between what he is told to do from above and what he knows will cause trouble, frustration, anxiety, or insecurity among those below, rarely would he himself sense internal conflict. He would not likely feel reponsibility to ask for a review of the decision in the light of the "smoke" he knew it would generate. Rather, he would *act* under instruction and "let the chips fall where they may."

Another way of saying it is, if faced with a conflict of interests, the manager under 9,1 would identify with the position of greater authority and power; the more so if the issue involved centered on action to promote production at the expense of people. It is for this reason that layoffs frequently have such a cold, arbitrary quality. Their only goal is "getting rid of people," without more than passing thought to corporate responsibility for the welfare of people who have given effective service for 15, 20 or 25 years, and for whom other means of livelihood are not in sight. Though in the light of corporate economics, new product development, and production technology, layoffs frequently are inevitable, the way they are conducted—the amount of notice given, provision of severance pay, early retirement arrangements, job-seeking assistance in the labor market, etc.—can do much to aid affected individuals to make transitions from one employer to another. Such planning and legitimate welfare assistance would be reacted to by a manager with a 9,1 orientation as "molly coddling" and "soft."

Leverage—The Muted 9,1 Approach

In the absence of the unrestrained capacity to exercise unilateral managerial control (*i.e.*, through "firing," etc.), techniques of *leverage* may be applied to accomplish the result. This is done by creating situations which offer the person with the lesser hierarchical authority no real alternative but to "accept or else."[47] A typical example is where a job is declared to be no longer necessary, with its occupant thereby made surplus. But since he cannot be fired, he is offered an equivalent job at a distance which, for many reasons (family, etc), he cannot possibly accept. His only option is to resign.

Leverage strategies are widely used in business, government and politics to settle differences in points of view in one's own favor. Though sometimes described as gentle persuasion, the thinking behind them might better be described as subtle coercion. Regardless of how described, the mental attitude involved is difficult to distinguish from 9,1; therefore, it is pictured here as a *muted* 9,1 approach. The gruffness is eliminated, but the effect is identical.

From the Subordinates' Perspective

Because of the emphasis on comparative evaluation between organization units in terms of production results, win-lose competitiveness *among those at the same level* is likely to develop under 9,1. The reason is that each vies with the others in terms of a "good showing" for advancement to higher positions. Such competitiveness is likely to go on outside the formal work system and to result in politics, maneuvering, etc.[48] Unleashing intercomponent competition—to "separate the men from the boys"—can result in spirited disagreement. Genuine disagreement is indispensible where differences are legitimate, but the 9,1 use of competition to spur effort often does not contribute to organization purpose. When it becomes intense and invidious it may work against achieving organization goals.[49]

When the disagreement that is producing conflict does arise with his peers or with his boss, the goal of the manager with 9,1 assumptions is to end the conflict by proving himself right and others wrong. A win-lose approach is taken in order to show the weaknesses in the opponent's point of view.[50]

The approach is to win by proving the rightness of one's position when the disagreement is between two people who have a parallel relationship, *i.e.*, where neither has authority over the other. The aim is not necessarily to develop a meeting of minds; indeed, if win-lose is underway, the objective is to bring one's adversary to his knees. The 9,1 element involves getting a result, with little or no regard for the other *as a person*. That he may be frustrated, degraded and, in the extreme, feel he has been "had" (and, therefore, rendered *more* ineffective in carrying out his job) is not given serious consideration as a part of the overall problem of resolving disagreement.[51]

When there is an issue with one's boss, the 9,1 approach is to prove the rightness of one's position. However, win-lose is tempered by the subordinate because of his lower level and, as such, he is likely to go "underground." The subordinate may "throw the sponge in." It is not unknown for him to seek to vindicate his position by drawing others into his camp, even though doing so only results in broadening the arena of conflict. By more passive resistance, he may allow events to take place that can cause the boss' course of action to falter.[52]

When subordinates are in conflict, another way to resolve the conflict is to appeal to a common boss—a third party who can adjudicate the conflict and rule a winner and loser. Appealing to the expert is straight use of authority to resolve differences. When the boss is bent on suppressing a subordinate and the subordinate is trying to win over the boss, the result—for the subordinate—is most likely to be that he loses. With the loss is likely to come, at least temporarily, a subordinate response of 1,1. All of these procedures, at least, solve the problem of *open* conflict. When open conflict is relieved through one person's demonstrating that he is right and that others are wrong, however, as has been said, a *victor* and a *vanquished* are produced. Feelings rooted in victory and defeat are not a particularly sound basis for establishing relationships that promote cooperation and mutually productive effort among managers or between supervisors and subordinates.[53]

Both the use of suppression and the emergence of win-lose power struggles contain assumptions about the in-

evitability of disagreement and about the lack of necessity, or perhaps the impossibility, of achieving true
agreement. Both indicate that disagreements, when they
arise, are to be managed by controlling the *expression*
of disagreement rather than by approaching and resolving the cause underlying the disagreement.

IMPACT OF 9,1 ON CREATIVITY AND CHANGE

Creativity, that is, finding new—or better—ways of
doing old things, or finding new things that are useful
and profitable to do, surely is an indispensable ingredient
in a competitive economic society. It is mainly from such
innovation that material progress toward better living is
possible.

How supervision is exercised determines to a great extent, how much creativity is unleashed and mobilized for
organizational application. It is also a determining factor in how much antiorganizational creativity—ways of
beating the system—is generated as a way of resisting
supervisory pressures and organizational requirements.[54]

As has been found in other aspects of the impact of a
9,1 managerial philosophy on actual results, it is important to consider creativity separately and to look at it from
the boss level and from the subordinate level.

At the Boss Level

At levels of managerial action, where emphasis is on
planning and devising ways in which organization accomplishments can be achieved, the amount of creativity
demonstrated is likely to be higher than at levels where responsibility is limited to executing plans devised by others.
The pick up of innovation can be immediate and changes
can be quickly authorized by those who have the authority to make such decisions.

However, the situation is likely to be quite different
and even less creative down the line.

At the Subordinate Level

A symptom associated with 9,1 management, particularly at the worker level, is the absence of organizationally relevant and creative ideas by people who work

at these levels. Some suggestions may help in explaining why. Their jobs most often are defined in terms of doing or executing; people are not considered in terms of contributing to the thinking aspects of the task; rather, they contribute by "turning out results." A primary advantage of work simplification and the division of activities into manageable pieces, for example, is that judgment and decisions, which concern anything more than simple motions or procedures, are reduced to a minimum.[55] By these arrangements, people do not need to think. And, as a result, they do not. At least they do not think in terms that contribute toward organization purpose(s).

If suggestions are passed up the line, the 9,1 action is likely to be that of immediate judgment, often with resentment, of the suggestions themselves.[56] Rather than taking an experimental attitude, the supervisor is likely to say, "We've tried that," or simply, "It won't work." To himself he may say, "New ideas go down; not up."

Frequently, it is said that low level jobs offer little opportunity for creativity. Just because a job does not *require* novelty in executing a routine task does not mean that possibilities of creativity are not present. In any event, if creativity and thinking are totally stifled, a result *may* be that a 1,1 orientation is taken.[57] Then interest is withdrawn and feelings of involvement minimized. Another consequence may be that if opportunity to participate actively in the thinking aspects of work is denied and this is coupled with strong output pressures, people will find ways to be creative, applying their talents to slow down production and to frustrate the goals of the organization.[58] Even assembly line work, where creative team-work is possible when disruptions occur, productive effort can effectively be reduced by people waiting for the problem to be solved (by others).

As a result, the creative abilities of people in the middle and at the bottom of such organizations are not always stifled, but rather they may be stimulated. *Then creative thinking goes into how to defeat the system and to prevent it from working well.* At the least, suggestion systems seem to wither on the vine under 9,1 and much good grass-roots experience and thinking goes begging. Quicker and more efficient ways of getting sound results are buried. In turn, discovery of ways to work more efficiently are used to the advantage of the individual worker in ways contrary to organization purpose. He learns to expend less energy in the same amount of time, rather than contributing to increased production. Successful application of incentive systems such as the Scanlon Plan[59] (which does reward worker creativity), and studies where computations of lost time are made, give evidence of the actual reduction in contribution that can be attributed to 9,1 management relative to what is possible. In some 9,1 based organizations there are dramatic examples of antiorganizational creativity—the "innocent" and unidentifiable causes of destruction of machinery and equipment, hiding tools, short-circuiting assembly lines, and so on. Many are highly creative.

Efforts by 9,1 management to thwart the antiorganization creativity efforts of subordinates seem always to be countered with even more ingenious and devious blockages.

The silent but powerful creative resistence of subordinates to changes designed to promote productivity is a barrier 9,1 has yet to deal with effectively. And, when large numbers of workers join in concert, they can form a chain of resistance that defies breakage.[60]

COMMITMENT UNDER 9,1

Commitment in a 9,1 organizational system is likely to vary, depending upon one's level of responsibility.

The Boss' Commitment

The following can be said of commitment to organizational purpose(s) of an individual whose own boss does not prevent him from managing in a 9,1 way. If his production ethic is to achieve results by whatever means, a circumstance *not* uncommon in 9,1, then it is possible his performance results are likely to be up, particularly in the short term. Another way of saying it is that if the organization gives reward only to production and shows little consideration for people, then a person with a 9,1 managerial orientation is likely to be committed. He feels no tension, he is in harmony with the organization. He is free to drive himself, and others, according to his own personal preferences.

Commitment of Subordinates

From the standpoint of those in subordinate roles under 9,1 supervision, however, the results in terms of organization commitment are likely to be quite different. 9,1 represents high centralization of planning, directing and controlling. Others are little more than agents of production. From the subordinate's angle, such managerial behavior is seen as thoughtless and arbitrary. He is being "used."

From a longer term perspective, 9,1 supervision is likely to generate one of three different reactions:

1. One reaction to 9,1 is a 1,1 compliance.[61] Then individuals do the minimum required of them, no more, no less.[62] In this way, they can avoid being "used" because they are able to maintain a kind of isolation and withdrawal, and yet execute those requirements necessary to retain their membership. The reaction described here is not restricted to the "working man," but occurs among persons at all levels of organization.

This 1,1 reaction to 9,1 condition of work has been amply described but frequently incorrectly interpreted by management.[63] Under such supervision, it is "obvious" that people are "lazy, apathetic and indifferent." The misinterpretation is that this is what they truly are. There is failure to recognize that such behavior is unnatural. The role of supervision in *causing* the lazy, apathetic and indifferent behavior is not recognized.

2. Another impact of 9,1 takes a stronger antiorganizational direction. Men who find themselves offended, and who are unable to redress directly what they regard as injustices, may then take another, more militant, orientation to correcting the problem. Given effective leadership, 1,1 is counteracted and they are aided to achieve through numbers what none was able to accomplish by

himself. The resulting formation of the strength of unions dedicated to *security* can be traced to reactions against 9,1 managerial conditions of work. Tannenbaum is emphatic in the point that unions come about in the way described above.[64] In recognizing their individual helplessness, he says, workers join together to enforce upon employers recognition of their common strength. The trade union, Tannenbaum indicates, "was the visible evidence that man is not a commodity and (simultaneously) that he is not sufficient unto himself."[65]

There are many reasons for men joining unions. The above description depicts one of the most significant ones. It is said here that this commitment is antiorganizational. This is meant to indicate that the reason for joining the union is to *resist* the organization.

3. A third reaction to 9,1, also involving antiorganization commitment, has been referred to in the section concerned with supervision. There it was said that slowdowns and other forms of work hinderances, such as damaging equipment, etc., are frequently practiced at lower levels as a means of discharging resentment.

Which of the three possible reactions, or what combination of them will occur, cannot be predicted without further information. The critical factor in the response to 9,1 is tensions of resentment and hostility. Whether it provokes 1,1 apathetic compliance, retaliation through destructiveness, or unionization, is partly due to the individual's make-up and partly to whether there is effective leadership to lead him into a union.

MANAGEMENT DEVELOPMENT UNDER 9,1

Another important organization and personal consideration is management development as a means of furthering individual capabilities to contribute to the organization. Encompassed are several aspects, including selection, induction, formal training, and performance appraisal. All are ways of increasing organizational capability through more effective people.

The 9,1 managerial orientation contains definite views

about management development. They take the following directions:

Selection

Selection is all important because "you can't make a silk purse out of a sow's ear." Get good people *first*. Then you don't have to train them to do what they should already know.[66]

There are several rules of thumb that might be considered. For example, young people with good military records are a good bet. So are people who have worked in college. They've had to sacrifice a little for what they've got. Unmarried men are a better bet than ones with families. But most of all, what you want is men with ambition—who want to get "to the top" and are willing to make the sacrifices to get there.

Induction

The 9,1 orientation contains at least two ideas about inducting the newcomer. One is this: "The best way to measure a man's calibre is to throw him into the thick of things. The strong ones will swim and the weaker sink. There's not much you can do better than to put a man to the acid test. You might as well find what you've got, quick."[67]

Along with this notion of "testing a man's mettle," is another. "Have a trial period, where you don't commit yourself to the man before you know what he's got. Then if you need to, you can separate him early. Your hands are not locked with promises."

Management Training

Another consideration is management training; the use of educational methods to further the ability of individuals to serve the organization.

A manager with a 9,1 orientation is likely to have definite views about "management training." Basically, he is likely to see supervisory talent as unlearnable.[68] "Either you have it or you don't." As a result, training—particularly human relations training—is likely to be seen as worthless, or even harmful.[69] The latter point of view is based on the fear that "training in human relations will make people soft."

If any management training is thought useful under a 9,1 orientation, it is likely to be training concerned with company objectives, rules and policies, with a little background information on the system for administering and promoting personnel. This kind of orientation or indoctrination training, as it might be said, "can keep a youngster from running amok, and getting into trouble before he learns the ropes."

Performance Reviews

Another aspect of management development is through performance reviews. Here the 9,1 approach is, "You let a man know." This is done clearly and without qualification. The supervisor's obligation, in other words, is to evaluate those under him thoroughly and to point out the ways in which improvement is to be achieved.[70] The subordinate is told what his weaknesses are and what he can do to correct them. "It is the man's responsibility, in the final analysis, to shape up or ship out."

9,1 PERSONAL BEHAVIOR

The adoption of any given dominant managerial orientation may represent an individual's choice from among several styles because of "basic" personality trends.[71] These personal characteristics may represent strong predispositions which make the expression of one set of managerial attitudes and assumptions seem more natural than another.[72, 73]

Outstanding Personal Characteristics

The key for understanding of the person whose personal behavior is oriented in a 9,1 direction is his drive toward mastery and proving himself through performance.[74] An inner sense of direction is maintained which is *achievement oriented*.[75] Opinions of others which might demand a shift from his course of action are disregarded. He tends to be impervious to criticism. Rejecting others who disagree with him is no cause of alarm.

The 9,1 oriented person places high value on making decisions that stick or on doing things his own way because it is "his" way. In terms of convictions, he is ready to stand up for his own ideas, opinions, and attitudes and to press forcefully for their acceptance, even when others are pushing for their own against him.[76] Because he tends to have strong convictions, he is likely to initiate action, take the ball and run in his own direction and under his own steam. The basic attitude is that, although he may not always be right, rarely is he in doubt. Once a conviction, opinion or attitude is adopted, it is likely to be clung to, tenaciously.[77] Given these attitudes, a person who is acting out of 9,1 assumptions is more inclined to "interpret" facts in order to uphold his own views than to modify his conclusion in line with the objective situation. He is directed-from-within himself.

Furthermore, he is oriented toward proving himself through performance or the validity of his position, even at the expense of friendly relations with people. Frequently, his momentum builds up to such a point that it is difficult even for his boss to stop him. Rather than gaining acceptance through being a "good guy," he seeks to gain control by winning for his point of view, even if it results in stepping on toes.

From the standpoint of personal attitudes towards conflict, he finds little reason to shy away. With either boss or peers, he is inclined to enjoy a fight and to try to win if doing so will prove himself. With a subordinate, the 9,1 approach to conflict and disagreement is to *prevent* it from occurring by suppressing disagreement. It is weak to let yourself be challenged by those reporting to you. Having learned obedience to paternal authority, challenge to his own authority is "heresy."[78] Acting according to 9,1 attitudes, his temper can well up when things are not going according to his wishes. His humor, like his approach to conflict, is hard hitting. It tends to carry a sting.

To the degree that 9,1 assumptions about how to manage represent a way of life for an individual, another question needs to be dealt with. The question is, "What kind of underlying motivation causes an individual to adjust in this manner?"

Childhood Origins of 9,1

The inner directed, tough-minded, hard-hitting kind of orientation to problems and people depicted in 9,1 is a way of behaving which has had a long history within the cultures of men.[79] However, in modern times, the underlying motivation of 9,1 would be understood in the following way.

Its origins can be traced to childhood.[80] Parents may, quite unwittingly, place demands for acceptable conduct on their children.[81,82] Such demands come, not from paternal consideration and thoughtfulness towards children and what is best for their growth, but from tension and anxiety within the parents themselves for achievement and hard work, as a means of proving oneself. Criticism, feelings of low self worth, and lack of respect for others tend to flourish under such circumstances. The child, though seeking love and approval, rarely finds it. Actually, he finds that punishment is the swift consequence of idleness and misconduct. He may find it impossible to get love and approval, but he can avoid disapproval through obedience, diligent effort, and achievement. As a result, the child can become overly preoccupied with concern to keep busy, to avoid wasting time, and to master and control himself and his environment.[83]

An individual can avoid the anxiety that parental disapproval produces and that comes from thinking about his deeper lying problems by keeping busy in some kind of activity. In this way, anxiety about one's own acceptability to parents may be relieved. Thus, reduction or avoidance of guilt becomes a powerful motivating force that may persist throughout a lifetime.[85]

A 9,1 oriented adult may think these objectives of "proving himself through hard work" to be his own, but in fact, he has taken them from his parents.[86] By adopting his parents' concerns, the child, in a sense, becomes a carbon copy of those who drove him toward personal mastery and achievement, even at the expense of others.[87] In other words, he develops a concern for getting things done, for producing, for proving himself through his own competence.[88] Power to win over others is a test of his strength. To be challenged by his own subordinates is a sign of weakness.

The more 9,1 are the assumptions of parents regarding child rearing, the greater the likelihood that because of their own needs, they compel their children to work, to save, to clean house, to study, and so on—to prove themselves.[89] While all may in themselves be desirable child activities, *it is the way that parents demand them that produces the results being described.* The result is that, 9,1 parents tend to want their boys to be manly, and with the same driving intensity, their girls to be feminine.

Sense of Direction

By the time a person who has been reared according to 9,1 assumptions becomes adult, he has adjusted more or less in the manner just described. Now, rather than feeling pangs or qualms of guilt at his failures to be productive, which are already related to his relationship with his parents, he feels qualms of guilt at his failure to discipline himself, to accomplish the results he had set himself toward. His parents' attitudes "live within him"; they have become his own. As Riesman says, "parents who discipline and provoke guilt-ridden anxieties in children serve effectively to set a gyroscope in motion in a child's early life. The child, as an adult, continues to take his orientation towards life from the gyroscope which had been set many years before."[90]

This kind of inner-directed person is not free to analyze the present situation and to take a studied empirical approach to it.[91] He has the direction that he must take already thrust upon his mind. 9,1 as a source of direction is likely to be inflexible when situations demanding rapid adaptation appear.[92] It is for this reason that in the 9,1 kind of adjustment, deeper lying factors of character and personality structure seem to compel an individual to continue in a direction once taken. Just because the direction in which the person is impelled turns out not to be the best, it does not automatically mean that the direction will be shifted adaptively to meet the awareness of an altered situation. Rather, it is more likely that the individual will try to adapt the situation to be consistent with his own direction.[93]

CONDITIONS AND CONSEQUENCES OF 9,1 ORGANIZATION STYLES

Of importance is a consideration of the circumstances and conditions that lead to and promote widespread utilization within organizations of one managerial orientation over another. Of equal importance is an understanding of the long-term consequences for organization development of the widespread application of one or another, or some combination of the various managerial theories.

Conditions and Circumstances Promoting 9,1

Many organizations of today, especially in the United States and Europe, have evolved from an industrial society founded on the concepts of 9,1 management.[94] Historically, 9,1 assumptions are rooted in cultural attitudes toward work and the nature of man, typified in the extreme as master-slave, baron-serf, etc.[95]

Although considerably altered over the years, managerial attitudes, values and assumptions regarding people remain, to a large extent, embedded in these traditions, which means that much current managerial thinking and practice is guided by explicit and implicit assumptions from the past.

Involved is the question from a 9,1 view of how best to achieve organization purpose(s) through people who are seen to be more or less truculent, unwilling, resistant agents of production.[96] In a word, then, a considerable number of organization practices today are based in past thinking—a quality of thinking that has not yet been seriously challenged by a system that can produce as well and not generate some of the secondary side effects already noted. Argyris questions, however, whether 9,1 thinking is not, in fact, "self-fulfilling" thinking that triggers 9,1 managerial actions. "Directive leadership creates dependence, submissiveness, and conformity. Under these conditions, subordinates will tend to be afraid to use their initiative. Consequently, the superior will tend to fill in the vacuum with directive leadership. We now have a self-fulfilling prophecy."[97]

Significant factors such as changing social values, widespread increase in the level of general education, and unionization, have begun to shift management thinking in a different direction than 9,1. Yet, until a theory of management is found that can do better than 9,1, it is likely that organizations which have a history of 9,1 management will not seek vigorously for more effective alternatives. In this connection, it is widely recognized that management *can* achieve high production results by 9,1 methods.[98]

What are some of the conditions that promote and maintain 9,1 concepts of management within an organization? One is related to education. Despite educational advantages available today, a large segment of our population still lacks the level of competence that would permit them to deal in work situations with a high level of technical knowledge and judgment. One consequence is that management still finds it necessary to exercise a great degree of planning, directing and controlling in the work situation, especially at the lower levels. Technically trained managers plan; up-from-the-ranks management supervise implementation, and others execute. Such an arrangement fosters 9,1 and 1,1.

Related to education is the fact that economic conditions are still such that a large number of people are almost wholly dependent for livelihood upon the work situation. Because of their limited skills and as a result of little fluidity in the work market, they are compelled to endure 9,1 close supervision of the kind often found in the lower reaches of organizations.[99] Of course, this situation is less true today than it was only 20 or 30 years ago.

Also, a related consideration is the fact that if mass

production is to be achieved efficiently, the need is for managements to simplify jobs into routine and simple segments. This need sustains the more general necessity described—to plan, direct, control and to coordinate the activities of workers who are performing low-level jobs. In order to adequately control such large numbers of workers in geographically dispersed organizations, it becomes even more necessary to centralize and move higher into the hierarchy of the organization the responsibilities for planning and coordination.

Another factor that promotes 9,1 is the keen competition between industrial organizations. As a result there is an even greater pressure today for tighter, more efficient controls over organization performance.

All of these make 9,1 a common style of management in a competitive industrial society.

Long-Term Consequences of 9,1 Management

Detailed analyses are available concerning the organizational consequences of 9,1 management. It would not be worthwhile to repeat them here except by way of summary.

Many of the long-term consequences of 9,1 already have come to fruition during this generation. The greatest of these has been unionization.[100] This is not to say that unionization in and of itself is a sole result of 9,1 management. But win-lose struggles between unions and managements frequently center on aspects of 9,1 management that are resisted and resented by wage personnel. Another consequence is that management's inability to cope effectively with its own problems of competition and the economic problems of the nation, continue to lead to more and more government intervention and control.

The gradually increasing skills and knowledges of people frequently fail to be tapped for their full potential under 9,1 long term. This could result in full advantage not being realized from managerial competence.

The most general, yet far-reaching, impact of 9,1 is the gradual shift of many working and managerial persons in the direction of a 1,1 accommodation to organization work.[101] As human performance potential increases but is not utilized, the greater is the shift to 1,1.[102]

SUMMARY

In this chapter the 9,1 style of managing people has been examined. Under 9,1 managerial assumptions, people are regarded as instruments of production.

Supervision of production under a 9,1 orientation places heavy emphasis on task and job requirements, on a "produce or perish" philosophy. People are bent to fit the job and are more or less disregarded except as they demonstrate themselves to be tools of production. The use of hierarchical power, in the authority-obedience sense, is the basis of control. One-to-one boss-subordinate relationships are the key linkages within the system. Human relationships and interactions are minimized except as work dictates the flow of orders and information through the system.

The relationship between a manager and his subordinates is based on the exercise of authority and obedience. Subordinates are for the purpose of implementing plans assigned to them. This they are expected to do with unquestioning obedience. Little concern is given to the development of subordinates or to communicating with them beyond issuing instructions or procedural changes.

When conflict erupts between subordinates, the 9,1 style is to suppress it because of the effect conflict can have on work. If the conflict is between peers, or with one's boss, the goal is to win.

The 9,1 motto is, "Nice guys finish last."

References

1. In their early work with small groups, Bales and others identified two distinct roles assumed by various members in problem-solving groups—"task" role and "social" role. Both sets of role behavior are rarely observed in the actions of any one individual, *i. e.*, a person is either concerned for the task (production) or his concern is for the social (people) aspects of a group's activities—seldom both *at the same time*. Representative experimental work and discussion of theory is contained in R. F. Bales, The Equilibrium Problem in Small Groups. In T. Parsons, R. F. Bales & E. A. Shils,

Working Papers in the Theory of Action. Glencoe, Ill.: Free Press, 1953, 111-161. (Also abridged in A. P. Hare, E. F. Borgatta & R. F. Bales (Eds.), *Small Groups.* New York: Knopf, 1955, 424-456.) Also, see Slater, P. E. Role Differentiations in Small Groups. *American Sociological Review,* 20, 1955, 300-310; Bales, R. F. & Slater, P. Role Differentiation. In T. Parsons, R. F. Bales, *et al. Family, Socialization, and Interaction Process.* Glencoe, Ill.: Free Press, 1955; Slater, P. E. Role Differentiations in Small Groups. *American Sociological Review,* 20, 1955, 300-310.

2. A recent study by Moment and Zaleznik is in line with the early work of Bales, *et al.* In addition to Task (Technical) and Social roles, Moment and Zaleznik identify a detached, sometimes passive, sometimes hostile and competitive role (Underchosen) and a Fusion role (Star), the latter being high on both task and "congeniality." *Stars* demonstrated a higher combination of task *and* socially relevant behavior. However, a partial dichotomy rather than an integration (Fusion) in the two concerns is suggested in some aspects for the roles of the Stars: "Satisfaction comes from engagement in the social-technical process in a way that *balances* progress toward improvement with the disruptions of change." p. 121. Moment, D. & Zaleznik, A. *Role Development and Interpersonal Competence.* Boston: Harvard University, 1963. (Italics, *i. e., balances,* ours).

As will be seen in Chapter 6, this book, a split between production and people concerns is still assumed under *5,5* and is contrasted with an *integration* of these two concerns under *9,9.* (Chapter 7). Since 5,5 (balancing), *per se,* is not treated by Moment and Zaleznik, it appears that both 5,5 and 9,9 (integration) fall into the category of "Stars."

3. Maier, N. R. F. *Psychology in Industry.* (2nd Ed.). Boston: Houghton, 1955, 139-140.

4. Marrow, A. J. *Making Management Human.* New York: McGraw-Hill, 1957, 73.

5. Barnard, C. I. *The Functions of the Executive.* Cambridge: Harvard University, 1938, 67; Urwick, L. *The Elements of Administration.* New York: Harper, 1953, 36-39.

6. Davis, R. C. *The Fundamentals of Top Management.* New York: Harper, 1951, 14-15, 244, 281, 294; Newman, L. E. Some Philosophies of Management. *Advanced Management,* 24, (7), 1959, 6-8.

7. The needs of the "formal" organization for production and the needs of individuals for mature growth and "self-actualization" are treated extensively by Argyris. Production and people needs are viewed as incongruent. See Argyris, C. *Personality and Organization.* New York: Harper, 1957; Argyris, C. *Understanding Organizational Behavior.* Homewood, Ill.: Dorsey, 1960; and, Argyris, C. *Interpersonal Competence and Organizational Effectiveness.* Homewood, Ill.: Dorsey, 1962.

"Theory X" as discussed by McGregor also provides a fundamental analysis of 9,1 assumptions and organizational behavior. McGregor, D. *The Human Side of Enterprise.* New York: McGraw-Hill, 1960 (see esp. pp. 33-43.). McGregor sees a need to integrate the needs of organizations and the needs of people. (See McGregor's concept of "Theory Y." McGregor, D., op. cit., 45-57.)

8. *The Managerial Grid: A Self-Examination of Managerial Styles.* Austin, Tex.: Scientific Methods, Inc., 1962.

9. Riesman, D. *The Lonely Crowd.* New Haven: Yale University, 1961, 111-126. (The behavior and concerns of "inner-directed" "Men at Work" as described by Riesman is characteristic of 9,1 assumptions and actions in the organization and society.)

10. David C. McClelland and his associates have investigated in great depth the personal behavior and characteristics, latent motives, early childhood origins, and socialization processes characteristic of individuals with high needs for achievement *(n ach).* Those individuals with high achievement needs, high fear of failure and relatively low regard for social interaction are most like the 9,1 behavior patterns described here. Theory and research investigations are contained in D. C. McClelland, J. W. Atkinson, R. A. Clark, & E. L. Lowell, *The Achievement Motive.* New York: Appleton-Century-Crofts, 1953; J. W. Atkinson (Ed.), *Motives in Fantasy, Action, and Society.* Princeton: D. Van Nostrand, 1958; and, D. C. McClelland, *The Achieving Society.* Princeton: D. Van Nostrand, 1961.

Moment, D. & Zaleznik, A., *op. cit.,* 122-123, also capture the orientations and actions of the 9,1 managerial style in their description of the "Technical Specialist."

11, Taylor, F. W. *The Principles of Scientific Management.* New York: Harper, 1947. (Argyris and McGregor have examined extensively the concept of authority and obedience in the work situation. Argyris, C., *op. cit.,* 1957; McGregor, D., *op. cit.,* 15-32. See also Roddick, P. M. *Authority, Responsibility, Leadership. Advanced Managment,* January, 1960, 12-15.)

12. Davis, R. C., *op. cit.,* 16, 144; Urwick, L., *op. cit.*

Guest provides a detailed account of the 9,1 use of hierarchy in his description of "Plant Y" under a former plant manager during the plant's "Period of Disintegration." Guest, R. H. *Organizational Change: The Effect of Successful Leadership.* Homewood, Ill.: Dorsey, 1962, 17-37 (see esp. p. 23).

13. The work of Likert, Katz, Kahn, Maccoby, Morse and others at the Institute for Social Research, University of Michigan, has brought to light many of the basic assumption underlying the concerns and actions of "Job-Centered" supervisors (9,1). A comprehensive review and summation of this group's experimental investigations is contained in Likert's *New Patterns of Management.* New York: McGraw-Hill, 1961. (See esp. p. 20.) Also see McGregor, D., *op cit.,* 33-34.

14. Zaleznik, A., Christensen, C. R. & Roethlisberger, F. J. *The Motivation, Productivity, and Satisfaction of Workers: A Prediction Study.* Boston: Harvard University, 1958, 415.

15. Freud, S. *Group Psychology and the Analysis of the Ego.* New York: Liveright, 1949; Menninger, W. C., A Prescription for Executive Mental Health; *Advanced Management,* 10, 60, 16-17.

16. Murphy, L. Key Questions on General Management Tasks. *Advanced Management,* 24, (10), 1959, 9-11.

17. Brown, M. *Effective Work Management.* N.Y.: Macmillan, 1960.

18. Marrow, A. J., *op. cit.*, 75-78; Argyris, C., *op. cit.*, 1957, 79-80; Maier, N. R. F. & Hayes, J. J. *Creative Management.* New York: Wiley, 1962, 5.

19. Bellows, R., Gilson, T. G. & Odiorne, G. S. *Executive Skills: Their Dynamics and Development.* Englewood Cliffs, N. J.: Prentice-Hall, 1962, 6; Guest, R. H., *op. cit.*, 29-30, 62.

20. Whyte, W. F. *Money and Motivation.* New York: Harper, 1955, 3-5.

21. Bellows, R., et al, *op. cit.*, 76-77; Whyte, W. F., *op. cit.*, 3.

22. Argyris, C., *op. cit.*, 1957.

23. In the early experimental work of Lewin, Lippitt and White (although with groups of children) goal setting (the imposition of group tasks by the leader) under the "authoritarian" leadership style, corresponds to the 9,1 approach. The reactions of subordinates (the children) are discussed. This early work also led to increased experimental work and better understanding of the concepts of group locomotion, productivity, cohesiveness, creativity, the effects of varying degrees of participation, as well as individual commitment, involvement, conflict and related personal and interpersonal phenomena. (See Lewin, K., Lippitt, R. & White, R. K. Patterns of Aggressive Behavior in Experimentally Created "Social Climates." *Journal of Social Psychology*, X, 1939, 271-299; Lippitt, R. An Experimental Study of Authoritarian and Democratic Group Atmospheres. *Studies in Topological and Vector Psychology, I. University of Iowa Studies in Child Welfare*, 16, 1940; Lippitt, R. Field Theory and Experiment in Social Psychology: Authoritarian and Democratic Group Atmospheres. *American Journal of Sociology*, XLV, 1939, 26-49; and, Lippitt, R. & White R. K. An Experimental Study of Leadership and Group Life. In E. E. Maccoby, T. M. Newcomb & E. L. Hartley (Eds.), *Readings in Social Psychology.* (3rd Ed.). New York: Holt, 1958, 496-511; Lewin, K. Group Decision and Social Change. In E. E. Maccoby, et al, (Eds.), *op. cit.*, 197-219.)

24. Whyte, W. F., *op. cit.*, 55.

25. Granick, D. *The Red Executive.* New York: Doubleday, 1961. (See esp. pp. 229-234.)

26. Roy, D. Quota Restrictions and Goldbricking in a Machine Shop. *American Journal of Sociology*, 1952, 427-442; Whyte, W. F., *op. cit.*, 11-49.

27. For a further discussion and the citation of related writings, see Argyris, C. *op. cit.*, 1957.

28. Likert, R., *op. cit.*, 106-107; Taylor, F. W., *op. cit.*

29. Taylor, F. W., *op. cit.;* Cartwright, D. & Zander, A. *Group Dynamics: Research and Theory.* Evanston, Ill.: Row, Peterson, 1953, 420

30. Likert, R., *op. cit.*, 106.

31. Mooney, J. D. & Reiley, A. C. *Onward Industry.* New York: Harper, 1931, 31; Urwick, L., *op. cit.;* Argyris, C., *op. cit.*, 60-61.

32. Tannenbaum, R. & Schmidt, W. H. How to Choose a Leadership Pattern. *Harvard Business Review*, 36, (2), 95-98. (The pattern or range of alternative leadership behavior available to a boss is

described. In terms of the *Grid*, this continuum runs from 9,1—
"boss-centered"—through varying degrees of 5,5 to 1,9—"subordinate-
centered." 1,1 and 9,9 are not considered as alternative modes of
leadership behavior.)

33. Likert, R. *op. cit.*, 107.

34. Guest, R. H., *op. cit.*, 20-21. Also see the work of Lewin, *et al*,
previously cited.

35. Experimental investigations have been conducted to investigate
the impact of various patterns of organization and networks of
communications on the behavior, reactions, productivity and satisfaction of members in the hierarchy. The results of this work are
significant in understanding the effectiveness of alternative managerial approaches to the use of hierarchy and authority. (See
Leavitt, H. J. Some Effects of Certain Communication Patterns on
Group Performance. *Journal of Abnormal & Social Psychology*, 46,
1951, 38-50; Kelley, H. H. Communication in Experimentally Created
Hierarchies. *Human Relations*, 4, 1951, 39-56; Heise, G. A. & Miller,
G. A. Problem Solving by Small Groups Using Various Communication Nets. *Journal of Abnormal & Social Psychology*, 46, 1951, 327-
336; and Bavelas, A. Communication Patterns in Task-Oriented
Groups. *Journal of the Acoustical Society of America*, 22, 1950,
725-730. Also in D. Cartwright & A. Zander (Eds.), *Group Dynamics: Research and Theory*. Evanston, Ill.: Row, Peterson, 1956,
493-506.

36. Guion, R. M. Some Definitions of Morale. In E. A. Fleishman
(Ed.), *Studies in Personnel and Industrial Psychology*. Homewood,
Ill.: Dorsey, 1961, 301-304.

37. McNair, M. P. Thinking Ahead: What Price Human Relations?
Harvard Business Review, 35, (2), 1957, 15-39.

38. Some of the relevant experimental work in communications
was cited previously in f. 35.

39. Guest, R. H., *op. cit.*, 17-37.

40. Blake, R. R., Shepard, H. A. & Mouton, J. S. *Managing Intergroup Conflict in Industry*. Houston: Gulf Publishing Company, 1964.

41. One of the early studies designed to measure the disruptive
effects of interpersonal competitiveness was conducted by Deutsch.
Also investigated was the facilitative effect of members perceiving
themselves to be interdependent in cooperative effort. Deutsch, M.
An Experimental Study of Effects of Cooperation and Competition
Upon Group Process. *Human Relations*, 2, 1949, 199-231. (In Chapter
7, more will be said concerning the effect of feelings of shared
goals and responsibilities on group productivity.)

42. Simmel, G. *Conflict* and *The Web of Group Affiliation*. (Translated by K. H. Wolff & R. Bendix.) Glencoe, Ill.: Free Press, 1955.
57-85.

43. Boulding, K. E. *Conflict and Defense*. New York: Harper,
1962, 309; Metcalf, H. C.; Urwick, L. *Dynamic Administration: The
Collected Papers of Mary Parker Follett*. New York: Harper, 1940,
31-32.

44. Thibaut, J. W. & Kelley, H. H. *The Social Psychology of
Groups*. New York: Wiley, 1959, 105.

45. Boulding, K. E., *op. cit.*, 313.

46. Riesman, D., *op. cit.*, 111-113.

47. McMurry, R. N. The Case for Benevolent Autocracy. *Harvard Business Review*, 36, (1), 1958, 82-90. Also in I. L. Heckmann, Jr. & S. G. Huneryager (Eds.), *Human Relations in Management*. Cincinnati: South-Western, 1960, 106.

48. Deutsch, M., *op. cit.*

49. Lippitt, R. & White, R. K. The "Social Climate" of Children's Groups. In R. G. Barker, J. Kounin & H. Wright (Eds.) *Child Behavior and Development*. New York: McGraw-Hill, 1953, 485-508; White, R. & Lippitt, R. Leader Behavior and Member Reaction in Three "Social Climates." In D. Cartwright & A. Zander (Eds.), *op. cit.*, 1953, 585-611; Mowrer, O. H. Authoritarinaism *vs.* Self-Government in the Management of Children's Aggressive Reactions as Preparation for Citizenship in a Democracy. *Journal of Social Psychology*, 10, 1939, 121-126.

50. Lewin, *et al*, *op. cit.*, 1939; Boulding, K. E., *op. cit.*, 309; Simmel, G., *op. cit.*, 113-114.

51. Blake, R. R. Psychology and the Crisis of Statesmanship. *The American Psychologist*, 14, 1959, 87-94. Also in W. G. Bennis, K. D. Benne & R. Chin (Eds.), *The Planning of Change*. New York: Holt, Rinehard & Winston, 1951, 466-477.

52. Simmel, G., *op. cit.*, 113-114; Blake, R. R. & Mouton, J. S. Reactions to Intergroup Competition Under Win-Lose Conditions. *Management Science*, 7, 1961, 420-435.

53. Thibaut, J. An Experimental Study of the Cohesiveness of Underprivileged Groups. *Human Relations*, 1950, 3, 251-278; Deutsch, M., *op. cit.;* Sherif, M. & Sherif, C. *An Outline of Social Psychology*. (Rev. Ed.). New York: Harper, 1956, 280-332; Blake, R. R. & Mouton, J. S. The Intergroup Dynamics of Win-Lose Conflict and Problem-Solving Collaboration in Union-Management Relations. In M. Sherif (Ed.), *Intergroup Relations and Leadership*. New York: Wiley, 1962, 94-140. (Laboratory studies and extensive field observations by the authors and others have shown how the "loser" dynamic can become a critical barrier to vertical and horizontal communications, problem solving and cooperation.)

54. Roy, D., *op. cit.;* Whyte, W. F., *op. cit.*, 11-49; Argyris, C. The Individual and Organization Structure. In K. Davis & W. Scott (Eds.), *Reading in Human Relations*. New York: McGraw-Hill, 1959, 60-68.

55. March, J. G. & Simon, H. A. *Organizations*. New York: Wiley, 1958, 12-13.

56. Fromm, E. The Creative Attitude. In H. H. Anderson (Ed.), *Creativity and Its Cultivation*. New York: 1959, 48.

57. Anderson, H. H. Creativity as Personality Development. In H. H. Anderson (Ed.), *op. cit.*, 131.

58. Roy, D., *op. cit.;* Whyte, W. F., *op. cit.;* Argyris, C., *op. cit.*, 1957, 95-102; Tannenbaum, R., Weschler, I. R. & Massarik, F. *Leadership and Organization: A Behavioral Science Approach.* New

York: McGraw-Hill, 1961, 81; Maier, N. R. F. & Hayes, J. J., *op. cit.*, 32.

59. Lesieur, F. G. (Ed.). *The Scanlon Plan*. New York: Wiley, 1958.

60. Stotland, E. Peer Groups and Reactions to Power Figures. In D. Cartwright (Ed.), *Studies in Social Power*. Ann Arbor: Institute for Social Research, 1959, 53-68.

61. Simon, H. A. *Administrative Behavior*. New York: Macmillan, 1947, 127; Festinger, L. An Analysis of Compliant Behavior. In M. Sherif & M. O. Wilson (Eds.), *Group Relations at the Crossroads*. New York: Harper, 1953.

62. Stouffer, S. A., Suchman, E. A., De Vinney, L. C., Star, S. A., & Williams, R. M., Jr. *The American Soldier*. Princeton: Princeton University Press, Vol. I, 1949, 410-429.

63. Argyris, C. Understanding Human Behavior in Organizations: One Viewpoint. In M. Haire (Ed.), *Modern Organization Theory*. New York: Wiley, 1959, 143; Argyris, C. *Understanding Organizational Behavior*. Homewood, Ill.: Dorsey, 1960, 17-18; McMurry, R. N., *op. cit.*

64. Tannenbaum, F. *A Philosophy of Labor*. New York: Knopf, 1951.

65. Tannenbaum, F., *Ibid.*,

66. Drucker, P. F. *The New Society*. New York: Harper, 1950, Ch. 22.

67. Drucker, P. F., *op. cit.*

68. Orth, C. D., III. More Productivity from Engineers. *Harvard Business Review*, 35, March-April, 1957, 54-55.

69. Fryer, D. H., Feinberg, M. R., & Zalkind, S. S. *Developing People in Industry*. New York: Harper, 1956, 30-35.

70. McGregor, D. An Uneasy Look at Performance Appraisal. *Harvard Business Review*, 35, May-June, 1957, 89-94.

71. For a comprehensive study, analysis and research into a personality syndrome, characteristic of many 9,1 aspects of behavior, see T. W. Adorno, E. Frenkel-Brunswick, D. J. Levinson & R. N. Sanford, *The Authoritarian Personality*. New York: Harper, 1950.

72. Bass, B. M. *Leadership, Psychology, and Organizational Behavior*. New York: Harper, 1960.

73. See Moment, D. & Zaleznik, A., *op. cit.*, for a description of 9,1 (Technical Specialist) personal behavior and characteristics.

74. Miner, J. B. Personality and Ability Factors in Sales Performance. *Journal of Applied Psychology*, 46, 1962, 6-13.

75. McClelland, D. C., *et al, op. cit.*, 1953; Riesman, D., *op. cit.*

76. Moment, D. & Zaleznik, A., *op. cit.*, 122-123.

77. Rogers, C. R. Toward a Theory of Creativity. In H. H. Anderson (Ed.), *op. cit.*, 75,

78. Frenkel-Brunswick, E. A Study of Prejudice in Children. *Human Relations*, 1, 1948, 295-306.

79. McClelland, D. C. The Use of Measures of Human Motivation in the Study of Society. In J. W. Atkinson (Ed.), *op. cit.*, 518-552; Child, I. L., Storm, T. & Veroff, J. Achievement Themes in Folk Tales Related to Sociolization Practice. In J. W. Atkinson (Ed.), *op. cit.*, 479-492.

80. McClelland, D. C., *et al*, *op. cit.*, 1953.

81. Barker, R. G., Dembo, T. & Lewin, K. Frustration and Regression: An Experiment with Young Children. *University of Iowa Student Child Welfare*, 18, (1), 1941; Meyers, C. E. The Effect of Conflicting Authority on the Child. *University of Iowa Study in Child Welfare*, 20, 1944; Bishop, B. M. Mother-Child Interaction and the Social Behavior of Children, *Psychological Monograph*, 65, (11), 1951; Watson, G. Some Personality Differences in Children Related to Strict or Permissive Parental Discipline. *Journal of Psychology*, 44, 1957, 227-249; Baldwin, A. L. Socialization and the Parent-Child Relationship, *Child Development*, 19, 1948, 127-136; Whiting, J. W. M. & Child, I. L. *Child Training and Personality*. New Haven: Yale University, 1953.

82. For a comprehensive review and discussion of experimental work in child-rearing practices as related to overt 9,1 behavior as well as other orientations to be discussed, see Sears, R. R., Maccoby, E. E. & Levin, H. *Patterns of Child Rearing*. Evanston, Ill.: Row, Peterson, 1957.

83. Rosen, B. C. The Achievement Syndrome: A Psychocultural Dimension of Social Stratification. *American Sociological Review*, 21, 1956, 203-211; Riesman, D., *op. cit.*, 40-50.

84. Slater, P. E. Parental Role Differentiation. *American Journal of Sociology*, 67, (3), 1961, 296-311.

85. Gordon, J. E. *Personality and Behavior*. New York: Macmillan, 1963, 292-293.

86. Shibutani, T. *Society and Personality*. Englewood Cliffs, N. J.: Prentice-Hall, 1961, 513.

87. McClelland, D. C., *et al*, *op. cit.*, 1953, 275-318.

88. Rosen, B. C., *op. cit.*

89. Winterbottom, M. R. The Relation of Childhood Training in Independence to Achievement Motivation. In J. W. Atkinson (Ed.), *op. cit.*, 453-478; Hoffman, L. W., Rosen, S. & Lippitt, R. Parental Coerciveness, Child Autonomy, and Child's Role at School. *Sociometry*, 23, 1960, 15-22.

90. Riesman, D., *op. cit.*,

91. Riesman, D., *op. cit.*, 47.

92. Erikson, E. H. Industry Versus Inferiority. In M. L. Haimowitz & N. R. Haimowitz (Eds.), *Human Development*. New York: Crowell, 1960, 249.

93. Gordon, J. E., *op. cit.*, 399-400.

94. Taylor, F. W., *op. cit.;* Fayol, H. *General and Industrial Management*. New York: Pitman, 1949; Mooney, J. D. & Reiley, A. C., *op. cit.;* Anderson, E. A. The Meaning of Scientific Management. *Harvard Business Review*, 27, 1949, 678-692; Gellerman, S. W.

People, Problems and Profits. New York: McGraw-Hill, 1960, 164. (Also see Urwick, L., *op. cit.*)

95. Simon, H. A., *op. cit.*, 127; McGregor, D., *op. cit.*, 1960, 25; Broom, L. & Selznick, P. *Sociology.* (3rd Ed.). New York: Harper, 1963, 627-635.

96. Blansfield, M. G. The Challenge of Executive Appraisal. *Advanced Management*, April, 1960, 20-24.

97. Argyris, C. In Defense of Laboratory Education. *Training Directors Journal*, 17, (10), 1963, 29.

98. Katz, D., Maccoby, N. & Morse, N. C. *Productivity, Supervision, and Morale in an Office Situation.* Part I. Ann Arbor: Institute for Social Research, University of Michigan, 1950; Gibb, C. A. An Experimental Approach to the Study of Leadership. *Occupational Psychology*, 25, 1951, 233-248; Likert, R. Measuring Organizational Performance. In K. Davis & W. Scott (Eds.), *op. cit.*, 276-277; Likert, R., *op. cit.*, 1961, 59.

99. Goode, W. J. & Fowler, I. Incentive Factors in a Low Morale Plant. *American Sociological Review*, 14, 1949, 618-624.

100. McGregor, D. Conditions of Effective Leadership in the Industrial Organization. *Journal of Consulting Psychology*, 8, 1944, 55-63; McGregor, D., *op. cit.*, 1960; Argyris, C., *op. cit.*, 1957, 103-107.

101. Riecken, H. W. Some Problems of Consensus Development. *Rural Sociology*, 17, 1952, 245-252; Argyris, C., *op. cit.*, 1957, 77-100.

102. Thibaut, J. W. & Kelley, H. H., *op. cit.*, 173.

CHAPTER FOUR

The 1,9 Managerial Style

In the upper left hand corner of the Grid is the 1,9 managerial orientation. Here a low functional concern for production, *1*, is coupled with high concern for people, *9*. As with 9,1, the 1,9 managerial orientation also is rooted in the assumption that production requirements are contrary to the needs of people.[1] To a manager with a 1,9 style, however, the attitudes and feelings of people *are* important. They are valuable in their own right. They come first. Within this context, conditions are arranged so that personal, social and welfare needs can be met.[2]

MANAGEMENT UNDER 1,9

When asked to describe his hierarchical responsibilities, a person operating under 1,9 assumptions is likely to use the same *words* as those the manager operating under 9,1 might use. He would say that his job is to plan, direct and control the activities of *his* subordinates. His aim as a manager, however, is to avoid pressuring for production at a rate higher than that which would win acceptance from organizational members. He leads by following. By deemphasizing production, the 1,9 approach avoids some of the conflict that arises from production decisions that disturb people.[3] A deeper 1,9 attitude is seen in the feeling that, "You can't *push* people for production because if you do, they balk and resist," or "You can lead a horse to water, but you can't make him drink." "When people have turned against you, they are in trouble and you are, too." How he plans and directs subordinates and the way in which follow-up takes place are briefly outlined below.[4]

Planning. "I give broad assignments to my subordinates and convey my confidence by saying, 'I'm sure you know how to do this and that you will do it well.' "

Work Execution. "I see my people frequently and encourage them to visit with me as their time permits. My door is always open. My goal is to see to it that they are able to get the things they want. That's the way to encourage people."

Follow-up. "I hold a meeting with those who are on the job where I place emphasis on congratulating the group as well as individuals. We have fun and when we get down to business our wrap-up sessions usually revolve around why we did as well as we did do and how we can help things to go as smoothly or more so in the future. Criticism rarely helps. My motto is 'Don't say anything if you can't say something nice.' "

The 1,9 managerial style, in other words, focuses on how to arrange conditions of work which will permit people to fit them with comfort, ease and security.[5] Under the 1,9 set of assumptions, it is felt that organizational demands for production often are harsh, overdemanding and unnecessary. When his people become disturbed, the manager with a 1,9 orientation also becomes disturbed. To counter-balance the demands of the organization, the manager can lighten work conditions by emphasizing the positive aspects of work, or by giving a bonus of some sort.[6] Informal conversation, a joke, an understanding pat on the back, a smile, coffee together—all help the task to pass a little easier and to make life a little more enjoyable.[7]

1,9 DIRECTION AND CONTROL

When it comes to actually directing the performance of subordinates, a manager who employs the 1,9 approach frequently adopts one of two ways. This particular phase of managerial responsibility may be less tasteful than other aspects of work, but subordinates, of necessity, look to him to establish conditions of work.

One attitude toward work direction that the 1,9 managerial approach might adopt can be described in the phrase, "I lead rather than push." (What he means is, "I find out how they want it and then help it happen that way.") The assumption here is that people should be shown rather than commanded. They should be supported and aided in their efforts rather than goaded.[8] This is evidenced where a supervisor, by taking over for them and doing it himself, helps subordinates in those difficult parts of the job for which he (the supervisor) has more technical knowledge or skill. It would be out of character for this manager to leave his subordinates to struggle for themselves or to push them to find out how. Under these 1,9 conditions, a manager insures willing and appreciative followers. (As they might say, "While I can't really respect him, I do like him.")

In contrast to 9,1, where accountability and responsibility are demanded of subordinates, with the 1,9 approach a manager gives warmth, acceptance and understanding.[9] His hallmark is to help. In return, he expects to receive devoted loyalty and, therefore, to be able to avoid difficulties connected with irresponsibility. Believing that devoted people will do what is needed out of their own desires and without being harshly directed, he is inclined to feel that there is little reason to be concerned with accountability and responsibility. In this way, matters that are of such great concern to a manager with a 9,1 orientation appear of little significance under the 1,9 orientation.[10]

Another way in which a manager with a 1,9 style deals with his subordinates is through gentle persuasion.[11] An inflexible order may become an apologetic request. A favor is promised in return for the inconvenience incurred. He avoids rejection by coating with sugar those required inconveniences that cannot be prevented.

Mistakes and Violations

Under 1,9, a supervisor might react to mistakes in obtaining production by saying, "Don't take it too hard. We all make mistakes. Maybe we'll have better luck next time. Are you going to the show tonight?" The assumption here is that harrassment, pressure and disciplinary action only stir up subordinates. They produce tension, and, in the long run, cause more errors.[12] Rather than calling attention to poor performance or the way in which it was done, the supervisor believes that if people are not crossed, they will correct themselves. Turn the topic away from the disagreeable toward the more pleasant. "Every cloud has a silver lining."

Thus, a 1,9 manager might say, "My approach to errors is to avoid blaming or placing responsibility, but to support the person by saying something like, "Well, I know you did the best you could. Don't worry. Things will turn out for the best." His motto is, "Forgive and forget." The blame is not placed on the person, even though the problem may be seen to be a consequence of his individual action. Rather, the assumption is that either people naturally want to do what is right so it is only disturbing to put emphasis on error, or that personal antagonisms might be stirred if he censures or rejects. The general result is "to accentuate the positive and eliminate the negative."[13]

Not causing embarrassment or resentment carries over into concern for rules, policies, etc. Under 1,9, policies and procedures are not rigid fences that you must force people to stay within. Rather, they are viewed as guidelines for action rather than as fixed requirements. In this way, you do not have to keep checking on people. Furthermore, when the deviation is slight or the policy not too important, the supervisor with a 1,9 orientation overlooks the action. ("Everyone else is winking, too.") If the violation is more severe, he is likely to feel that the person will usually straighten up, and a gentle reminder helps him know you want him to.

As a result, under 1,9, there frequently is a "looseness" in the organization in terms of formal aspects of performance such as arrival time, extended coffee breaks, social visiting, lunch hours, and an occasional absence, etc.

It can be said that the manager who manages according to 1,9 assumptions is anxious to be nice to people. If he should make a decision or issue an order which his group does not like, he probably would try to pull it back, or if impossible, to follow through with a "soft-sell,"[14] or then to persuade by encouraging sympathetic understanding of his problem. If these approaches meet failure he is likely to ask their understanding and compliance by shifting the problem. It becomes "what his boss wants." Using the 1,9 approach a manager must keep making peace with people at all levels in order to win support.[15] Bosses in particular can make it difficult. Frequently, the demands placed by a boss on a subordinate, who practices 1,9, are for more drive, greater output—higher production. How this manager copes with this dilemma will be discussed further on. For now, it might be said that 9,1 attitudes are abhorred by a 1,9 oriented manager, and vice versa, and each threatens the other.

THE CONCEPT OF GOALS UNDER 1,9

Goal setting under 1,9 takes an interesting turn. In its application, management, by goal setting, produces a democratic atmosphere which tends to be of a pseudo character.

To impose quotas or goals on others is, from a 1,9 angle, objectionable. Yet, to "manage by objectives" is attractive, because then you do not have to apply close supervision. The aim, then, is to get the people to set general goals which everyone can support.[16] Even more important is the consideration that self-set personal goals can guide the individual's own effort. Free and unguided discussion at all management levels is the preferred method for achieving the results being discussed.

By this way, a number of organization-wide goals that everyone can embrace are identified. Trending toward the lowest common denominator, they often take the form of improving organization by developing a program for getting better management-at-all-levels, or improving community relations. The goals set tend to be quite general, but everyone can support them.[17]

Personal goals under such an approach run the full gamut from learning to listen to others, to taking a grammar improvement or public speaking program at the local high school. When such goals are set, the supervisor can constructively offer help and encouragement.[18] With such shared positive motivation for improvement, a basis for positive thinking has been set. There is no reason people should have misunderstandings or fights.

The pseudo quality present here is from getting involvement and participation of personnel around issues that are not directly work connected. As a result there is no strong sense of "stake" in organization success and "how to make it happen."

BOSS-SUBORDINATE RELATIONSHIPS UNDER 1,9

1,9 stands in rather dramatic contrast to 9,1 in its orientation to boss-subordinate relationships. Whereas the password of 9,1 is isolation of subordinates from one another, in 1,9 the key is *togetherness*. The person operating according to a 1,9 managerial orientation is more likely to see his work unit as *one big happy family*. Boss-subordinate relationships are essentially one to all, rather than one to one.[19]

The boss with a 1,9 orientation sees subordinates as his most important product. He will go all out to see that they are satisfied with working conditions and with him. "Subordinates are important. My job is to provide for them and keep their spirits up."

If subordinates do become unhappy with work arrangements, diligent effort is made to meet their complaints. Use is made of breaks in the daily routine to lighten the atmosphere. Whereas the controlled coffee break of a 9,1 manager is tolerated by him because of its contribution to decreasing fatigue and thus increasing output, the 1,9 attitude is that coffee breaks provide a friendly, sociable basis for people to get together and to get away from performance tensions. The extended coffee break is likely to be found in a 1,9 atmosphere. Social dinners, parties, and picnics also contribute to *esprit de corps*.[20]

Office arrangements and decor, such as the accountant example described under 9,1, are fruitful media for analyzing grid orientations. Another example—the opposite extreme of the accountant example—that captures the essence of the 1,9 follows.

This particular office, in size and level of responsibility within its organization, is quite similar to that of the accountant section in the earlier example. The particular manager supervises the work of a unit in a large records section of an old-line, blue-chip organization. Over the years the tradition has become that managers control their own office furniture, desk arrangements, coffee breaks, lunches, etc.

Contrast the following description with that of the previous 9,1 example. It was one of efficiency, discipline, and near automation in the mechanical way in which work flowed and communications passed from one person to another.

Fourteen people work in this office, *including* the manager. There are no cubicles, partitions or screens. Floral decorations or pots of ivy sit on six of the desks. A radio is on another. When it is on, it is turned low to "not disturb others." It only becomes a center of attention during the World Series, the Memorial '500', the Kentucky Derby, and similar special attractions like a space shot. On ordinary days, though, it is set on soft music. (Piped music sometimes is 1,9, also.[21] "It helps people take their minds *off* their jobs!")

A coffee maker which operates all day, everyday, stands in one corner. Pastries and doughnuts are delivered each morning. In this way, the work day begins on a light note as people drift in for their coffee and sweets. For many, this is breakfast. Around ten, pairs and threes drift off to the cafeteria for 30 or 40 minute coffee breaks. The informal rule is "no work discussions during the breaks."

The usual work day, in other words, is at a comfortable pace. Few crises arise in an otherwise repetitive routine. Those that do are easily scheduled into the section's activities by the manager. If there are extra work demands, he pitches in wherever he is needed. He is one of "them."

"Many departments here have a high turnover," he once remarked. "We don't. Most of my people have been with me for four years or more. He has been with the company 33 years. He's been with me for twelve."

In a short time this section's duties will be assumed by another. Five can handle the work now assigned fourteen.

Meetings with Subordinates

The person with a 1,9 orientation is more likely to go overboard for groupness, not to achieve work purposes, but for sociability.[22] Members of the group get together for the main purpose of sharing their thoughts. They share thoughts of a non-critical work nature and do discuss, in a manner, routine issues that arise and require to be attended to. But, social relations motivation permeates many activities in the work situation, frequently under the guise of "consulting people to get their views."

As a result of the above, within a 1,9 work setting, the informal group flourishes. Each work nucleus has its own uniformity of opinion and attitude about a wide range of matters. Conformity is valued in order to "get along well" and to be "liked by people."[23] Deviation is likely to cause loss of acceptance.

A supervisor whose managerial assumptions are 1,9 might put it this way:

"Meetings get people together to share ideas. Good relations can be cemented by free discussion. Quick and easy decisions often happen. If disagreement and conflict arise, it is better to table the discussion than to force the issue."

Thus, points of similarity and agreement are brought to the fore under an atmosphere of sweetness and light.[24] Issues which are likely to provoke real disagreement and break up the group are tabled and eventually buried. Decisions are made by the group in most instances, particularly those which are of significance and where the benefit of group support is important.

Attitudes Toward His Boss

The aim of the 1,9 orientation with respect to his boss is in the same vein as his attitudes toward subordinates. Towards his boss, a manager with a 1,9 orientation is "responsive." He does not disagree or take issue. He wants to do what is expected in as good a manner as he can. His own security is increased if he is able to win his boss' support and understanding. He is careful to guard his boss against 'bad' news and to 'play down' or to keep problems that may exist below him quiet.[26] Negatives only create unnecessary tensions and strains in relations. In keeping with this frame of mind, then, the 1,9 approach is, "I try to keep my boss informed periodically . . . I emphasize my group's cooperative efforts and I do not burden him with occasional problems. If a problem needing his attention does arise, I give it to him one piece at a time, so he doesn't get upset. Also, I 'test' him to see when to tell him. It is important to be sure he got up on the right side of the bed."

Creating and Maintaining Morale

Through off-the-cuff chats and counseling with his people, the current state of employee morale is always at his fingertips. He does not need to worry, because it is up.

High morale is ever the focal issue of 1,9 management. When pressures for higher output come from above, the first thought is toward its effect on employee morale. When no other course is open and production must be stepped up, effort is made to ease the impact. But in a showdown, people come first.[27] A manager with a strong 1,9 orientation can be expected to plead the case of his subordinates' plight if things become too tough. His thoughts turn to getting more help, extending the schedule to give more time, etc.

Communication Activities Under 1,9

In the 1,9 managerial style, communication activities would be expected to be intense, with a high level of conversation in the informal system.[28] Communications in the formal system (*i.e.*, orders and reports, etc.) are minimized. Since concern for production is low at 1,9, it seems true that the discussions, scuttlebutt and grapevine of a 1,9 managerial style involve social matters, local politics, and personal elements to the exclusion of production or work-oriented information.[29] Negative attitudes, if they do exist, are driven underground. Rather than expressing antagonism directly, the third party route of "gossip" tends to be the rule. As women playing bridge discovered long ago, it is possible to vent one's frustration concerning a person or her actions, not directly on her but by talking about her to others. In this way, social steam leaks prevent pressure from building up.[30]

Communication upward in the hierarchy is "positive." It is the radarscope concept of "avoiding storms by watching the pips." In other words, to the degree possible, only what is going well is reported.[31]

The manager who runs a 1,9 show is likely to use the "house organ" as a means of highlighting social events, fellowship and other positive bits of communication that give people a sense of belonging and organization identification.[32] It brings to the attention of its readers the details of the human side of the organization. Sports activities, picnics, unusual vacation experiences, and other achievements are matters that receive emphasis.

Office bulletin boards contain cartoons, jokes about work, someone's latest vacation snapshots, notices of awards, and the like. Good news and happy times are what is communicated. In other words, the communication system provides a significant outlet for social and emotional aspects of relationships.[33]

1,9 APPROACHES TO MANAGING CONFLICT

Understanding how conflict is dealt with provides a latch string of insight into 1,9 in a way that no other concept does.

From a 1,9 orientation, disagreement, negative emotions, rejection and frustration are to be avoided.[34] Positive, harmonious and accepting relationships are sought.[35] The manager operating under a 1,9 orientation is very much concerned about his own acceptance. Unable to use stern and harsh methods of having his wishes acted upon by subordinates, this supervisor is likely to appeal to feelings and to reason. But, the insecurity behind his own adjustment is likely to show through. As a result, and after brief efforts at reasoning, reconciliation through appeasement is the likely next quick step. The management of conflict under 1,9, then, takes shape in the form of a supervisor tending to take whatever actions he can to maintain harmony.[36]

From the Boss' Perspective

When the boss manages subordinates according to a 1,9 style, his basic approach is to smooth over conflict.[37] The meaning of "smoothing over" conflict can be brought out by drawing distinctions between *smoothing over* conflict and *suppressing* it, as in 9,1.

Conflict is suppressed when its expression is prevented, whether by criticism, "cutting it off," or by punishment. In comparison, conflict is smoothed over by talking people out of it, or, in other ways, glossing over it.

People are likely to be cajoled and coaxed into agreement by looking at how good things are, relative to how bad they might be — accentuating the positive and eliminating the negative, in other words.[38] At a superficial plane, the mental attitude is that "every cloud has a silver lining"; or "every day, in every way, things are getting better and better," "a person should count his many blessings, and name them one by one." There just should not be fights and disagreements. People should accept one another. When disagreement does appear, the plea is, "Let's come together on those things that we can agree on and not fight one another on those matters that do not seem to be resolvable." The plea, "Don't say anything if you can't say something nice," comes through loud and clear.[39]

A supervisor always runs the risk that his decisions will not be well received by some or all his subordinates. If his decision is challenged by subordinates, the 1,9 approach is to present it once again. If he still gets questioned, he withdraws to keep harmony by saying, "OK. Do it your own way."

There are many ways in which the supervisor with a 1,9 orientation can promote harmony.[40] One is to bring up for discussion topics on which there is widespread agreement.[41] Another way to maintain harmony is to "pour oil on troubled waters." The conflict is smoothed over even though it may remain beneath the surface. Or, the

supervisor may treat divergent points of view in such a
general fashion that the group never comes to grips with
them. Real issues do not become polarized; they are not
brought into focus. Rather, they are put in such an abstract way that *everyone* can agree with them. Also, it
frequently is possible to table a decision until the accompanying tensions are reduced or until other issues become more pressing and the problem is forgotten. Alternatively, when issues do become polarized, a committee
can be appointed to look into the matter. By using a committee in this way, a 1,9 boss can avoid responsibility for
negative recommendations.

Another facet of the problem needs to be understood.
Conflict with one's peers is not likely to be brought into
the open in the sense of expressing negative attitudes or
disagreement directly. But the tensions are there nonetheless. A result is that much gossip takes place in interactions between people who are operating in a 1,9 setting.
The rationale is that, being overly concerned with people,
and not wanting to hurt them or to be hurt by them, and,
therefore, being unable to confront conflict directly, tensions toward others which cannot be expressed in such a
way as to clear the air inevitably leave their mark, and a
person feels a need to talk.[42] One way to relieve such tension
is simply to talk about those who are the cause of
them to others who can offer sympathy or understanding.[43]
Therefore, the 1,9 kind of orientation promotes talkative-
ness, because inability to confront conflict directly leaves
residual tensions which can at least be ventilated through
individuals' being able to talk to third parties about it.
Such talking does not make a person feel right, but it
often helps him feel better.[44]

This need for a chance to talk leads to another condition where a person operating under 1,9 assumptions does
act toward relieving negative emotions. This occurs, for
example, where some person is stirred up, or aggravated
at others or toward the situation. Rather than trying to
prevent the expression of emotions, the person under tension is given the chance to ventilate his feelings, sometimes through a professional counselor where people can

go for advice.[45] Indeed, in the extreme, such professional personnel as industrial psychiatrists and psychologists and ministers are employed to provide this service.[46] Then the person whose emotions are wrought up is encouraged to talk them out until he has calmed down. In this way disruptive emotions can be discharged and a fresh perspective on the problem taken.[47] The more serious consideration here is with respect to underlying causes, however. The causes which generate the conflict — often to be found in on-the-line supervision itself — are not examined and cleared out of the way. Indeed, the boss is eliminated from handling the problem when it is taken over by professional specialists.[48] One consequence is that many of the constructive contributions to improving supervision by involving it in the problems it is generating are more or less automatically lost under 1,9. Another consequence is that even though the momentary tensions are discharged, unresolved underlying causes linger to generate further and new areas of disagreement and tension.[49] Nevertheless, by this way a 1,9 approach usually can reestablish a spirit of friendly relations. The latter, it would seem, is a key motivating factor for the 1,9 approach.

From The Subordinates' Perspective

Under 1,9, a manager places high value on avoiding conflict with his boss. His basic approach is simple. He stays in such close contact with his boss' thinking that he rarely "gets out on a limb." Under these circumstances, he is able to parrot his boss' thinking. If effective in doing so, then occasions for dispute are few and far between.

But another factor should be emphasized in connection with 1,9 boss conflict. It is that the subordinate avoids giving the boss bad news that might place him (the subordinate) in a position of criticism; he glosses it over, making even bad news appear shiny and bright.[50] In addition, when challenged by his boss to explain circumstances which, if accurately described might promote controversy, his inclination is not to give all the facts. Although he may not *lie* outright, he can play down and in other ways shade the truth so as to make it more pleasing or acceptable.

The above considerations should give a boss, who manages a subordinate with a 1,9 orientation to conflict, serious basis for concern. This kind of withholding, glossing, shading, and playing down negative information can turn into a powder-keg situation. A result is that a boss can be unaware, blinded or fooled regarding situations that can lead to losses of production, a breakdown of people relations, or both, until the situation becomes chronic and explodes.[51] When the explosion occurs, the boss has no basis for knowing what produced it.

IMPACT OF 1,9 ON CREATIVITY AND CHANGE

Creativity also can be viewed in two ways. First to be examined is the creativity of a person whose managerial orientation is 1,9. Then, the impact of 1,9 supervision on *those who are managed within a 1,9 framework* provides a second area of examination.

At The Boss' Level

Creativity often is the product of strong mental independence, intellectual nonconformity, and the clashes of opinion, or all of these.[52] As a result, creativity is not likely to be a value toward which a manager with a 1,9 orientation strives. Thus, the creative aspirations of the individual whose orientation are 1,9 is likely to be low. He is likely to play down the conditions that can produce disagreement with resultant creativity.[53] Thinking in new, different or strange ways, or listening to the suggestions, ideas or proposals of subordinates that might lead to change, cannot help but upset people who are adjusted to a comfortable pace.[54] Thus, resistance to change initiated from *within* his own organization is likely to be high under 1,9. The resistance is not so much that of an active foot in the aisle, but more in terms of foot dragging.

If a suggestion comes up from below to a person managing according to a 1,9 orientation, his approach is to compliment the subordinate so as not to dampen enthusiasm. Rather than evaluating it himself, he is likely to go to his boss without taking a position on it, to get agreement or disagreement. If the boss agrees, he takes credit for "getting it through"; if not, his inclination is to say, "I liked it, and tried, but the boss couldn't see it."

At The Subordinates' Level

There is, however, one facet of pseudo-creativity which is likely to be characteristic of the 1,9 orientation. As discussed elsewhere, a 5,5 orientation takes its direction essentially from tradition. In contrast, a 1,9 adjustment takes its primary anchorage from what other people presently are doing and thinking, especially their bosses and other higher-ranking individuals.[55] In other words, 1,9 is anchored in the present and "what others think." One's acceptance by superiors and associates is important.[56] Hence, it is predictable that individuals whose adjustments are in the 1,9 direction *are likely to respond favorably to changes and to fashions and fads once others have begun to do so.*[57] The response is that of following respected models who themselves are responsible for new ideas, fads and fashions. In other words, the 1,9 adjustment is *copying*. If an individual's copying behavior is seen out of context and as a single example, it can appear as innovation and creativity. The point being made here, however, is that the opposite — copying behavior — is true.

A 1,9 climate frequently is found in research segments of an organization where, in one sense, creativity is the intended form of production, but where creativity is absent. But, if 1,9 is likely to be stifling of conflict and unresponsive to change, as just indicated, a contradiction seems to appear. What can account for it? The general answer goes something like this. Creative people, or those whose jobs are in the scientific-engineering area, are unlikely to accept 9,1 with its authority-obedience assumptions, because it is said to "stifle creativity."[58] When resistance and antagonism are generated, management, in an effort to avoid losing people, swings in the 1,9 direction. The assumption then becomes that the best way to manage is to create good working conditions and to declare hands off with respect to work direction, especially in creative areas. Thus, a country club atmosphere is produced, where the kind of disagreement, intellectual nonconformity and clash of ideas needed for creative and innovative work is absent. Thus, institutions designed to promote creativity become quite comfortable and uncreative places to work.

COMMITMENT UNDER 1,9

1,9 having as it does the soft human relations motif with little functional concern for production, defines a circumstance which can generate high social commitment. There may be high identification with the work group and enjoyment in its activities, both on the job and beyond.[59]

The Boss' Commitment

If a person is asked about his managerial position, he is likely to say, "I would not want to change jobs." When asked why, he might reply, "Because I enjoy the people with whom I work. I couldn't ask for better conditions or for more security." The point here is that the commitment is high, but the commitment is in the human dimension. The production dimension, or tasks accomplishment, is more or less eliminated. This is the situation where high morale and low actual productivity are coupled.[60]

At The Subordinates' Level

To make it clear, managers with a 1,9 orientation are likely to be good company men, loyal to their boss, and proud of the company. Here people "who care," meet a company which looks after them and gives them security, now and for the future.

MANAGEMENT DEVELOPMENT UNDER 1,9

Under 1,9 management development and other formal personnel programs take on quite a different character than that of other orientations. This is particularly true with respect to the selection and induction of "new hires."

Selection

The 1,9 managerial style in screening and selecting new employees is keyed to those aspects of a person's character and background that best indicate that he will "fit in" harmoniously with the existing organization culture.[61] Indications of active participation and leadership in campus social organizations, fraternities and the like are values that receive considerable weight in the selection of college graduates. Weighted application blanks and interview guides contain judgments on personality, sociability, dress, neatness, manners, hobbies and many other social variables that may predict one's ability to accept and conform to the values and norms of present employees. Decentralized hiring insures that the person's potential immediate supervisor can look him over and judge the individual against a subjective group standard of likes and dislikes.

Induction

New personnel experience an introduction to the new organization that is warm and unhurried. The 9,1 induction is "sink or swim," but the 1,9 goal is to insure that new employees have the best possible picture of the organization in terms of preinduction[62] at the point of coming to work. This involves visiting the job location and bringing one's wife along. During the visit, coffees or teas or other social affairs are planned. They insure that people get acquainted informally.

During the first year or two there are frequent social affairs, where there is opportunity to get together with old timers. In this way, the culture of the past generation flows informally into the minds, feelings, attitudes and emotions of the new one. By this approach, adjustment problems are reduced and security increased.

Management Training

As touched on in the beginning, 1,9 places heavy emphasis on the personal growth and development of people.[63] However, there is no necessary correlation between this growth and development and organizational contribution. As a consequence, 1,9 management development is likely to lack a clear cut concept of organization purpose on the production side.

1,9 does have the concept of personal worth of the individual. There are two different aspects of personal development which appear in 1,9.

One is in terms of the concept of the direction of individual growth. This is described in a proposition which states that if individual growth and development is not warped or prevented, then the direction of growth is toward maturity and personal fulfillment.[64] Therefore, organization demands which prevent an individual from freedom of self-expression are, in a certain sense, adverse to the attainment of individual maturity.

A related concept which is prevalent in 1,9 managerial development is that of "self-actualization."[65] Here, the idea is that given autonomy, and freedom from pressure, the direction of individual motivation is toward actualizing oneself. Organizational supervision should, as a result, be in the direction of aiding an individual toward self-actualization or toward becoming his complete "self." On-the-job help is good management development.

Examples of 1,9 individual management development, where the goal is personal growth without any necessary relation to the work situation can be found in company sponsored Great Books Clubs, music appreciation clubs, fine arts education, philosophical discussions, inspirational messages, and the like.[66] Here the intent is to help broaden the total person. Such activities are of value in and of themselves. But, where the motivation is to give people what they want, to put work and effort in the background and to subordinate learning that could have production impact to cultural pursuits, then the goal is embedded in a 1,9 orientation.

Performance Appraisal

Beyond on-the-job aid, performance appraisals primarily are geared to helping people get along with others and counseling with them on personal matters by listening, to private help and encouragement. The goal of the boss with a 1,9 orientation, in other words, is to see how he or the company can help the individual to live in a more personally rewarding way.

1,9 PERSONAL BEHAVIOR

Outstanding Personal Characteristics

The personality basis of 1,9 as a managerial style seems to reflect an individual's concern for how he is reacted to by others in an acceptance-rejection way.[67] He is so responsive to what others think that he wants to be liked by them and to gain their approval. In a word, the motivation of the person who is oriented in a 1,9 fashion is to gain acceptance by others, sometimes regardless of the personal expense involved.[68]

As a result, the person with a 1,9 predisposition places high value on good relationships, on being a "good guy." To avoid being rejected, he seeks to avoid rejecting others. How is this done under a 1,9 orientation? It is possible by accepting the opinions, attitudes and ideas of others in preference to pushing his own. He avoids "locking horns," or "crossing them up." As a result, when convictions are expressed, they are more likely to be reflections of what his boss, or his peers, or his subordinates think and want than of his own convictions and desires. He is rarely in an initiating role on issues which call for exerting positive leadership. He does actively initiate contacts and moves in to establish bonds of friendship. He rarely generates conflict, but when it does appear, either between himself and others, or between others, he tries to soothe bad feelings. When tensions between people do arise, his humor attempts to reduce them.[69] He is patient and his temper is not easily triggered. 1,9 is a friendly, likeable, orientation. *It is other directed.*[70] It takes its cues from outside, not from inside.

Childhood Origins

What is it that prompts an adjustment to life like that described here? Again, as with 9,1 this orientation can be best understood by tracing evolution from childhood. In

9,1, parents confront children with punishment for being disobedient and unproductive, thereby instilling the compulsion to performance, no matter the cost in personal effort or strain. Parents who rear children who lean toward 9,1 are *sure*. Parents who rear 1,9 children are *unsure*.[71] They do not know, in themselves, how the child should develop. Being insecure about exerting control and discipline on the one hand, and wishing to avoid rejection, even by their own children on the other, such parents are likely to turn to others for advice.[72] Regardless to where the search turns, however, such parents show their children how anxious they are and how little they depend upon themselves and on their own convictions as sources of direction for what they do. The family situation, then, is likely to be one where parents are insecure and anxious about what to do. Wanting their children to be loved, it is likely that parents who act according to 1,9 give affection as a means of molding the child to their wishes. Wanting to be loved himself, the child comes to feel secure only when acting in a way that brings him parental love. This is by the child's giving love to his parents. Then he feels secure.[73]

Under such circumstances, children are likely to learn that fighting is bad, but that acting in ways to please parents and others is good. Thus, the child learns that to be loved, he must be good.[74]

Sense of Direction

The kind of a parental model just described results in the child also learning to be anxious as to what he should do, as to how he should relate. From his parents he learns to lean on others for judgment as to what is appropriate and best and will lead to his being loved. He might be expected to develop great skill in *accommodating* his thoughts and attitudes to insure that they conform with what others think and expect of him. From the very beginning, in Riesman's terms, such a child is launched in an other-directed way, or 1,9.[75] Being so responsive to the wishes of people and wanting to avoid feelings of anxiety and rejection that might be stimulated by doing things that would hurt them, it is clear why a 1,9 person shows very high concern for people and a minimum concern for production.[76]

1,9 assumptions appear to be the other side of the coin of 9,1. In terms of Maslow's need hierarchy, the dominant orientation of both a 9,1 and 1,9 person stem from the need for love and acceptance by parents.[77] However, 1,9 is an adjustment whereby a person tries to obtain approval by being responsive to what others think and do —to be liked by them, in other words—so as not to be rejected. The 9,1 adjustment is one where love of parents can be obtained through self discipline and mastery; that is, through performance. The same childhood needs— for security and acceptance—lead to opposite results, depending on how parents use them to control their children.

The question can be asked about the extent to which 1,9 simply represents conformity with the requirements of the situation. In the manner in which 1,9 is described here, it represents a step beyond the concern to conform to the standard pattern. That is to say, 1,9 represents an individual's desire to achieve love and acceptance even though it leads to overconformity. The 1,9 person's anxiety and doubt about his own acceptance contribute to an *oversensitivity* to the desires and wishes of others.[78] The anxiety connected with fear of rejection, then can produce a person whose attitudes are characterized as 1,9— solicitous, acquiescent to others, malleable, and easily subject to changing attitudes to conform to situations, even though they themselves may be contradictory.[79]

CONDITIONS AND CONSEQUENCES OF THE 1,9
ORGANIZATION STYLE

As is true for 9,1, there exist in many organizations certain conditions that tend to promote 1,9 as a style of management. An understanding of these conditions and the consequences of a predominant orientation toward 1,9 can aid in the evaluation of this style as an organizational approach to obtaining performance through people.[80]

*Conditions Promoting 1,9 as an Organization Style of
Management*

There are at least two situations in which the "country
club" style can become a company way of life. One is
where a company is operating on a cost plus basis, or in a
situation of such high demand that profits are inevitable.
In this instance, competition does not force the company
to operate effectively. In fact, the company can return a
profit with little attention placed on minimizing costs of
production. As a result, it becomes unattractive to make
efficiency moves because these might spread anxiety
among organization members and lead to dissatisfaction.
It is simpler to take the easy way out and to just let
things go as they may. Of course, this is a negative decision and will not attain maximum production. It does
support feelings of personal security, however, as no one
feels unwanted.

A second situation in which 1,9 occurs is in quasi-
monopolistic organizations. Such actions as efficiency
moves which call for layoffs, tight controls, etc., that
would disturb the feelings of people do not need to be
taken. It is primarily concerned with maintaining what
is believed to be good human relationships.

A dramatic example of 1,9 as an organizational way of
life is contained in the following situation: A large manufacturing establishment, up to several years ago, maintained a practice, built up over years, of employing an
extra group of temporary laborers during summer
months. This was done to compensate for the absence of
regular work force members on vacation. Vacations for
permanent organizational members were *not* scheduled
with production objectives in mind. Instead, the organization "picked up the bill" through employing substitutes.
The result was that each member of the wage force was
able to have his vacation exactly when he wanted. A
dramatic conclusion from this 1,9 way of life occurred,
however. Because its product became hopelessly non-com-
petitive, the plant shut down. *With this luxury style of
management—not facing the problem of involving people in solving the real issues of production — everyone
then had 52 weeks of vacation per year!*

Long-Term Consequences of 1,9 Management

The "be nice" approach, which smothers conflict and seeks to avoid the conditions that produce it, can lead to harmony in human r e l a t i o n s. However, production suffers. The 1,9 organization, which is prepared to maintain a comfortable sum of well-being among its managerial and work force is unlikely to obtain the creative thinking needed to accomplish the best out-put. Not only is the 1,9 approach ineffective in achieving high out-put, it does not really achieve any lasting human relationships since conflict and frustration are not dealt with and relived. They are merely smoothed over or buried.[81]

Decisions *against* efficiency moves, such as in the example above, that are motivated by a desire *not* to disturb people in order to maintain personal security, are negative. They do not accomplish the productive purpose of the organization. While such decisions *seem to* favor the development or maintenance of good relationships, such relationships are not sound, in any basic sense. Looked at from a broader time perspective, they are built on a foundation of toothpicks. The reason is that, in a profit-motivated economy, those organizations that *are* responsive to economic pressures can (and should) overtake a "fat and happy" organization. Under such circumstances it can be seen why relationships motivated by togetherness are dangerous. More competitive organizations should run them out of business — because the *real* danger to cultural evolution of economic systems is that they *cease* to strive for change and improvement. They are weak, if for no reason other than that they contain the seeds of their own destruction; for example, the closing of the plant just described. More important is the threat they create toward the long-term erosion of a free enterprise way of economic life.

SUMMARY

Under a 1,9 orientation, the work tempo is a comfortable one. At best, people are encouraged rather than driven. Subordinates are expected to turn out some work to avoid trouble and because of loyalty and acceptance. The boss is more of a big brother than the stern parental figure. Human relationships, in the sociable meaning of the phrase, are important, in and of themselves. The *group*, not the individual, is the key unit of the organization, with friendliness and harmony among its members the desired atmosphere.

The 1,9 motto is "nice guys don't fight."

References

1. McNair, M. P. Thinking Ahead: What Price Human Relations? *Harvard Business Review*, 35, March-April, 1957, 15-39.

2. Walker, C. R. & Guest, R. H. *The Man on the Assembly Line.* Cambridge: Harvard University Press, 1952, 141-163.

3. Mayfield, H. The Counseling Function in Management. *The Personnel Administrator*, 3, (1), 1958, 23-24. Also in I. L. Heckmann, Jr., & S. G. Huneryager (Eds.), *Human Relations in Management.* Cincinnati: South-Western, 1960, 513-519.

4. *The Managerial Grid: A Self-Examination of Managerial Styles.* Austin, Tex.: Scientific Methods, Inc., 1962.

5. Gellerman, S. W. *People, Problems and Profits.* New York: Mc-Graw-Hill, 1960, 165; Cleeton, G. U. The Human Factor in Industry. *The Annals of the American Academy of Political and Social Sciences*, 274, March, 1951, 17-24. Also in I. L. Heckmann, Jr., & S. G. Huneryager (Eds.), *op. cit.*, 17-26.

6. Stagner, R. *Psychology of Industrial Conflict.* New York: Wiley, 1956, 327-329.

7. Sabsay, N. From the Worker's Point of View. *Harvard Business Review*, 25, 1947, 339-347; Likert, R. *New Patterns of Management.* New York: McGraw-Hill, 1961, 7-8.

8. Likert, R., *op. cit.*, 101-104, 174.

9. Fiedler, F. E. Assumed Similarity Measures as Predictors of Team Effectiveness, *Journal of Abnormal & Social Psychology*, 49, 1954, 381-388; Given, W. B., Jr. The Engineer Goes Into Management. *Harvard Business Review*, 33, January-February, 1955, 43-52; French, E. G. Motivation as a Variable in Work-Partner Selection. *Journal of Abnormal & Social Psychology*, 53, 1956, 96-99.

10. Simmel, G. The Sociology of Sociability. *American Journal of Sociology*, 60, (3), 1949, 254-261. Also in T. Parsons, E. Shils, K. D. Naegele & J. R. Pitt (Eds.), *Theories of Society. Vol. I.* Glencoe, Ill.: Free Press, 1961, 157-163.

11. Fromm, E. *The Sane Society.* New York: Holt, Rinehart & Winston, 1955, 294.

12. Representative experimental work related to the effect of tension, anxiety, threat, negative feedback and similar interpersonal conditions may aid the reader to place in perspective the underlying assumptions and concerns of 1,9 "supportive" and conflict-free be-

havior, *e. g.*, see Shaw, M. E. Some Effects of Problem Complexity Upon Problem Solution Efficiency in Different Communication Nets. *Journal of Experimental Psychology*, 48, 1954, 211-217; Lanzetta, J. T., Haefner, D., Langham, P. & Axelrod, H. Some Effects of Situational Threat on Group Behavior. *Journal of Abnormal & Social Psychology*, 49, 1954, 445-543; Festinger, L. & Hutte, H. A. An Experimental Investigation of the Effect of Unstable Interpersonal Relations in a Group, *Journal of Abnormal & Social Psychology*, 49, 1954, 513-522; Cervin, V. Individual Behavior in Social Situations: Its Relation to Anxiety, Neuroticism, and Group Solidarity. *Journal of Experimental Psychology*, 51, 1956, 161-168; French, E. G. & Chadwick, I. Some Characteristics of Affiliation Motivation. *Journal of Abnormal & Social Psychology*, 52, 1956, 296-300; de Charms, R. Affiliation Motivation and Productivity in Small Groups. *Journal of Abnormal & Social Psychology*, 55, 1957, 222-226; Harvey, O. J., Kelley, H. H. & Shapiro, M. M. Reactions to Unfavorable Evaluations of the Self Made by Other Persons. *Journal of Personality*, 25, 1957, 393-411; Pepinsky, P. N., Hemphill, J. K. & Shevitz, R. N. Attempts to Lead, Group Productivity, and Morale Under Conditions of Acceptance and Rejection. *Journal of Abnormal & Social Psychology*, 57, 1958, 47-54; Schachter, S. *The Psychology of Affiliation.* Stanford, Cal.: Stanford University, 1959; Likert, R., *op. cit.;* Herzberg, F., Mausner & Snyderman, B. B. *The Motivation to Work.* New York: Wiley, 1959, 87, 113-114, 125.

13. The 1,9 behavior and orientation toward others is consistent with the "Social Specialist" role identified by Moment and Zaleznik. See Moment, D. and Zaleznik, A. *Role Development and Interpersonal Competence.* Boston: Harvard University, 1963, 123-124.

14. Fromm, E., *op. cit.*

15. Roethlisberger, F. J. The Foreman: Master and Victim of Double Talk. *Harvard Business Review*, 23, 1945, 283-294; Zentner, H. Morale: Certain Theoretical Implications of Data on The American Soldier. *American Sociological Review*, 16, 1951, 297-307.

16. Maier, N. R. F. *Psychology in Industry.* (2nd Ed.). Boston: Houghton, 1955, 409-410.

17. Smiddy, H. F. Managerial Decision-Making. *Advanced Management*, 23, (11), 1958, 5-18.

18. Menninger, W. C. A Prescription for Executive Mental Health. *Advanced Management*, September, 1960, 16-17.

19. Watson, J. A Formal Analysis of Sociable Interaction. *Sociometry*, 21, 1958, 269-281.

20. Bass, B. M. *Leadership, Psychology, and Organizational Behavior.* New York; Harper, 1960, 50; Speroff, B. J. Job Satisfaction and Interpersonal Desirability Values. *Sociometry*, 18, 1955, 69-72.

21. Maier, N. R. F., *op. cit.*, 480-481.

22. Bass, B. M., *op. cit.*, 49.

23. Schachter, S., *op. cit.;* Blake, R. R. & Mouton, J. S. Conformity, Resistance, and Conversion. In I. A. Berg & B. M. Bass (Eds.), *Conformity and Deviation.* New York: Harper, 1961, 19.

24. Tannenbaum, R., Weschler, I. R. & Massarik, F. *Leadership and Organization: A Behavioral Science Approach.* New York: McGraw-Hill, 1961, 109.

25. Shibutani, T. *Society and Personality.* Englewood Cliffs, N. J.: Prentice-Hall, 1961, 289.

26. Appley, L. A. *Management in Action.* New York: American Management Association, 1956, 194-197; Stagner, R., *op. cit.,* 329.

27. Guion, R. M. Some Definitions of Morale. In E. A. Fleishman (Ed.), *Studies in Personnel and Industrial Psychology.* Homewood, Ill.: Dorsey, 1961, 301-304.

28. Horsfall, A. B. & Arensberg, C. M. Teamwork and Productivity in a Shoe Factory. *Human Organization,* 8, 1949, 13-26.

29. Homans, G. C. *The Human Group.* New York: Harcourt, Brace, 1950.

30. Wilensky, J. L. & Wilensky, H. L. Personnel Counseling: The Hawthorne Case. *American Journal of Sociology,* 57, 1951, 265-280; Stagner, R., *op. cit.,* 316.

31. Stagner, R., *op. cit.,* 329.

32. Dover, C. L. Silence—An Employee Relations Pitfall. *Advanced Management,* 22, 1957, 7-10.

33. Stagner, R., *op cit.,* 319-330; Kelley, H. H. Communication in Experimentally Created Hierarchies. Human Relations, 4, 1951, 39-56.

34. Fromm, E. The Creative Attitude. In H. H. Anderson (Ed.), *Creativity and Its Cultivation.* New York: Harper, 1959, 51; Riesman, D. *The Lonely Crowd.* New Haven: Yale University, 1961, 268.

35. Guetzkow, H. & Gyr, J. An Analysis of Conflict in Decision-Making Groups. *Human Relations,* 7, 1954, 367-382.

36. Purcell, T. V. Observing People. *Harvard Business Review,* 33, May-June, 1955, 90-100.

37. Himler, L. E. The Counseling Interview. In I. L. Heckmann, Jr. & S. G. Huneryager (Eds.), *op. cit.,* 552-554.

38. Given, W. B., Jr. *op. cit.;* Newman, L. E. Human Values for Management Engineers. *Advanced Management,* 24, (2), 1959, 15-17; Tannenbaum, R., *et al, op. cit.,* 109.

39. Boulding, K. E. *Conflict and Defense.* New York: Harper, 1962, 171.

40. Jennings, E. M. *The Executive: Autocrat, Bureaucrat, Democrat.* New York: Harper, 1962, 215; Boulding, K. E., *op. cit.,* 166-188.

41. Smiddy, H. F., *op. cit.*

42. Stagner, R., *op. cit.,* 330.

43. Mayfield, H. The Counseling Function in Management. *The Personnel Administrator,* 3, (1), 1958, 23-25.

44. Wilensky, J. L. & Wilensky, H. L., *op. cit.*

45. Mayfield, H., *op. cit.*

46. Menninger, W. C., *op. cit.*

47. Maier, N. R. F. *The Appraisal Interview: Objectives, Methods, and Skills.* New York: Wiley, 1958, 10.

48. Dickson, W. J. The Hawthorne Plan of Personnel Counseling. *American Journal of Orthogenic Psychology,* 15, 1945, 343-347.

49. Simmel, G. *Conflict* and *Web of Group-Affiliations*. (Translated by K. H. Wolff and R. Bendix:) Glencoe, Ill.: Free Press, 1955, 19-20, 121-123.

50. Stagner, R., *op. cit.*, 329.

51. Appley, L. A., *op. cit.*, 194-197.

52. Simmel, G., *op. cit.*, 1949; Anderson, H. H. Creativity as Personality Development. In H. H. Anderson (Ed.), *op. cit.*, 119-141, and, Creativity in Perspective., *Ibid.*, 236-267.

53. Fromm, E., *op. cit.*, 1959, 51; Shibutani, T., *op. cit.*, 313; Jennings, E. M., *op. cit.*, 206.

54. Mead, M. Creativity in Cross-Cultural Perspective. In H. H. Anderson (Ed.), *op. cit.*, 225.

55. Asch, S. E. Effects of Group Pressure upon the Modification and Distortion of Judgments. In H. Guetzkow (Ed.), *Groups, Leadership, and Men*. Pittsburgh: Carnegie, 1951; Hurwitz, J. I., Zander, A. F. & Hymovitch, B. Some Effects on the Relations among Group Members. In D. Cartwright & A. Zander (Eds.), *Group Dynamics: Research and Theory*. Evanston, Ill.: Row, Peterson, 1953; Lippitt, R., Polansky, N. & Rosen, S. The Dynamics of Power: A Field Study of Social Influence in Groups of Children. *Human Relations*, 5, 1952, 37-64; Cole, D. "Rational Argument" and "Prestige-Suggestion" as Factors Influencing Judgment. *Sociometry*, 17, 1954, 350-354.

56. Berg, I. A. & Bass, B. M. (Eds.), *Conformity and Deviation*. New York: Harper, 1961, 13.

57. Riesman, D., *op. cit.*, 73-76, 118.

58. Given, W. B., Jr., *op. cit.*

59. Watson, J., *op. cit.*

60. Likert, R. Patterns in Management. In E. A. Fleishman (Ed.), *op. cit.*, 350.

61. French, E. G. Motivation as a Variable in Work-Partner Selection. *Journal of Abnormal & Social Psychology*, 53, 1956, 96-99; Fiedler, F. E. Assumed Similarity Measures as Predictors of Team Effectiveness. *Journal of Abnormal & Social Psychology*, 49, 1954, 381-388.

62. Stone, C. H. & Kendall, W. E. *Effective Personnel Selection Procedures*. Englewood Cliffs, N. J.: Prentice-Hall, 1956, 383.

63. Likert, R. A Motivational Approach to a Modified Theory of Organization and Management. In M. Haire (Ed.), *Modern Organization Theory*. New York: Wiley, 1959, 184-217.

64. Maslow, A. H. *Motivation and Personality*. New York: Harper, 1954, 91-92; Argyris, C. *Personality and Organization*. New York: Harper, 1957, 53; McGregor, D. *The Human Side of Enterprise*. New York: McGraw-Hill, 1960, 39.

65. Maslow, A. H., *op. cit.*, 92; Argyris, C. *Understanding Organizational Behavior*. Homewood, Ill.: Dorsey, 1960, 8-10.

66. Ohmann, O. A. "Skyhooks" With Special Implications for Monday Through Monday. *Harvard Business Review*, 33, 1955, 33-41.

67. Schachter, S., *op. cit.*

68. Moment, D. & Zaleznik, A., *op. cit.*, 123-124.

69. Bradley, P. The Joking Relationship in Industry. *Human Relations*, 10, 1957, 179-187.

70. Riesman, D., *op. cit.*, XX, 19-24.

71. Levy, D. M. Maternal Overprotection. In M. L. Haimowitz & N. R. Haimowitz (Eds.), *Human Development*. New York: Crowell, 1960, 399-407; Watson, G. Some Personality Differences in Children Related to Strict or Permissive Parental Discipline. *Journal of Psychology*, 44, 1957, 227-249; Whiting, J. W. & Child, I. L. *Child Training and Personality*. New Haven: Yale University, 1953; Fenichel, O. *Psychoanalytic Theory of Neurosis*. New York: Norton, 1945.

72. Riesman, D., *op. cit.*, 47; Shibutani, T., *op. cit.* 313.

73. Horney, K. *Neurosis and Human Growth*. New York: Norton, 1950; Hall, C. S. & Lindzey, G. *Theories of Personality*. New York: Wiley, 1957, 130-134.

74. Leary, T. *Interpersonal Diagnosis of Personality*. New York: Ronald, 1957.

75. Riesman, D., *op. cit.*

76. Moment, D. & Zaleznik, A., *op. cit.*, 67.

77. Maslow, A. H., *op. cit.*, 80-106.

78. Bowers, D. G. Self-Esteem and the Diffusion of Leadership Style. *Journal of Abnormal & Social Psychology*, 47, 1963, 135-140.

79. Watson, J., *op. cit.;* Shibutani, T., *op. cit.*, 289.

80. Blau, P. M. *Bureaucracy in Modern Society*. New York: Random House, 1956.

81. Likert, R. Patterns in Management. In E. A. Fleishman (Ed.), *op. cit.*

82. Mead, M., *op. cit.*

CHAPTER FIVE

The 1,1 Managerial Style

Low concern for production, *1*, is coupled with low concern for people, *1*, in the lower left hand corner of the grid, where the 1,1 managerial pattern is located. Like 9,1 or 1,9, an incompatibility is assumed to exist between production requirements and needs of people. However, since concern for both is low, the manager with a 1,1 orientation experiences little or no dilemma between production and people — he is more or less "out of it." But, the person managing 1,1 has learned to "be out of it," while remaining in the organization. Little is expected of him, and little is given by him in return.[1] 1,1 as an approach is rare in organization situations of non-repetitive action where each situation presents a different set of problems to be solved. It is far more common in routine operations, and in various staff functions.[2]

The phrase 1,1 management of people is an anomaly. A person who has adopted a 1,1 orientation might better be described as "lost among," rather than managing people.[3] Anomalous though it may seem, there are, today, many persons in managerial ranks whose supervision is best pictured as 1,1.

The 1,1 approach is unnatural. It comes to those who have accepted defeat. To permit oneself again to become involved and concerned over what happens in the work situation can only lead to deeper frustration and discouragement.[4] It is an approach characterized, then, by low involvement with people and the contribution of minimum effort toward organization purpose.[5]

MANAGEMENT UNDER 1,1

The supervisory approach under 1,1 is to put people on jobs and to leave them alone. He does this by letting people do their work as they see fit. He does not pester them. "Don't put your hand in a hornet's nest," is a motto characteristic of a manager who operates in the 1,1 direction. His administrative responses are of minimum movement, enough to get the pressure off his back, but little more. The following show how a 1,1 supervisor views his managerial responsibilities.[6]

Planning. "I give broad assignments though I don't think in terms of goals or schedules. I do little planning. A way that you might describe my job is I'm a message carrier. I carry the story from those one level above to those one level below me. I put as little 'embroidery' or interpretation on what I pass as possible. I do what my job description requires."

Work Execution. "If I make the rounds, I take little on-the-spot action. People are free to solve their own problems. They like it that way. I do, too."

Follow-up. "If he inquires, I talk to my boss who tells me what is to be done next and to find out how he wants it done and who he wants to do it."

With a 1,1 orientation, a person takes responsibility for filling his position, but only in a superficial way. His imprint is like a shadow on the sand. It passes over the ground, but leaves no permanent mark. Before judging whether such a prospect is unattractive, however, consider first what this can mean. A person may leave no mark in the organization of which he is a member, but neither does the organization leave its mark on him — a mark which, otherwise, could inflict the pain of anxiety and the frustration of failure.[7]

DIRECTION AND CONTROL UNDER 1,1

Since the manager who has adopted the 1,1 approach does only the minimum in *both* directions, he is not likely to be found exercising power, as in the 9,1 orientation.

Nor is he concerned with the affection of his people, as is true for 1,9. In comparison with the 5,5 style, his goal is not that of using precedent and established practice to orient his action. Rather, the 1,1 orientation is of minimum exposure and accountability. He sticks by the rules, so as not to stand out from the crowd.[8]

By way of exerting direction on others, the 1,1 approach is one of message carrying. He passes orders down the line from above so as not to get caught short.[9] When supervision is required, he does enough to be able to report, "I told them what to do — if they haven't it's because they didn't listen. It's not *my* problem."

The following is a literal description of an incident which may serve to picture the 1,1 style of direction and control. The supervisor had just returned from a weekly staff meeting, where changes in procedures, policies and the like are discussed so that each subordinate can initiate appropriate changes within his own area of responsibility. The supervisor, as was his usual custom, called his five subordinates to his office. When all were seated, he read mechanically a copy of a memorandum and notes he had taken as it had been presented earlier and had been discussed. He checked off each topic as he read it, careful that none could say later that he had not "communicated." When he had completed this recitation, he filed the memo and his dated notes in his desk drawer.

Without looking up, he said, "I'm going to the record shop. Who has the (company car) key?" The keys were located. As he turned to leave, one subordinate ventured a question concerning how and when a particular change was to be effected.

"They didn't say," was the supervisor's reply.

Another raised a question about fifteen large boxes of materials in the hallway.

"They just said to order them. They didn't say what to do with them when they got here. Let them set. Somebody will come get them when they start looking for the stuff." With that, he left.

Little more needs to be said about 1,1 direction and control. This incident adequately describes the approach.

The "facts" as the supervisor heard them were carried down to his subordinates—no more, no less.

Mistakes and Violations

The 1,1 approach to mistakes by subordinates is to ignore them, unless the magnitude of the mistake is such that he himself will "catch it." However, routine errors are overlooked—in fact, they are expected. "Who cares?" When subordinates make mistakes, he places the blame on them in such a manner as to relieve himself of responsibility for their actions.[10] When a mistake is made by a subordinate, a supervisor with a 1,1 orientation is likely to say, "Oh! *They* are always causing trouble, but what can I do?"

This feeling of lack of responsibility for mistakes is an outstanding characteristic of a manager with a 1,1 orientation. He is as slippery as a cake of soap when trying to pin him down—the responsiblity can always be placed elsewhere—on someone else, the system, on the organization, or on "breaks."

Consistent with the assumption that it is best not to "shake the trees" and perhaps wind up with a "hornets' nest," the 1,1 approach is to shrug one's shoulders and to hope subordinates will not be called to account.

As mentioned, from a personal standpoint, an individual with a 1,1 orientation finds security in knowing the rules. Knowledge of what is required to prevent infractions by others allows him to make the rules known and be safe. He wants to avoid involvement in others' areas or problems so as not to be held accountable himself.[11] Then, when policies and procedures are violated by others, he is likely to say, "It's better to turn your head than to cause a furor unless the situation is one which is actually dangerous, or will get you in trouble." If they get caught it is not his fault, as he can prose, "They knew they were not supposed to. It's no skin off my back."

CONCEPT OF GOALS UNDER 1,1

There is no concept of goals as ordinarily understood under 1,1. The reason is that goals, if present in 1,1, are unrelated to concern for production or to concern for how people should be used in gaining production. Rather, the purpose of 1,1 behavior is a self-centered one.[12] It is that of personal survival within the system to get the pay and, eventually, retirement benefits. No more. Goal accomplishment in other words is personal—it has no sense of either organization contribution or of concerns of others present within the organization. The general attitude is not far away from reactions to the dole of depression days.[13]

At this point, however, another distinction should be made. It separates the sociological concept of anomie from 1,1 kinds of organizational behavior. Under anomie personal behavior has lost any aim except subsistence, with others, like social agencies taking over responsibility for that by giving food and shelter.[14] One does not retain membership of any sort. The difference is clear as it relates to an individual's real goal or purpose in 1,1; that of maintaining organizational membership and continuity for one's own personal survival advantages.[15] This concept is absent in anomie. The organization, in a 1,1 sense, becomes the means for maintaining the socially acceptable role of citizen by discharging the very minimum of citizenship requirements. Position and status lose meaning but pay is sought within the organization.

If one can speak of 1,1 goals within the organization, then those goals related to organization survival are the only ones appropriate to discuss. A goal of 1,1 then is to hold one's position—to "make" retirement. This means keeping one's nose clean, and doing just good enough to hold on. This can mean that in the event of a burden or manpower reduction, if the person with the 1,1 orientation has been successful in remaining inconspicuous, the odds are in his favor that he will be overlooked.

BOSS-SUBORDINATE RELATIONS UNDER 1,1

A 1,1 managerial orientation is similar to the above in the relationships area. Whereas the 9,1 aim is to enforce isolation among subordinates as a means of control, and the aim of 1,9 is to foster togetherness, also a means of control, the aim of the manager with a 1,1 orientation is to *isolate himself from both his boss and his subordinates.*[16] The fewer contacts with either, the better. Then he is less likely to become involved in work problems requiring decisions or other managerial actions.[17] He wants to avoid the control of others.

A manager under 1,1 assumptions makes little effort to isolate others or to get others together, either on a one-to-one or a one-to-all basis. He does so only when it is unavoidable. Under the 1-1 orientation, the following remarks are typical of a person in the lower levels of an organization:

"My goal is to keep my nose clean. The best way is to stay out of sight. When I can't escape, I do enough to get by and to keep people off my back."

Under the 1,1 orientation, subordinates are viewed as a necessary evil, to be fended off, or if necessary, tolerated.

"Subordinates can be a source of problems. If job descriptions fixed individual responsibility more clearly, there wouldn't be so much commotion."

Meetings with Subordinates

In terms of meetings, the 1,1 orientation is "to hold regularly scheduled meetings which are a matter of company policy." Obviously, the meetings are ones where decisions are not made but communicated down as in the previous example, which gives the flavor.

The concern of a person whose characteristic style of management is 1,1 is turned inward.[18] Only required production or social contacts which, if ignored, could place his position in jeopardy, are maintained. Other events seem to pass unnoticed. Another way of picturing the 1,1 approach is in the "count me out" attitude. In the extreme, he often is able to find reasons for not attending department functions, informal meetings, or even regularly scheduled work meetings. He does not initiate contacts. When unavoidably caught in a group of two or more, he seldom participates in the topic of discussion. Neither words nor expressions reveal his thoughts about what is being said. The degree to which he can remain passive, non-responsive and uninvolved is governed by the acceptable minimum others will tolerate without frustration.

1,1 Attitudes Toward His Boss

Attitudes toward his boss are consistent with that just described.

"The less I see the boss, the more comfortable I feel."

To be there without being noticed, as is a chameleon, is the secret of 1,1. Interacting with one's boss, whether in work-related functions or socially, can expose him to unwanted notice. Looking upward, 1,1 assumes it is best to limit the relations with one's boss to receiving instructions, without question or comment.[19] In this way, the boss can only assume concurrence and commitment. Under 1,1 assumptions, then, the pattern is to "complete all reports and communications, accurately and on time."

A manager, once the president of a subsidiary company, was transferred to the legal department of the parent organization. The reason given was "health." It was the nature of the company to guarantee job security, so the manager was "set" until retirement. For twelve years, until his retirement, he was seldom seen. This manager came and went quietly and unnoticed. His secretary, who rarely did typing, saw him infrequently. Incoming and outgoing calls were few in the beginning and continued to shrink. Meeting attendance became irregular until for the two years prior to retirement he went to none. He had been "shelved" and he knew it. To this treatment his response was 1,1. And, the organization carried an item of expensive deadweight for twelve years.

Creating and Maintaining Morale

The manager with the 1,1 style prefers to be left to himself and so lets his subordinates create their own conditions of morale. Since he is not interested in them, he leaves them alone to fend for themselves. They can handle their problems in whatever way they please.[20]

Several rather different morale reactions to 1,1 then tend to appear. One is from the subordinate who is eager for "leg room." For him, the 1,1 boss may fit the bill to a

"T." Looking upward, the subordinate is able to see nothing but "delegation." If he is a competent self-mover, the withdrawal of the boss is almost unnoticeable, at least for a period of time. Furthermore, if the boss' boss two levels up understands the situation and gets pay increases, etc., for the subordinate two levels down, the 1,1 intermediate layer is likely to have little or no negative influence. The boss two levels up is likely to supply the guidance needed but unavailable one layer up.

A second and more common morale response to 1,1 is finding a way to get "out" from under it, by leaving, transferring, etc.[21]

A third morale response to 1,1 supervision is that of subordinates of a 1,1 oriented supervisor moving in the same direction—reacting to 1,1 with a 1,1 reaction. There are two reasons. One is from the feeling of inability to "get anything done" through the boss, leading to one's own eventual withdrawal of effort. The other is 1,1 clusters tend to form, with others "moved in" to be supervised by a manager who also is of a 1,1 mind.

Thus morale reactions under 1,1 are more complex and difficult to predict when supervision follows some other managerial style.[22]

Inverted 1,1

When situations have arisen that prevent efficiency moves (in some countries, where U.S. firms operate, government regulations prevent manpower reductions through layoff, etc.), 9,1 management actions have, on occasion, taken a diabolical form. One way is through the inverted 1,1 approach. Given a surplus of clerical personnel, for example, 10 of them are assigned, within a large office space, to individual desks. To complete the picture, all work is withheld so that no one has any activity to occupy his attention. Strict discipline insures that no conversation takes place. The result is that people cannot avoid a 1,1 situation. There is no escape, save through resignation, a solution that all but the very strongest come to quickly. Thus, in the inverted 1,1, the aim is to destroy morale to the point where people leave the organization.

Communication Activities Under 1,1

The characteristic of "isolation", typical of the 1,1 managerial style, holds for communications as well as other areas. Isolation extends across groups from his own to another, and between levels—between himself and his boss or subordinates. In other words, communication is at a minimum level.[23] Another way of saying it is that the 1,1 motive of organizational accommodation can best be protected when communication is maintained at a low level. As a general rule, communication, except for the strictest quality of message carrying, characteristic of 1,1, tends to involve the person communicating in the content of the message being passed. The 1,1 goal does not include generating interest in the content in the person communicated to. The generation of interest is contrary to the goals of 1,1 orientation. Obviously, then, the 1,1 managerial orientation is geared to restrictive communications.[24]

Another word should be said here regarding the concept of the 1,1 orientation as involving the message-carrier role. Say, an individual is accommodating to organizational circumstances in a 1,1 way and communications between levels are required where he constitutes the link. The best description of this role is that the 1,1 oriented person engages in message carrying of a "high fidelity" character. That is, his goal under these circumstances is to know the message he is expected to pass downward and to do so in such a manner that criticism does not involve him. He wants to avoid criticism for inadequacy of communication.[25]

It would be out of character for a manager with a 1,1 style to promote or even to utilize mechanical news media such as those commonly found in organizations. If they exist and are promoted, it is through the efforts and contributions of others.

1,1 APPROACHES TO MANAGING CONFLICT

In dealing with conflict, the solution for the manager operating under 1,1 is to *avoid* it.[26] This is accomplished in many ways. One way, literally, is to withdraw from situations of conflict where physical flight is possible. By getting out of the situation, the danger of an individual's getting into trouble can be missed. The way to deal with a disturbing memo, for example, is to defer an answer, or file it and forget where it was filed. To a query, the answer is, "Sorry, I've not received it." An alternative, which is often available when withdrawal is not possible, is to maintain *strict neutrality* by not voicing any personal opinion.[27] Maintenance of isolation and neutrality in many organization settings is easy to accomplish when interest in production and people is low. Other ways such as speaking with "double talk" or "gobbledygook," meet the requirements of an answer without any commitment.

From the Boss' Perspective

The boss operating from a 1,1 orientation can remain free of conflict with his subordinates simply by not acting as a boss. In a way, this can be viewed as the "ostrich dynamic." By keeping his eyes closed, he does not see conflict. If a disagreeable situation is ignored, in time it is likely to disappear.[28] From another point of view, this manager, by turning himself into a message carrier—a communication link between two levels—is merely carrying out orders from a higher level, as seen from the point of view of his subordinates. Thus, any appearance of conflict with a subordinate can be shunted up the line.[29] Conversely, if subordinates question a decision, he pulls back or does not insist, leaving responsibility on them. If the situation should come to such a state as to jeopardize him, he would carry the message up for action.

From the Subordinates Perspective

Under a 1,1 managerial orientation, a subordinate manager is likely to avoid conflict with his boss and peers by not disagreeing. He is outwardly, at least, compliant with his boss, and he makes little or no demands on peers. His chief response to directions is likely to be, "If you say so." Whenever possible, a manager with a 1,1 orientation remains out of sight. If it is necessary to be counted, he still seeks to maintain strict neutrality.[30] Under conditions of controversy, where asked by his boss to take a position, he might deflect the pressure by saying something like, "There has not been time to study the problem fully," or, "I would need more facts before making a judgment." If pressured still more, a final appeal likely is, "Perhaps the best way is to proceed as you think best." If pressured still more, a final appeal likely is, "We had better continue as has been done in the past."

If results fail to be accomplished and he is asked to account for his actions, the subordinate passes the blow on down by saying, "I told them, but they didn't follow through."

IMPACT OF 1,1 ON CREATIVITY AND CHANGE

The person with a 1,1 managerial style is likely to give the appearance of lacking creativity. However, he frequently may be highly creative, as evidenced by his superior ability to appear uncreative and to blend invisibly into the background, like a chameleon.

At the Boss' Level

The creativity of which 1,1 truly is capable is directed toward self preservation. Thus, 1,1 actions are not exactly anti-organizational. They are survival-based and, in a sense, non-organizational.

Are people who have adjusted to 1,1 incapable of constructive creativity? A striking observation points to the fact that many individuals whose organizational adjustment is 1,1 actively pursue interests in community life, at home through hobbies, or in their families.[31] One manager who might truly be characterized as having a 1,1 orientation in his work setting, is an active member of the city council in the city where his plant is located. Another is choir director of a large church. Though not in the creative category, these examples suggest that a person adjusted to 1,1 has not "run out of steam."

To think creatively within the organizational setting, to explore for new concepts and areas of investigation or to stimulate change through the involvement of others is, in a real sense, anti-1,1. For this reason, one would not expect, and indeed, one cannot find a manager with a 1,1 style who engages in these kinds of activities in the work setting.

His reaction to change suggested from below is likely to be that of deadweight. If subordinates do make suggestions, he either buries them or passes them up one level. He rarely follows up unless it is easier to respond to those from either above or below than to do nothing.[32]

At the Subordinate Level

A 1,1 managerial orientation, because of the lack of interest, enthusiasm, etc., it contains, is likely over-all to dampen the efforts of those operating in a subordinate capacity.[33] Although he may not prevent, in an active way, creativity and innovation, neither does he support it. Creativity or change initiated by a subordinate often needs to be carried up the line for further action. What happens to it is determined two, not one, layers up. And frequently it only gets that high if the subordinate short-circuits in the intermediate layer. Here again, since the goal of 1,1 is to avoid involvement with *his* boss, this is sufficient inducement for him to "lose" or "overlook" the ideas or suggestions of subordinates. Then, as one hears from subordinates under these conditions, "I got tired of beating my head against the wall and talking to a 'sponge'— so I said, 'to heck with it.' "

COMMITMENT UNDER 1,1

As indicated previously the 1,1 commitment involves a different dimension of consideration than the two already presented. In 1,1, the commitment of an individual is minimum with respect to organization purpose of production or with respect to people. But a maximum is sought after with respect to self and survival. Self-commitment for the purpose of achieving the survival, from financial security, benefit programs, retirement, and so on, is high.[34]

The Boss' Commitment

It should be emphasized that commitment of any kind is not necessarily absent in the person whose orientation is 1,1. This is especially true in the 1,1 accommodation to the organization.

The behavior of an individual may swing from 1,1 on the job to any other style away from work. Years of 1,1 accommodation to the job, however, is likely to lead to 1,1 or 1,9 or perhaps 5,5 outside the organization. Where 9,9 or 9,1 or even 5,5 is a fundamental component of a person's psychological underpinnings and personal value system, it is unlikely the individual would remain long in an organization and come to 1,1. In other words, it appears there must be present in a person a predisposition to move in a 1,1 direction. Of course, many situational factors, compounded, can produce an "impossible" situation and a shift to 1,1 for anyone, despite his basic orientation.

As touched on earlier, involvement has a spontaneous quality. Given favorable conditions, it does not need to be "produced." Involvement needs only to be *released.* Once released, people cannot avoid becoming committed to and identified with the problems facing them. As such, involvement has a motivational quality—the characteristic of tension. Like other tensions, then, involvement must find expression—a channel or an outlet.[35]

In the event conditions are such that 1,1 accommodation to the work situation is preferable to withdrawal from it, other outlets for involvement and commitment outside the organization are possible.[36] Certainly, among more highly professional people, salaries, bonus plans, stock purchasing plans, status, and the like may make it highly desirable to remain with an organization; even when 1,1 appears to be the only course of action in the "psychological vacuum" within which one works.

Once resigned to a 1,1 life in the work situation, individuals with healthy capacities for involvement and commitment must seek expression elsewhere.[37] Obviously, such activities are found primarily outside the organization.[38] However, some are to be found in the organization, and convert a 1,1 to something else such as the 1,9 orientation below. There are examples of people who spend countless hours and needless amounts of energy "serving" company sponsored clubs and similar activities. An example is one person who was the social and program chairman of a company recreational club. Once he did get involved, he participated in the activities generated from a budget of over $20,000. This "job" required the time from many of his nights and week-ends, and several hours a day of his regular work day also were used in this way. He did superbly in this capacity, but it should be noted that it was a pleasant job, almost completely free from pressure.

"Moonlighting," owning one's own small business, providing off-the-job services, or holding city offices, etc., are examples of what may be commitment that is placed outside the organization. Often, so much effort is expended in this direction that many individuals find it difficult to return to something else from 1,1 on the job even if they so desired.

An attorney in the legal division of one large company had a private practice, "unknown" to others. From it he grossed in excess of $18,000 annually. His practice was so demanding that much of his regular working hours, vacation time, sick-leave time, accumulated leave-of-absence, and so forth was applied to his practice. He was known in legal circles as an energetic, hard-driving and "helpful" man behind the public scenes. He was maintained on the company rolls as the law librarian—a job he "came to" in a recent reorganization. The rationale for permitting him the freedom was that it gave the company "useful" contacts and a certain professional relations advantage.

The Subordinate Commitment

Commitment of the subordinate managed according to 1,1, as with creativity, generally is likely to be dampened or low because of the lack of leadership and enthusiasm of the supervisor.[39] It can be very frustrating to have only a neutral, indifferent ceiling on one's activities, where influence from below is not responded to. On the other hand, some people prefer a boss with a 1,1 orientation to one with a 1,9 or 5,5 orientation. The reason given is that under the 1,1 style with the delegation phenomena, the person is more free to pursue his own work activities to which *he* is committed.

MANAGEMENT DEVELOPMENT UNDER 1,1

Selection

Selection under a 1,1 approach would involve finding ways to insure that others made the employment decision. There are numerous ways.

Consider the possibility that a 1,1 person is involved in college recruiting. How would he do it? With interviewees, he would restrict himself to being factual, giving requested information about the company and employment opportunities in a disinterested "matter of fact" way. If the person's *vita* corresponded with the job description, he would invite an on-site visit, if authorized, or report back that, "at least on paper," the applicant qualified. He would avoid positive or negative recommendations and would withhold his subjective opinion.

Under the circumstances described, he would have fully abdicated the employment decision, leaving it in the candidate to make his own decision, or to his boss to initiate further action.

Induction

If required to host inductees, his approach would not be programatic, in the 5,5 sense, nor would it be social, in the 1,9 way, nor would it be "sink or swim," in the 9,1 fashion. Rather, he might orient an inductee by giving him free reign to explore, visit whom he wishes, and get acquainted and oriented "in his own way." The extreme of it would be, "come back when you're through."

Management Development

The concept of 1,1 is so inconsistent with the constructive thinking possible in management development, that it is difficult to picture or to discover a 1,1 management development approach. One can accurately say that the idea of development is nonexistent in 1,1 thinking. If standardized training programs are a part of the organization's over-all development program, 1,1 fills his quota when requested from above or when subordinates automatically become eligible. Or, subordinates under him find their way into training on their own hook—he neither encourages nor discourages them. If nominated himself, he would go. There would not likely be an effort to get out of it.

Performance Appraisal

Performance appraisal is attended to as a matter of policy. For example, if the Personnel Department sends appraisal forms to supervisors on a periodic basis, the manager with a 1,1 orientation completes and returns them mechanically. Little thought goes into the ratings. He is careful, of course, not to rate anyone too high or too low —just about average. To do otherwise, could bring attention to his subordinates, and to him. If an interview is required as a matter of policy, he is likely to call the subordinate to his office, give a mechanical explanation, ask if he has any questions, and, if appropriate, ask that he sign the rating form. If there are no questions, the interview is over.

1,1 PERSONAL BEHAVIOR

The person who has adopted a 1,1 orientation is anchored neither to mastering the work environment nor to being loved by the people in it. His motivation is turned inward. Survival within the system is his dominant theme. Passive satisfaction has become his state of adjustment.

Outstanding Personal Characteristics

The person who adopts the 1,1 orientation goes along, in a passive way. He does not respond positively and enthusiastically. Furthermore, he does not search out a middle position. The 1,1 approach does involve going through the expected motions.[40] Because of this, a person operating under a 1,1 style frequently appears to follow rules of conduct in much the same way as does one with a 5,5 approach. The reason for it, though, is far different. When disagreement arises as to course of action, a 1,1 approach *avoids* taking sides, so much so that a person acting 1,1 is likely to be described as colorless because he rarely expresses convictions and does not search out those held by others. But, while one may not know where he stands, it does not seem to matter. When conflict does arise, he tends to remain neutral and, to the degree possible, to stay out of it. For as he says, "Bullets that fly over you don't hurt." Because of his neutrality, he rarely gets stirred up. If he does participate with humor, it is likely to be seen by others as rather pointless.

In the sense of his relationships within the work organization, the best description of the 1,1 approach is that of *nondirection*. It is nondirection from an outside point of view because there is little feeling of active pursuit of a path of interest or achievement.[41] Rather, the behavior is more like a jelly fish which floats, responding to the motion of the waves without a direction of its own.

Childhood Origins

Why do some adults adjust to frustration and failure by "fighting back" or trying to solve it by correcting the causes, etc., while others resign themselves, accepting it in a passive self-protective way?

Childhood factors undoubtedly predispose one direction or another of responding.[42]

When as a child one solved his problems of the frustrations of parental authority by sulking, or running away, and was allowed to do so, the underpinnings for an adult, 1,1 adjustment were being set.[43] For some parents, the *best* way to deal with a child who has been punished is to "let him sulk," by leaving him alone, or even, to put him in "solitary" ("Go to your room and *stay* there!"). Should the child continue to cry and be annoying, there is more spanking on top of the isolation.

Depending on how thoroughly this approach to child rearing is applied by parents, it is possible for the sulking, withdrawal pattern to become a strong back-up style for the child. Whenever frustrated, he withdraws—either physically, or by leaving the game, or by daydreaming, etc.[44]

It is only one step beyond for a frustrated adult to accommodate to organizational pressures and tensions in a similar fashion. Of course, it is more sophisticated, however, because it involves maintaining the outer decorum of institutional life, *i.e.*, being on the job, while being withdrawn from its demands and activities.[45]

Sense of Direction

In trying to understand various modes of adjustment, sociologists have described behavior which is, in some respects, like 1,1, similar to that depicted here. Durkheim used the word *anomie* as a way of characterizing the 1,1 adjustment, or that person who has no entity, who is rootless and drifting and who in his own behavior reveals no direction.[46] The word *anomie* catches one of the deeper characteristics contained in the 1,1 type of adjustment to an organization. The *a* (away from) is placed before *nom* identity. *Anomie* means "away from identity."

The individual who is acting according to a 1,1 orientation, though, is different in an important aspect from a state of *anomie* as portrayed in sociology. The difference is this. On Christmas Eve, a bum in skid row—dirty, ill attired, unshaven, sitting quietly, not communicating with other bums, aptly describes anomic people—rootless, drifting, not trying to influence the environment and, in turn, living in an environment that makes no demands on him. Respect for others is absent. So is self-respect. There is, therefore, an important difference between anomie and 1,1.

The 1,1 orientation is better understood as typical of a person who has beat a strategic withdrawal from active participation. In doing so, however, he has maintained the cast and form of acceptable behavior. His withdrawal is within him, but the exterior trappings remain as they were. He by no means would allow himself to become disheveled or dirty. He maintains the physical and functional appearances that put his behavior into conformance with that of the many others with whom he is associated. The withdrawal is interior only.[47]

CONDITIONS AND CONSEQUENCES OF A 1,1 ORGANIZATIONAL
STYLE

Circumstances Promoting 1,1 as an Organization Style

1,1 as an organization style, is too contradictory with
evolution to be actively striven for as a positive goal. However, there are conditions within organizations themselves
which promote the emergence of 1,1 in some large segments of the industrialized population.[48]

One circumstance likely to produce 1,1 in an individual is the simple matter of failure to be able to meet the
demands placed on him in an organizational setting. For
example, sometimes, in both industry and government a
1,1 orientation can be found where a person repeatedly has been by-passed for promotions. Rather than looking elsewhere, he adjusts in the work setting by doing as
little as possible, seeking satisfaction elsewhere.[49] He might
say, "The work isn't too bad. We like the town. We have
a comfortable house. I'm marking time until my retirement. I hope my chair doesn't break down."

A widespread 1,1 reaction is found in various work activities where task simplification and division of labor have
been carried to the extreme and where goals and expectations are not known or considered.[50] In situations of monot-
onous, repetitive, unchallenging work, it has been esti-
mated that as many as one-third of an organizational work
force can be apathetic, bored, disinterested, withdrawn, and
uninvolved in the job itself. In other words, a 1,1 adjustment has occurred.

One or two circumstances of truly total 1,1 organization existence can be envisioned. One is a circumstance
where work is "made for people." An example
might be the *WPA* during the depression of the 30's.[51] Although not necessarily 1,1 in the actual sense of the word,
it is possible that such a situation could produce a 1,1
organization. The other circumstance is a similar one—
it is one in which prices are fixed and commodities are
prescribed or where work is completely contracted. Such
circumstances might well result in a 1,1 organization.

Many a manager has risen to his present level by tough,

hard-minded managerial practices of driving, pushing and shoving to get productivity out — in a word, a true 9,1 managerial style. But, at the same time unions have gained strength. Progressively, the union has placed more and more restraints on some managements through contract bargaining. The kind of tough, coercive management that previously was applied is prevented from presently being employed.[52] To a tough 9,1 manager, it frequently appears as though the organization has gone hopelessly 1,9. As a result, the 9,1 manager is caught in a double-bind. He can no longer manage in a 9,1 way because of constraints placed upon him, but he can not tolerate, in his own conduct and value system, to manage in a 1,9 "soft" manner.

One consequence can be that he takes the withdrawal route of throwing up his hands and abandoning the effort, slipping into the 1,1 corner. Because he may be reasonably well aware of what he is doing, he does not "abandon ship." Rather, he "stays aboard," living by organizational rules and regulations and maintaining appearances in his exterior relationships. Nonetheless, he withdraws his emotions and convictions from the job in a manner which says, "I couldn't care less."

Technological innovations coupled with either self-imposed or union-imposed restrictions against firing, can lead to a 1,1 adjustment. Featherbedding or filling a paper job description which has no functional utility—is only likely to emphasize more the personal survival aspects of behavior.[53]

Long-Term Consequences of 1,1 Management

Certainly the 1,1 style of managing, or of personal or organization adjustment, is not the most common. In a competitive economy, a business operated under 1,1 concepts would be unable to continue very long. On the other hand, many individuals and organization segments may perform in the 1,1 manner, and survival may be possible for long periods of time. This is true especially in production situations that have become bureaucratic in nature and where "no one is ever fired."

As noted in the introduction, the 1,1 behavior of individuals is unnatural behavior. It is a situation of personal defeat that an individual comes to instead of begins with. 1,1 behavior is really an indication of failure for the individual and for the organization as well.[54] It is failure in that he has accepted defeat and has withdrawn from participation to the degree that even criticism no longer carries a sting. It is failure for the organization in that individual productive efforts are not integrated with sound human relationships.[55] 1,1 organization adjustment is also a situation of failure in that potential productive contribution is wasted.[56]

SUMMARY

A manager with a 1,1 orientation exerts minimum influence in his contacts with others. Little concern for production or people is expressed. In a supervisory position, he is most likely to be found executing messenger-carrier functions, communicating orders from the layer above to the layer below. The supervisor is an expert at passing blame for failures along in such a way as to absolve himself from responsibilities, yet he rarely initiates criticism spontaneously. His criticism is strictly in the interest of self-defense. Being allowed minimum involvement in the organization's purpose and with its people is all he asks.

The 1,1 orientation toward supervision is message carrying with minimum contact. Through minimum contact and non-involvement, 1,1 reduces the need to take more active steps with respect to managerial responsibilities. The less he sees of his boss the better. Subordinates or members of other groups are left to fend for themselves, even when action on his part may be appropriate. Being present, yet absent, is the 1,1 accommodation.

References

1. Shaw, D. M. Size and Share in Task and Motivation in Work Groups. *Sociometry*, 23, 1960, 203-208.

2. Blau, P. M. *The Dynamics of Bureaucracy*. Chicago: University of Chicago, 1955, 172-179, 184-88; Collins, O., Dalton, M. & Roy, D. Restriction of Output and Social Cleavage in Industry. *Applied Anthropology*, 5, (3), 1946, 1-14; Whyte, W. F. *Money and Motiva-*

tion. New York: Harper. 1955; Argyris, C. *Personality and Organization*. New York: Harper, 1957.

3. McGee, R. *Social Disorganization in America*. San Francisco: Chandler, 1962, 66-78.

4. Experimental studies and observations of children and adults have demonstrated the reactive and accommodative behavior of individuals to situations of prolonged frustration. The adaptive behavior described in these studies is most like the 1,1 orientation discussed in this chapter. Representative studies include: Eisenberg, P. & Lazarsfeld, P. F. The Psychological Effects of Unemployment. *Psychological Bulletin*, 35, 1938, 358-390; Lewin, K., Lippitt, R. & White, R. K. Patterns of Aggressive Behavior in Experimentally Created "Social Climates." *Journal of Social Psychology*, 10, 1939, 271-299; Dollard, J., Doob, L. W., Miller, N. E. Mowrer, O. H. & Sears, R. R. *Frustration and Aggression*. New Haven: Yale University, 1939; Barker, R. G. Dembo, T. & Lewin, K. Frustration and Regression: An Experiment with Young Children. *University of Iowa Studies in Child Welfare*, 18, I, 1941; Merrill, M. A. *Problems of Child Delinquency*. Boston: Houghton, 1947; Marquart, D. I. The Pattern of Punishment and Its Relation to Abnormal Fixation in Adult Human Subjects. *Journal of Genetic Psychology*, 39, 1948, 107-144; Wright, M. E. The Influence of Frustration Upon the Social Relations of Young Children. *Character & Personality*, 12, 1943, 111-112; Maier, N. R. F. *Frustration: The Study of Behavior Without a Goal*. Ann Arbor: University of Michigan, 1949; Heber, R. F. & Heber, M. E. The Effect of Group Failure and Success on Social Status. *Journal of Educational Psychology*, 48, 1957, 129-134; Pepitone, A. & Kleiner, R. The Effects of Threat and Frustration on Group Cohesiveness. *Journal of Abnormal & Social Psychology*, 54, 1957, 192-199; Moment, D. & Zaleznik, A. *Role Development and Interpersonal Competence*. Boston: Harvard University, 1963, 124-125. (Lewin, *et al*, speak of "laissez faire" leadership and Moment and Zaleznik speak of an "Underchosen" role.)

5. Drucker, P. F. *The New Society*. New York: Harper, 1950, 83; Vitalis, M. *Motivation and Morale in Industry*. New York: Norton, 1953, 51; Argyris, C., *op. cit.*, 89-95; Schutz, W. C. The Interpersonal Underworld. *Harvard Business Review*, 36, (4), 1958, 123-135.

6. *The Managerial Grid: A Self-Examination of Managerial Styles*. Austin, Tex.: Scientific Methods, Inc., 1962.

7. Maier, N. R. F., *op. cit.*

8. Guest, R. H. *Organizational Change: The Effect of Successful Leadership*. Homewood, Ill.: Dorsey, 1962, 17-38.

9. Guest, R. H., *op. cit.*

10. Guest, R. H., *op. cit.;* Lippitt, R. & White, R. K. The "Social Climate" of Children's Groups. In R. G. Barker, J. S. Kounin & H. F. Wright (Eds.), *Child Behavior and Development*. New York: McGraw-Hill, 1943, 485-508; Lippitt, R. & White R. K. An Experimental Study of Leadership and Group Life. In G. E. Swanson, T. M. Newcomb & E. L. Hartley (Eds.), *Readings in Social Psychology*. (2nd Ed.) New York: Holt, 1952, 340-355.

11. Schutz, W. C., *op. cit.*

12. Blau, P. M. Patterns of Interaction Among a Group of Officials in a Government Agency. *Human Relations*, 7, 1954, 337-348; Fouriezos, N. T., Hutt, M. L. & Guetzkow, H. Measurement of Self-Oriented Needs in Discussion Groups. *Journal of Abnormal & Social Psychology*, 45, 1950, 682-690; Moment, D. & Zaleznik, A., *op. cit.*

13. McGee, R., *op. cit.*, 34-41.

14. Broom, L. & Selzinick, P. *Sociology*. New York: Harper & Row, 1963, 717.

15. Hickson, D. J. Motives for Workpeople Who Restrict Their Output. *Occupational Psychology*, 35, 1961, 111-121.

16. Argyris, C. Human Relations in a Bank. *Harvard Business Review*, 1954, Sept.-Oct., 63-72.

17. Lawrence, P. R., Bailey, J. C., Katz, R. L., Seiler, J. A., Orth, C. D., Clark, J. V., Barnes, L. B. & Turner, A. N. *Organizational Behavior and Administration: Cases, Concepts, and Research Findings*. Homewood, Ill.: Dorsey, 1961, 237-238.

18. Moment, D. & Zaleznik, A., *op. cit.*

19. Kipnis, D. & Lane, W. P. Self-Confidence and Leadership. *Journal of Applied Psychology*, 46, 1962, 291-295.

20. Guion, R. M. Some Definitions of Morale. In E. A. Fleishman (Ed.), *Studies in Personnel and Industrial Psychology*. Homewood, Ill.: Dorsey, 1961, 301-304.

21. Marrow, A. J. & David, G. Why Do They Really Quit? *Management Review*, 41, 1952, 157-158; Argyris, C., *op. cit.*, 1957, 76-122.

22. Pelz, D. C. Influence: Key to Effective Leadership in the First Line Supervisor. *Personnel*, 29, 1952, 209-217.

23. Hurwitz, J. I., Zander, A. F. & Hymovitch, B. Some Effects of Power on the Relations Among Group Members. In D. Cartwright & A. Zander, *Group Dynamics: Research and Theory*. Evanston, Ill.: Row, Peterson, 1953, 483-492.

24. Kelley, H. H. Communication in Experimentally Created Hierarchies. *Human Relations*, 4, 1951, 39-56.

25. Roethlisberger, F. J. *Management and Morale*. Cambridge: Harvard University, 1952. (See esp. 89-105.)

26. Blake, R. R., Shepard, H. A. & Mouton, J. S. *Managing Intergroup Conflict in Industry*. Houston: Gulf Publishing Company. 1964.

27. Guion, R. M., *op. cit.*

28. Guest, R. H., *op. cit.*, 35.

29. Guest, R. H., *op. cit.*, 25.

30. Appley, L. A. *Management in Action*. New York: American Management Association, 1956, 127-128.

31. Argyris, C., *op cit.*, 1957, 116-118; Schutz, W. C., *op. cit.*

32. Schutz, W. C., *op. cit.*

33. Kelley H. H., *op. cit.*; Guest, R. H., *op. cit.*; Smith, E. E.

The Effects of Clear and Unclear Role Expectations on Group Productivity and Defensiveness. *Journal of Abnormal & Social Psychology,* 55, 1957, 213-217.

34. Roy, D. Quota Restriction and Goldbricking in a Machine Shop. *American Journal of Sociology,* 57, 1952, 427-442; Whyte, W. F., *op. cit.;* Hickson, D. J., *op. cit.*

35. See Chapter 7 (9,9) for more complete discussion of tensions, goals, involvement, etc.

36. Blum, F. H. *Toward a Democratic Work Process.* New York: Harper, 1953, 94-99.

37. Weschler, I. R., Kahane, M. & Tannenbaum, R. Job Satisfaction, Productivity and Morale: A Case Study. *Occupational Psychology,* 26, 1952, 1-14; Argyris, C., *op. cit.,* 1957, 116-118.

38. Schutz, W. C., *op. cit.*

39. Pelz, D. C., *op. cit.*

40. Riesman, D. *The Lonely Crowd.* New Haven: Yale University, 1961, 244.

41. Buber, M. Productivity and Existence. In M. P. Stein, A. J. Vidich & D. Manning (Eds.), *Identity and Anxiety.* Glencoe, Ill.: Free Press, 1960, 630.

42. Fromm, E. *Escape From Freedom.* New York: Holt, Rinehart & Winston, 1941, 29-32; Moment, D. & Zaleznik, A., *op. cit.,* 13-25.

43. Barker, R. G. *et al, op. cit.;* Sears, R. R., Maccoby, E. E. & Levin, H. *Patterns of Child Rearing.* Evanston, Ill.: Row, Peterson, 1957.

44. Maier, N. R. F. *Psychology in Industry.* (2nd Ed.) Boston: Houghton, 1955, 485.

45. Maier, N. R. F., *op. cit.,* 1955, 457-490.

46. Durkheim, E. *The Division of Labor in Society.* Glencoe, Ill.: Free Press, 1947; McGee, R., *op. cit.*

47. Schneiderman, L. *Repression, Anxiety, and the Self.* In M. P. Stein, *et al,* (Eds.), *op. cit.,* 157-165.

48. Argyris, C., *op. cit.;* Mills, C. W. *The Sociological Imagination.* New York: Oxford University, 1959, 165-176; Bensman, J. & Rosenberg, B. The Meaning of Work in Bureaucratic Society. In M. P. Stein, *et al,* (Eds.), *op. cit.,* 181-197.

49. Argyris, C., *op. cit.;* Schutz, W. C., *op. cit.;* Mannheim, K. Types of Rationality and Organized Insecurity. In C. W. Mills (Ed.), *Images of Man.* New York: George Braziller, 1960, 519.

50. Horwitz, M., Exline, R. V. & Lee, F. J. *Motivational Effects of Alternative Decision-Making Processes in Groups.* Urbana, Ill.: University of Illinois, 1953; Fromm, E., *op. cit.,* 295; Smith, E. E.. *op. cit.*

51. Marrow, A. J. *Making Management Human.* New York: Mc-Graw-Hill, 1957, 12.

52. Tannenbaum, F. *A Philosophy of Labor.* New York: Knopf, 1951.

53. Lincoln, J. F. *Lincoln's Incentive System*. New York: McGraw-Hill, 1946, 20; Riesman, D., *op. cit.*, 268.

54. Neumann, F. Anxiety and Politics. In M. P. Stein, et al, (Eds.), *op. cit.*, 270-271.

55. See Herzberg, *et al* for a thoughtful analysis and interpretation of work motivation in the industrial situation. Recommendations, consistent with 9,9, are put forward by the authors to replace 1,1 lack of interest and "hygienic" (1,9) concepts that are "... not related to the actual conduct of work [and] are the major sources of satisfaction, there is little motivation for the fulfillment of the highest potentiality in the work of each individual. When such a society has to cease living off the fat of earlier creativity, it may very well suffer the fate undergone by earlier societies now no longer in existence. The world is full of the dusty ruins of empires that were not resilient enough to cope with barbarian invaders." Herzberg, F., Mausner, B. & Snyderman, B. B. *The Motivation to Work*. New York: Wiley, 1959, 131. (For a summation of the consequences indicated by the authors' work, see especially pages 130-139.)

56. Hickson, D. J., *op. cit.*

CHAPTER SIX

The 5,5 Managerial Style

The middle of the Grid identifies 5,5. It is where intermediate concern for production, *5*, is linked with moderate concern for people, *5*. 5,5 also assumes conflict between organization purpose of production and needs of people.[1] Rather than resolving the issue in the direction of production as in 9,1, or of people as in 1,9, or 'leaving the field' as in 1,1, satisfactory or workable solutions are found through equilibrium or compromise processes.[2] Acceptable, even though not sound, production is possible from this approach without unduly disturbing people.[3] The 5,5 orientation assumes that people are practical, that they realize *some* effort will have to be exerted on the job. Also, by yielding some push for production and considering attitudes and feelings, people accept the situation and are more or less "satisfied."

The 5,5 approach is based on a persuasive logic. It says, "What person or movement has ever had its exclusive way? Extreme positions are to be avoided. Doesn't experience show, again and again, that steady progress comes from compromise, trading out, and a willingness to yield some advantages in order to gain others? Democracy, as it has come to be interpreted by many today, operates quite well by yielding to the many and mollifying the few."

Realistically, then, the guiding assumption of 5,5 is *not to seek the best position for either production or people* ("that would be too 'ideal' "), but to find the position that is in between both, about half-way.[4]

110

MANAGEMENT UNDER 5,5

The key to 5,5 is found in placing some emphasis on production. Since recognition is given to the fact that, realistically, people cannot be ignored or disregarded, some deliberate consideration is given to the people side. Yet, this is different than 9,1, as can be seen in the managerial examples that will follow; the 5,5 approach holds to the responsibility to plan, direct and control, typical of 9,1.[5] However, just as important, a major part of this responsibility is seen to be coupled with a need to communicate, to get understanding, and to elicit suggestions from subordinates.[6] This aspect is different from 1,9. In other ways the 5,5 style is designed to open up the possibility of subordinates' thinking about their job in more than a 1,9 social manner.[7]

The way in which combining and splitting is done in a 5,5 orientation can be seen in the following descriptions.[8]

Planning. "I plan work for each subordinate, more in a general way than down to details. After explaining aims and schedules, I make individual assignments. I insure that subordinates are agreeable with what is expected of them and that they feel free to come back if they need help in carrying my assignments out."

Work Execution. "I keep up with each man's job and review his progress with him from time to time or when he asks for it. I give positive suggestions if a subordinate is having difficulty."

Follow-up. "I meet with those involved in the job on a carrot-and-stick approach. I try to get discussion in order to point out good points as well as mistakes and to indicate how people can improve without *telling them*. Each individual gets the opportunity to discuss any reasonable suggestions he might have for improvement before I describe the next assignment."

In other words, there is a mixture, or balance, between taking people into consideration while still emphasizing the relevant aspects of work. In day-by-day activities, if either production or people are suffering, the 5,5 approach is to fix it, by finding a new position that can eliminate the imbalance. The flow of work through people under conditions of 5,5 is a delicate one. The 5,5 approach requires constant attention. It demands a delicate "balancing act," combined with the skills of a go-between.

DIRECTION AND CONTROL UNDER 5,5

Under 5,5 management, as under 9,1, people are seen as agents of production in relation to performance. However, for the 5,5 pattern, people are also termed "important." What this approach says is that, "You have more trouble in the long run if people are driven and disregarded than if you push for next best and, in addition, take some of their needs into account as you go. People are also an important product; they get equal consideration with production."

As a result of this 5,5 line of thinking, a manager does not *command* or *direct* in a 9,1 way so much as he *leads, motivates, and communicates* to get the job done.[9] The 5,5 managerial style does avoid exerting formal authority, in the strict 9,1 authority-obedience way of obtaining unquestioning obedience. Rather, this approach to leadership is to request and to sell, to try to get people to want to work.[11] As a manager whose orientation is a 5,5 approach explained, "I never give an order without explaining why and testing to see if people buy it. People are more likely to go along if you tell them the reason something has to be done and let them talk and even gripe a little."

The use of the "carrot and stick" approach is 5,5—a gentle prod if work falls behind, but an incentive or reward for 'satisfactory' accomplishment.[12]

Mistakes and Violations

For mistakes by subordinates, a similar attitude prevails. The fair but firm approach when errors occur is to give an employee the benefit of the doubt. The 5,5 approach is to insure the subordinate knows his job and what is expected of him. The "carrot" part is, "You can't blame him if he wasn't told differently. Give him another chance." The "stick" part is, "Make it clear a reoccurrence will require disciplinary action. This is the kind of mistake that can't be overlooked more than once. I'll have to take some (unspecified) action next time." In other words, the benefit of doubt is granted on a first occasion. However, conformity with what is expected has a high premium. When disciplinary action does become necessary, it is graduated according to the magnitude and seriousness of the error.[13]

The 5,5 style leans heavily on conformance with traditions, precedents and established rules and regulations for direction of day-by-day contacts with subordinates.[14] Authority is not likely to be experienced directly and in a personal way by subordinates, as in 9,1, but indirectly through reference to procedures, precedents and past practices. The manager might say, "Long years of experience have gone into the evolution of our procedures and practices. They have stood the test of time. I'm sure," he may joke, "that you would not want to kick a winner in the face." At a more general level, a 5,5 supervisor might say, "It is essential that our traditions, policies and procedures be conformed with and it is my responsibility to sell my people on following them. If they understand that rules are for the *good* of all, they generally will follow them willingly."

In other words, under 5,5 the premium is placed more on formal rules and precedents, for their own sake.[15] Achieving conformance with them is not done in a bullish way, but through a more sophisticated modern way, such as applying pressure on the man through his associates, *i.e.*, employing the sanctions through informal system, etc.

Because of the significance of traditions, precedents and past practices, authority is likely to be seen in the "rules" or "the way it's done." A manager with a 5,5 orientation will say, "It has to be this way because that's what the rules say," or, "that's the way the company wants it done."

Organizations that are managed by 5,5 orientations are likely to be viewed as quite bureaucratic since rules, regulations and red tape frequently appear to be an end in themselves.[16] They become "sacred cows." Under such conditions, managers are less free to interact to solve problems under their own personal authority. They have become "administrators" in the sense of interpreting procedures and regulations.[17] They, literally, manage paper rules and regulations; not people or problems of production.[18]

Often policies and regulations are ambiguous—the course of action is not clear. When this is true, the 5,5 way of resolving uncertainty is for the manager to scout around among his peers in other areas for what "they would do," or for a precedent.[19] Alternatively, he may tactfully tease an interpretation out of his boss without seeming to be unable to act in a competent and appropriate manner. In time he will have the answer. Whatever others are doing or what his boss thinks, then, becomes his own guideline for action.[20] This insures that he will not deviate from the expectations and organizational performance of others. By this way he can get results and yet not get himself "in a crack."

CONCEPT OF GOALS UNDER 5,5

Under 5,5, the relation between organization and individual purpose is explained in the following way: "There is a primary organization purpose, which is to return profit; but there also is another purpose which is to provide satisfaction and security to our people." These dual concepts catch the character of 5,5, getting a balance between individual and organization purposes.[21]

In the concrete work setting, perhaps the best phrase to catch the idea of goal orientation at 5,5 is the idea of a *target*. A target, in its ordinary industrial application, is something at which people shoot. Failure to hit the target is not necessarily something that is subject to ridicule or punishment, as in 9,1. Because it is important to keep people with him, the manager who operates with a 5,5 style sets achievable production goals— ones that can be reached in terms of the average ability of subordinates working under moderate supervisory pressures.

In this context, a target is not a do-or-die quota as in 9,1. Rather, a target is interpreted under 5,5 as a direction toward which people should set their sights. If one aims slightly higher than the average and efforts slip somewhat below, nothing really is lost in the long run. The objective, then, is to keep operations within the "acceptable" circles surrounding the bullseye.

Under 5,5 conditions, the manager takes pains to explain the reasons why the work is to be done according to his plan.[22] Furthermore, he is flexible in that he listens to others and alters plans to meet unforeseen objections and to avoid undue resistances. The manager with a 5,5 approach wants his plans to be acceptable and to conform with the thinking of those around him, both above and below. A target serves to define an area of orientation with respect to production results.

Many aspects of organization life encourage a target of mediocrity, particularly in larger, older, blue chip organizations. Young members are told, "pace yourself, don't shoot too high or, in the event of failure, you will stand out in comparison with the person who set attainable goals for himself." Pressures toward conformity surround the person or group who would, otherwise, strike out for higher goals of work performance.[23] The goal for a person is not to be a "flash (in the pan), but to be durable, to be with it for a long, long career; to be able to roll with the punches."[24]

BOSS-SUBORDINATE RELATIONSHIPS UNDER 5,5

The 5,5 orientation prefers a one-to-one relationship between boss and subordinates in terms of supervision and work direction. Unlike 9,1, however, the relationship is on more of a "regular guy" or give-and-take basis.[25]

A 5,5 manager has confidence in his subordinates when he feels they understand the organization and its system. "I insure that subordinates know the limits of what is acceptable. Within that framework I afford them the freedom of action to exercise their authority." But he is quick to spot deviations, particularly for those likely to reflect on him. He explains how observance of standard practices is for the good of all. In this way, the manager is able to prep subordinates for the coming years of good organization service expected of them.

Meetings with Subordinates

Group sessions and special groups such as committees or task forces are relied on extensively.[26] In this way, there is a heavy component of one-to-all interactions with a 5,5 orientation. He says, "I use a group meeting to give people a chance to participate. 1 am always open to suggestions. My group frequently makes recommendations that I give weight to in making the decision."

Committees serve several purposes. One is to give an opportunity for participation in discussions relevant to work, without giving authority away.[27] Another purpose is in a subtle way to avoid responsibility for, and negative reactions from, solo decisions.[28] This can be done by basing them on group recommendations. A third way is more genuine. It is to elicit ideas and suggestions which can then be further evaluated for merit and possible use, and for personal credit.[29]

Attitudes Toward His Boss

The supervisor with a 5,5 managerial orientation anticipates the expectations of his boss. He acknowledges the need for good relations and seeks to prove leadership qualities by getting production with minimum friction. His goal is to be a little bit above 'average,' but to avoid getting known as "gung ho."

Because of the need to be on middle ground, 5,5 is not likely to be conspicuously different in either an outstandingly good or poor direction. Rather, his actions with those higher in the hierarchy are likely to be characterized by doing what is politically expedient.[30] To a person with a 5,5 orientation, the question is not so much what is best, but what is sellable or workable. Thus, he takes the expedient action, frequently at the expense of a sounder way to go that might provoke discord. He is likely to embrace points of view which serve neither people nor production needs fully, but are taken because of politics. That is, they are possible.

The manager with a 5,5 orientation is likely to "report all exceptions and unusual occurrences to his boss, and enough day-by-day detail to give him the flavor of what is going on." He keeps a finger in the wind, though, to see which way it is blowing, in order to be close at hand.

Creating and Maintaining Morale

In the 5,5 philosophy, high morale is seen to be connected to work.[31] The satisfaction of personnel, as in 1,9, is not an end in itself. Rather, attention is given to morale in terms of its potential production contribution. Certainly, the loss of morale, by analogy to the friction in a machine, can be deleterious to production.

"The importance of morale as a contributing factor in production can't be overlooked. Morale can be kept high by striking a happy balance between emphasis on production and people's enjoyment of their work. People, as well as machines, need maintenance. Things must be kept oiled, if you want them to run smoothly."

Opinion surveys are likely to be used as indicators of a healthy level of satisfaction (see a later section concerned with this topic).

Communication Activities Under 5,5

Under the 5,5 managerial style, approximately equal weight is given to the formal and informal organization.[32] (The informal organization is made up of social relationships of liking and disliking, feelings and attitudes, expectations and values, etc., that people develop out of their formal organization membership.)[33] A person with a 5,5 style believes every formal organization should have its rules, regulations and policies. There also should be a chain of command, a span of control, job specializations, etc., and a communication system.[34] However, he acknowledges that, people being what they are, the formal organization also produces an *informal* organization. The informal organization has its own norms, standards and rules of conduct, its leaders and followers, its conformists and deviants, and its own channels of communication.[35] He knows that the informal organization can either support the goals of the formal organization or,[36] in a fantastically large number of ways, prevent their attainment in a manner which is very difficult for management to cope with. *Recognizing the inevitability of the informal organization, his way of adjusting to it is to use it.*[37] In this way, he can keep organizational goals for production from frustrating people while preventing people from shirking reasonable organizational demands for production and efficiency.

The character of communication at the 5,5 position, then, is likely to include the concept of "communications watcher." What is meant here is that the importance of the informal system as an indicator of morale and satisfaction is well known. In the extreme, the informal system is the source of information about morale and satisfaction, how people are reacting, union and management relations, and so on.[38] Thus, the informal organization can tell much about the "pulse" of people—about how people are feeling and what they are saying.[39] In this way, disturbing anti-organizational trends and individual pressure points can be traced. As a manager with 5,5 overtones says, "You have to keep your antenna out to know what's going on, that is, to get the signal."

The concept of *watching* comes in because the goal of 5,5 communications is to avoid generating organization tensions. Another way of saying it is that the timing of messages in the formal system is balanced against communications being received regarding morale and satisfaction from within the informal system. If an announcement would have a deleterious effect on morale, or if morale already were low, the announcement would be withheld, at least for a time. This would be done to avoid the dissonance or tensions that otherwise would be produced between the formal and informal if negative information were to be released before people were conditioned.[40] By "keeping in touch," the 5,5 manager frequently is able to recommend corrective actions concerning issues which, left unattended, might easily erupt into disturbing organizational conflict that could push production down.

In this, but also in many other ways, one aspect of the 5,5 orientation is the role of *go-between*. It involves running between the formal and informal, testing a course of action, first from one side, then from the other. By a series of approximations then, finally, a position emerges which "will get the job done *without* stirring up too much trouble."

Over a period of time, such compromises are likely to form a patchwork quilt of contradictions, reversals, starts and stops, etc. This is *practical* as opposed to *systematic* management.

The opinion poll and related kinds of surveys can provide a crutch, a source of information behind which a person with a 5,5 managerial attitude can hide, in the absence of a precedent, while at the same time making decisions. When a market survey or opinion poll points in a given direction, then the 5,5 manager can accept that course of action without exposing his own thinking or putting his own "judgment on the line." In effect, he can hide behind the expertise of the opinion poll without "sticking his neck out."

This criticism of opinion polls should not be interpreted as criticism of management measurement. The problem being discussed here is not in the nature of the measurement itself, but rather in the mechanics of its use and interpretation. A manager may make decisions by hiding behind an opinion survey result to avoid human judgments that involve risk and reservation. Then he leans on such measurement to avoid exposing his own judgment. If things go wrong, he always can avoid the blame by placing it on opinion polls.

The same kind of 5,5 organization attitude can be seen in casual conversation just as well as in the more mechanical and ritualistic use of test scores or survey results. Recently, in asking what course of action he would take on a given problem, a manager indicated that his way would be to test out in his own mind what it is that "most people" think or "most people" would do (or conduct his own personal poll). Then he would feel greater certainty because his decision coincided with the majority point of view. And so, if he were uncertain as to what course of action to take, he would not defer to the group decision as in 1,9. Nor would he risk holding to personal conviction in disregard of majority opinion, as might be true in 9,1. Rather, he would conduct his own survey and find out how most people look at the problem. He indicated that when he had found out what most people thought, the solution would be the one which he himself would also apply.

Another characteristic of 5,5 communications is with respect to the "trial-balloon" concept. Before taking a definite stand, the 5,5 approach is that of putting out a trial signal to anticipate what the reaction would be if it became official. In this way, the 'propriety' of a message can be assessed before any final commitment to putting it out is made.

But, the 5,5 manager does far more than monitor the radar screen of the informal organization, as is true for 1,9.[41] He may take active steps to correct contrary or anti-organizational trends by feeding the informal system confidential information on a not-to-be-repeated basis. In this way he is able to correct misguided rumors, to relieve tension and to calm troubled waters. At the same time, he is seen by influential members of the informal organization as a 'good guy' who comes through when the chips are down and lets you in 'on the know.'

Perhaps a more subtle aspect of the communication system in 5,5 is with respect to signals communicated by status grading.[42] Status grading provides a non-verbal way of calibrating the informal hierarchy and insuring one's appropriate place in it.[43] The concept of status grading can be seen in many 5,5 industrial communities. Each individual knows how large a car it is appropriate for him to drive and how large the house is he should live in. "How," the question must be asked, "does an individual know this?"

The answer is that an individual knows what is right because "right" is something between what applies for his boss and what applies for subordinates.[44] Another way of saying it is that if the boss drives a bigger car, say an Oldsmobile, and subordinates drive, say a Chevrolet, then the appropriate car for him to drive is perhaps a Buick or a Pontiac. It's in between — not as large and expensive as the Olds, nor as small and relatively inexpensive as the Chevrolet. The same reasoning applies in deciding where to live and what size house to live in. Here the answer is that one should live in a house the expense of which is equal in distance between that of the boss and those of subordinates — not so expensive as that of the boss, but more expensive than those lived in by subordinates. By keeping in touch with trends, one maintains his appropriate position within the informal status system.[45]

In keeping with this concept of communications, office or company news sheets feed into the informal communication system information which will bolster the formal system and acceptance of the company. In general, the internal publication is a potpourri of daily news—a little bit of sports on the back page, some local city news on pages 1 and 2, bits of company information on 1, 2 and 3, some social news on page 3, and, frequently, a question and answer section where queries are invited from those who would like information, with "studied" answers provided.[46]

5,5 APPROACHES TO MANAGING CONFLICT

To understand the 5,5 approach to managing conflict, it is important to touch back to the underlying 5,5 attitudes concerning production and people. People are considered as important as production under 5,5. Morale is important. Feelings and attitudes are not ignored. Disregarded, they are barriers which can hinder production. The two have to be kept together to prevent one disrupting the other. Here the manager's attitude might be:

"Human nature being what it is, you can't expect to really go all out for either production or for people. If you go all out for production, you lose the commitment and good will of people. You generate their active resentment. On the other hand, if you go all out for people, production falls by the wayside. What you have to do is yield, to twist, turn and bend to find a course down the middle that represents steady, even if not dramatic, progress. You've got to split the difference, but there's nothing bad about that. Progress, in this world, is made by people who know how to give something to get something. By going this route, you might not get a whole loaf but, on the other hand, neither do you starve."[47]

These attitudes are basic for understanding a 5,5 approach to conflict. The 5,5 approach is summed up as follows:

"Seldom is it wise to confront conflict head-on. If you do, someone wins and someone loses. A lot of people don't know it, but a loser in a fight is a potential enemy when the next battle shapes up. Furthermore, many conflicts represent hot emotions of the moment. If you back off and let the situation cool a while, you can usually find a basis for pulling the warring parties together. A little breathing time gives you a chance to think of an acceptable ground. Frequently, it's possible to take some of one man's ideas and a little of another's and to put them together. The solution you come up with may not be the perfect one, but it will probably get bought in that some of the thinking of each of the contending factions is represented in it.[48] Each gets something. Thus, everyone wins, at least a little bit, and is satisfied."

From the Boss' Perspective

There are a variety of ways to deal with conflict under a 5,5 approach. On the surface, each appears different from the others, but all have a common fundamental concept. It is *splitting* or separation. That is, conflict is managed by keeping parties in conflict apart until a solution can be found.[49]

One way of splitting, probably the most common of all, whether from the boss' perspective or from the subordinates' point of view, is compromise—finding a middle ground between two opposed alternatives.[50] In the 5,5 use of compromise, the final position does not meet the full requirements of either alternative, but it does provide a middle position that people with different positions find better to accept than to retain their own position and to continue the argument. There are some situations where the middle situation is the *best* solution, but 5,5 orientation is not aimed at this position because it is the best one. Rather, the middle ground is sought to *split the difference* and get a resolution. This permits an accommodation, even though it does not deal with the reservations and doubts that led to the difference.

A clear point of distinction should be emphasized with respect to compromise as a decision-making approach in a political as contrasted with a work and production setting. There are many reasons for believing that when other approaches fail, compromise is an adequate basis for the resolution of conflict in the context of political action. For example, under certain political circumstances, only rarely is it possible to confront conflict in a face-to-face setting. Each person is obligated to represent the interests of many divergent and diverse groups. The end position taken may be something intermediate between all of the positions represented.

Quite a different point of view applies with respect to conflict, however, when practiced in the setting of operational performance. Here the true goal of managerial competence is to achieve the best result in terms of production through people. The best is rarely defined by something which is in the middle, intermediate, or which represents a splitting of differences between divergent points of view. An adverse result is that though the problem is solved, the solution leaves the deeper-lying problem unresolved.

Another very common way of splitting involves a situation where there are two subordinates in an open conflict. When the boss happens on it, his immediate response is to talk to them one by one to understand the problem. Then he tries to find some middle ground to which they can both agree. Finally, he gives each one, separately, his decision. This is likely to result in some basis for agreement in terms of which subordinates can live together, at least administratively, even under conditions of mutual dislikes. The boss has handled the conflict by splitting it.[51] (Parents use the same approach in settling fights between children.)

With the 5,5 approach, splitting also can occur when disagreement is present among people who are called together to discuss an issue.[52] Here, though appearing to do so, the ranking person may have no intention of using group actions as the basis of decision. However, because of the popularity of the idea that people should discuss, deliberate, and debate, he may go through the motions of group decision making while subtly retaining personal control.[53] The technique is as follows: The ranking person sees *each* of the subordinates in private. He talks through with them the problem as he sees it. He gets their concurrence with the appropriate course of action as he sees it. When each person has given his commitment to the position, then he calls a meeting. The mechanics of deliberation and debate are present even though there is little likelihood that the decision will be anything different than the one that has been "seeded" through earlier private discussions. In this way, each of the persons who represents a potential position in a conflict of views has been neutralized by having been split from one another and tied down before coming together.

Splitting may also mean permanent physical separation of warring persons. One way is to move people who are in conflict so that they are not in direct contact with one another. This might happen, for example, in a large room where a number of people work. Here, the splitting strategy might be no more, for example, than separating the subordinates in disagreement. They are moved to opposite sides of the room, each to work in isolation from one another.

Another method of splitting that is common in 5,5 is that of using transfers to get rid of people who fight or in other ways "don't fit."[54] There is no effort to confront the reasons for the difficulty. Rather, by devious means arrangements are worked out to provide an assignment in another location to the person who seems to be the focus for a problem. (Then the problem child belongs to someone else.)

Another splitting mechanism that finds use in 5,5 is that of redrawing the organization chart.[55] The function of one of the contending parties is transferred, in terms of its reporting line so that the two individuals in conflict no longer have a common boss. Therefore, they have no basis for maintaining mutual relations. When the function is transferred, it sometimes is possible to work out a physical rearrangement to reflect the different reporting arrangement. This automatically separates the two people who were previously in conflict. It "solves" the problem.

All of these strategies for dealing with conflict are based on the concept of splitting—separating people and maintaining a separation among them as a basis for controlling conflict. The various procedures are classified here as 5,5. The reason is that they do not consider the conflict itself and take positive action towards its causes. The conflict is there but it is kept underneath the surface.

From the Subordinates' Perspective

From the point of view of a subordinate, who is in potential or actual conflict with his boss, the 5,5 approach is that of *balancing* and *tentativeness*. The subordinate does not follow his boss' thinking and take it blindly. Nor does he meet it with flat disagreement. Nor does he avoid taking a position at all. Rather, he remains tentative so that he can shift without being wrong and losing face or without being seen as inconsistent and vacillating. A hallmark of 5,5 in this connection is balancing the positive against the negative. For example, when asked to suggest a course of action, a subordinate with a 5,5 orientation can always balance a strength with a weakness, a recommendation with a reservation. A typical 5,5 phrase is "on the one hand ... *but, on the other ...*"

The premium placed on tentativeness as the basis for getting *workable* solutions to problems often results in his actions seeming quite acceptable. However, a contradiction is likely to appear between his own perception of the problem and those of his boss. The paradox is in the fact that whereas the subordinate sees himself as *realistic*, by shifting to reduce conflict, he is likely to be seen by his boss as a person lacking character, integrity, and internal strength. From the other person's perspective the person frequently is seen to move purposely away from the position that was generating conflict, not in terms of his altered understanding and convictions regarding the problem, but rather by making proposals which only solve the surface problem. It is just this kind of thinking that comes through to a boss, not as helpful, but as lacking in character and in intellectual strength.

When a subordinate is in conflict with other peers, resolution can be sought in several ways. Meeting the other person half-way is a 5,5 strategy at the peer level, equivalent to compromise. The other major stratagem is to appeal to authority in some manner. One is by seeking for a precedent in tradition to solve the problem without losing face or yielding status. In this way, the weight of impersonal authority can be brought to bear and no one is really "wrong." When subordinates are in conflict, another way is to appeal to a common boss—a third party who can adjudicate the conflict and rule a winner and loser.[56]

IMPACT OF 5,5 ON CREATIVITY AND CHANGE

Creativity is *not* likely to be part and parcel of the work interaction of managers whose orientation is 5,5.[57] Traditions and established practices as an orienting framework in itself is likely to insure that 5,5 will seek to maintain or preserve the *status quo* rather than to change it.[58]

At the Boss' Level

Not wanting to be criticized for stepping out of line, either by being forward or for blocking progress, the manager with a 5,5 orientation tests the informal system or uses other means, such as his boss' thinking, to ascertain how much is too much in terms of resistance, and to promote that which is within acceptable limits.[59]

However, the word "creativity" is valued. One is "for" it. Efforts to tap the potential contribution of people are made, at least in a superficial way.

How? To release the creative energies of people, various gimmicks and techniques are used. Brainstorming is one such example.[60] Since criticism is suspended during the brainstorming period, conflict is avoided. People do not feel their ideas to be rejected. Evaluation of them is not needed as the basis for just listening to new ideas. Here again splitting occurs between thinking and the exercise of reasoned judgment. The ideas produced by brainstorming are then carted away, for others to evaluate.[61]

In terms of suggestions or new ideas from subordinates, the manager with a 5,5 orientation knows that frequently a subordinate can make important operational improvements. He reviews each suggestion to be sure it has not been presented before. If it looks good—and is not too far out of the realm of possibility in line with current practices—he encourages the subordinate to write it up. Then it is submitted through appropriate channels for evaluation. Again, splitting is the means of avoiding disagreement.

At the Subordinate Level

Since supervisors "do not listen too well" to subordinates in either 9,1 or 5,5 the **administrative** solution to the creativity problem is likely to be a suggestion system.[62] Such a system gets around the problem of the supervisor who cannot hear the creativity of subordinates to whom he refuses to listen. Suggestion systems are initiated with a plan, they work well for a while, and then dwindle to a mediocre level. In time, they become "just another tradition" in a 5,5 organization. After several years of contending with red-tape "coin-your-ideas" programs or "Suggestion Boxes," the rare suggestions that do find their way to the boxes often are unsigned forms in quadruplicate, in the nature of "Drop Dead" suggestions.

COMMITMENT UNDER 5,5

Some of the descriptions given earlier will serve for examining a new facet of organizational adjustment. The goal of a 5,5 style is to avoid self-directed action in much the same manner as 1,1 avoids self-directed action. But what is absent in 1,1 and present in 5,5 is readiness to *take* action which is organizationally-based. A 5,5 manager, in other words, sees his task to be to get people to do what the organization wants of them by inserting himself as the go-between. He is the connecting rod between organization and man.

The Boss' Commitment

The commitment of 5,5 is that of getting acceptable results by working along, representing the system while avoiding actions that would upset the applecart and expose him to criticism. This commitment is one that, in comparison with a 1,1 low survival insurance, has high survival insurance. By being a good organization man, a manager insures regularized quasi-seniority based promotion. By operating acceptably within the requirements and expectations of the system, he eliminates the reasons for withholding reward of promotion or salary. Perhaps he has not shone and demonstrated particular reasons for outstanding reward, but this sure-footed approach provides every reason for intermediate reward. Moving at one's appropriate pace within the promotion grading system is a value toward which a person with a 5,5 orientation is committed. In other words, he is committed to the system as is, not so much to contribute to achieving organization purpose. To be a good "organization man," in other words, is the commitment of the manager with a 5,5 orientation.[63]

Commitment of Subordinates

A person managed in a 5,5 setting might say, "The company provides every opportunity I want. It's an old and respected company. Just say its name to anyone and you can get credit or any other consideration you need. They have a regular promotion plan and I have a boss who is fair but firm. The company rewards loyalty and long service, and that's what I'm going to give them. There are only five people near my age in my department. At a good, steady pace, I have an above average chance of becoming the department head or the assistant—or at least one of the section heads, which is not bad either. We have a nice home now. In fifteen years, we should be able to move into a $35,000 to $45,-000 home. I'll get a good retirement, and our two kids are assured a college education. My wife and I belong to several clubs and organizations in town. I've got it made—no ulcers for me."

What is the commitment here? It is to a just better than average life with its conventional values and status symbols. No burning involvement—no high commitment to accomplishment of the sort that requires striking out in experimental or innovative ways; just an uncomplicated, steady and progressive way. In this sense, com-

mitment to survival, as in 1,1, is high. The commitment
is one that demands no more than slightly above average
effort—stay up and maybe just a little ahead of the middle of the pack. As with the boss, so with subordinates.
Satisfaction in the form of prestige becomes a goal of 5,5
—prestige through external symbols of achievement, not
through an inner sense of contribution.[64]

MANAGEMENT DEVELOPMENT UNDER 5,5

Selection

Given selection responsibilities, a 5,5 oriented manager would examine candidates from the following point
of view. He would, first, want them to have the creden-
tials of competence—a college degree or high school
diploma, as appropriate, would be a must. Beyond that
consideration, though, his interest would be in extra-
curricular activities—wideness of leadership, and having
been active in the right organizations: student government, church, and other campus activities.

He would present the company in a positive light,[65]
pointing not only to its security and welfare advantages
(stock purchase plans, savings arrangements, health insurance, vacations, etc.), but also to its capacity to offer a
man a future, perhaps by describing, in a general way, a
few typical success stories. His approach would be the soft
sell, playing up the pros and playing down the cons.[66]

Induction

At the point of induction, the 5,5 approach to management development is likely to involve an extended
orientation program. The organization inductee is given
a period of two, five, seven or nine weeks, or even longer,
to become adjusted to the organization. Some orientation
programs are informal and involve tours of major facilities.
Others involve presentations by each of the major functions
to describe their roles. In addition, during this period, rules,
regulations, policies, procedures, mechanics of pay and vaca-

tions and so on, all are presented and discussed in detail. Toward the end of insuring that the individual's accommodations to the organization's mechanical system will be adequate, the pace is slow and not too demanding.[67]

Management Development

Beyond this approach to management development the 5,5 strategy is likely to involve short courses and night school work. Classes are conducted, often on an incompany basis using company facilities. In that case, the top man shows how important it is by kicking it off; he gives it his blessing. Completion is with certificates and a handshake. Everyone is successful. Alternatively, arrangements are made at nearby academic institutions. In the latter case, part or all the tuition is paid by the company. The tradeout is that the man spends his working time on the job in return for the company's paying the expense. Other than these arrangements, the attitude toward management development in 5,5 is likely to involve little more than lip service. Formalized training programs are designed to reinforce company traditions, policies and so forth—to make the person more knowledgeable of the organization and how to use it to get work done.[68]

Performance Appraisal

Another aspect of management development in 5,5 involves performance reviews. Under 5,5, the goal is to aid the individual by a sandwich review: pointing out some of his strong, then weak points, and then the remainder of his strong points (bread-meat-bread) in such a way as to compensate for discouragement that may be felt over weaknesses. Interviews close on a note of praise and encouragement. In this way, the score is kept approximately equal. Even under unfavorable circumstances, a subordinate is likely to come out of a performance review feeling a little better.[69]

5,5 PERSONAL BEHAVIOR

Outstanding Personal Characteristics

The person with a 5,5 predisposition does not work on the production side for excellence in performance, and he does not expect ideal relations with people.[70] He knows it is impractical to try for utopia because no matter how hard you try, you can only please some of the people some of the time. Thus, his realistic goals are to achieve workable solutions to problems that result, not in genuine gratification, but in good sound satisfaction. His preferred approach to conflict is to find out what the best course of action has been in terms of tradition and past practice or according to common sense or rules of thumb.[71] As a result, when ideas, opinions or attitudes different from his own appear, he searches for compromise positions representing majority thinking that can relieve the impasse; from compromise approved by others comes self-approval. When conflict does arise, however, he tries to be fair but firm, to get a fair solution that is equitable to as many as possible.[72]

When operating on the basis of convention, he is secure to move ahead, he feels self-confident. He starts the ball rolling—takes the lead—when precedent or past practice dictates the way to go. But he rarely moves out in front until a new direction has been established. When he does introduce humor into a situation, it is the kind that either sells himself in terms of increasing his acceptance by others or the position he wants to get bought.

What is the primary or motivational core in child development which leads an individual to adopt 5,5 approaches? Whereas avoidance of guilt associated with failure seems to motivate 9,1 types of action, and avoidance of social rejection, 1,9, and avoidance of contact the 1,1, it would appear that the motivation of 5,5 is concerned with approval and prestige, and avoiding the shame that comes from its loss. Prestige, in this sense, has to do with an individual feeling approved of for his own performance, not because he thinks himself successful, but because he is thought successful in the eyes of others. By respecting traditions and norms, supporting the *status quo,* and avoiding behavior that might be seen to deviate from established practices, one's behavior can steer him on down a path which is quite likely to win security, status and prestige.[74]

Childhood Origins

The person with a 5,5 disposition, then, can be understood in terms of the effort to anchor himself to the mode or *status quo.* In doing so he orients himself in two ways. One is in terms of what the majority does or thinks. By conforming with the majority he avoids being conspicuous and extreme. In this way he is responsive to contemporary pressures. Perhaps as much, or even more significant, is that security, direction and certainty can be had from adhering to social convention and codes of of conduct, represented by tradition, past practices and precedent.[75]

Children reared in such a way as to prefer 5,5, then, are likely to be ones who are concerned with what is right and wrong, good and bad, as defined by the local society of one's parents' environment. Self-esteem is possible by doing what others think is right or good. But one does not think it through; rather one looks at what others accept. Not to measure up provokes shame and disapproval.[76]

In the 5,5 orientation, right and wrong are defined in strictly social terms.[77] Child rearing places a premium on codes of conduct based on social morals, etiquette, and so on. These provide guidelines for behavior. Approval is extended to the child who lives according to traditions and standards set before him. Parents teach that shame and disgrace follow deviation from what is expected, *i.e.,* "what will people *think?*" Thus, the child learns to lean on tradition and precedent as guides to action. Esteem of others stems from ability to follow prescribed rules. He also finds that deviation from conventional standards or doing what is different or unusual can bring reproach and disparagement with loss of esteem and love from his parents, who then cover up or rationalize to hide their own embarrassment.

Where Does the Direction Come From?

The middle ground of the 5,5 orientation is not necessarily based on deliberate or rational choice. It may be
just as unreasoned as the guilt-motivated pressure for
production in 9,1 or the anxiety-ridden fear of rejection
of 1,9. The fear of shame, of deviating too far from the
conventional or expected toward one extreme or another,
may be what causes the 5,5 individual to search for pre-
scriptions from the environment of yesterday, to define
what would constitute the best thing to do today.[78] In
addition, a strategem often used by the parents of 5,5
children is that of bargaining. "Eat your vegetables and
you can have dessert," is an example of a tradeout in
the eating habits area. A child soon learns to bargain
back and expects a reward or desired object or action
from his parents in return for complying with their pre-
scriptions. Thus, the bargaining orientation of the parent is a critical ingredient in building the character of a
person with a dominant 5,5 orientation.

The 5,5 orientation, characterized as it is by seeking
prestige and status, has a number of strategies available
for achieving some measure of self-defined success. First,
when confronted with a problem requiring solution,
traditions, past practices and precedents become the
guides to action. According to the 5,5 approach, those solutions are ones which "have stood the test of time." Beyond that, from a practical point of view, "a half of a
loaf is better than none." A result is that a person
oriented toward a 5,5 approach is flexible. He can shift
and slide, twist and turn, with the demands of the situation. If a course of action can be found in tradition or
precedent, then the 5,5 person experiences no contradiction within himself. He is *tradition-directed.*[79]

In contrast with the 1,9 person, he is not so anchored
to personal feelings of acceptance-rejection that a few
disgruntled people are anxiety provoking. Rather, with
his wave length tuned to the majority and his skill in
looking for trends and middle positions, he can piece
together a fabric of action which is the least unacceptable to many. In many ways, then, the 5,5 orientation

can operate adequately when confronted with both production or people problems. However, it is unlikely to achieve true excellence or to result in full failure. Rather, it is likely to achieve a careful maintenance of the *status quo*.

CONDITIONS AND CONSEQUENCES OF THE 5,5
    ORGANIZATION STYLE

Circumstances Prompting 5,5

Circumstances prompting 5,5 as an organization style can be viewed best from an historical perspective.[80] Antagonistic and hostile reactions to 9,1 management produced for a brief period an overreaction into the 1,9 direction of excessive concern for feelings and attitudes. However, after a period of "the human relations binge," as in 1,9, counterforces developed to move people in the opposite direction.[81] Rather than an alternative of either 9,1 or 1,9, the pendulum got dampened and stopped in the middle of the 9,1-1,9 diagonal, where a *balance* was sought by hitting a happy medium.

Another social circumstance which continues to promote 5,5 as an organizational style is the transfer of concepts from politics to the industrial setting. The rightness of the majority; the significance of people being with leadership in a supportive sense; feelings of equality and respect for the individual and a sense of democracy are values which can be translated into 5,5 or 9,9 managerial philosophy. Emphasis on lawful, orderly behavior, rooted in tradition and past practices, when the *rule* is the critical element, rather than on experimentation, leads most pronouncedly into 5,5 as a managerial style.

Long-Term Consequences of 5,5 Management

Whyte, in his popular book, *The Organization Man*, offered a scorching, but quite accurate, analysis of 5,5 as the general American approach to management today.[83] In the absence of a truly sound managerial base, 5,5 is seen as superior to a 9,1 system, which can generate intense warfare that disrupts organizational and individual

goals.[84] 5,5 is also seen to be superior to the 1,9 approach
of sweetness and light that results in people becoming
contented and happy but which, in the extreme, can produce a flat, fat, flabby and ineffectual organization.

Many large organizations, whether industrial, government, military, or academic, have been unable to gear
their membership to any greater accomplishment or
commitment than that represented by 5,5. 5,5 management is here to stay and for a long time to come. It is
entrenched.[85] It is able, over long periods, to endure as a
way of life in large, massive organizations.

Yet, the challenge confronting modern management
is to *set higher goals* than 5,5 as the basis for future
accomplishment.

A 5,5 reliance on norms and traditions can, for many
of the repetitive problems of management, provide effective mechanical guidance that fits adequately a large
majority of situations. But, there are many management situations where reliance on tradition is insufficient
for getting the job done. Thus 5,5 provides a poor basis
for promoting innovation, creativity, discovery and novelty.
All of these are likely to be sacrificed by the adherence to
tradition and "majority" standards of conduct. Long term,
then, the 5,5 or *status quo*, results in a gradual slipping behind as more movable, progressive organizations take advantage of new opportunities of better management
practices.

SUMMARY

The *people* dimension in the work situation is as important in the 5,5 orientation as is the *production*
dimension. 5,5 seeks to maintain a balance between the
two. A basic assumption of 5,5 is that people will work
willingly and do as they are told if the reasons for doing
so are explained. Thus, 5,5 communicates freely with
subordinates. Both the formal and the informal systems
are used for this purpose to keep people in the know.
However, just enough is communicated so people have
a general sense of what is going on. If too much is told, they
might resist when fully known plans or decisions need

to be shifted. Enough concern is shown at the *people* level so that adequate production can be achieved. This is seen in 5,5 approaches to management development, communication, performance reviews and the use of meetings. Meetings are to cut in the people, to hear suggestions and to convey a sense of having had a hand in the making of decisions.

One other aspect of 5,5 again concerns the informal system. 5,5 does not just monitor the grapevine and oversee how things are being done, but actively uses the informal system toward organizational purposes. Here is an example. If a particular informal procedure, method or technique emerges from the informal system and it is a good organization action, 5,5 takes steps to formalize the informal action through policy or writing so that it can become a part of formal operations.

The 5,5 managerial orientation places some concern on both the production and people aspects of supervision. The carrot-and-stick approach is a key to supervision, in which the 9,1 substance of work direction is mellowed by a realistic consideration that friction among people is just as costly to production as it is to poorly maintained machines. Rather than integration, however, there tend to develop two counter-balancing systems, a formal and an informal one which tell how work really gets done, and who, in fact, has power and influence. Energy toward work accomplishment is likely to be drained as it is utilized to keep the two systems from getting out of step with one another.

References

1. Shull, F. A. Administrative Perspectives of Human Relations. *Advanced Management*, March, 1960, 18-22; Roethlisberger, F. J. The Foreman: Master and Victim of Double Talk. *Harvard Business Review*, 23, 1945, 283-298.

2. Shull, F. A., *op. cit.*

3. Davis, R. C. *The Fundamentals of Top Management*. New York: Harper, 1951, 72-73.

4. Pfiffner, J. M. & Presthus, R. V. The Role of Human Relations. In K. Davis & W. Scott (Eds.), *Readings in Human Relations*. New York: McGraw-Hill, 1959, 253; Davis, R. C., *op. cit.*

5. Drucker, P. F. Integration of People and Planning. *Harvard Business Review*, 33, 1955, 35-40; Urwick, L. F. The Purpose of a Business. In K. Davis & W. Scott (Eds.), *op. cit.*, 85-91.

6. Katz, R. L. Skills of an Effective Administrator. *Harvard Business Review*, 31, 1955, 33-42; Allen, L. A. *Management and Organization*. New York: McGraw-Hill, 1958, 43-44; Tannenbaum, R. & Schmidt, W. H. How to Choose a Leadership Pattern. *Harvard Business Review*, 36, 1958, 95-101.

7. McCauley, B. G. Accent the Man in Management. *Advanced Management*, August, 1960, 24-27.

8. *The Managerial Grid: A Self-Examination of Managerial Styles*. Austin, Tex.: Scientific Methods, Inc., 1962.

9. Allen, L. A., *op. cit.*

10. Smiddy, H. F. Managerial Decision-Making. *Advanced Management*, 23, 1958, 5-18.

11. Levine, J. & Butler, J. Lecture Versus Group Decision in Changing Behavior. *Journal of Applied Psychology*, 36, 1952, 29-33; Maier, N. R. F. *Psychology in Industry.* (2nd Ed.) Boston: Houghton, 1955, 138-139.

12. McGregor, D. M. *The Human Side of Enterprise*. New York: McGraw-Hill, 1960. Strauss, G. & Sayles, L. R. *Personnel: The Human Problems of Management*. Englewood Cliffs, N. J.: Prentice-Hall, 1960, 116.

13. Strauss, G. & Sayles, L. R., *op. cit.*, 115-117.

14. Merei, F. Group Leadership and Institutionalization. *Human Relations*, 2, 1949, 23-39; Riesman, D. *The Lonely Crowd*. New Haven: Yale University, 1961. (See Riesman's discussions of the *Tradition-Directed* individual.)

15. Beach, D. S. An Organizational Problem—Subordinate-Superior Relations. *Advanced Management*, 1960, 12-15.

16. Blau, P. M. *The Dynamics of Bureaucracy*. Chicago: University of Chicago, 1955, 172-179, 184-188; Jennings, E. M. *An Anatomy of Leadership*. New York: Harper, 1960, 27.

17. Mills, C. W. *White Collar*. New York: Oxford, 1953, 80-81.

18. Herzberg, F., Mausner, B. & Snyderman, B. B. *The Motivation to Work*. New York: Wiley, 1959, 125; Jennings, E. M. *The Executive: Autocrat, Bureaucrat, Democrat*. New York: Harper & Row, 1962, 90.

19. Festinger, L. *A Theory of Cognitive Dissonance*. Palo Alto, Cal.: Stanford University, 1957, 1-31; Thomas, W. I. & Znaniecki, F. Three Types of Personality. In C. W. Mills (Ed.), *Images of Man*. New York: George Braziller, 1960, 408.

20. Riesman, D., op cit.; Tannenbaum, R., Weschler, I. R. & Massarik, F. *Leadership and Organization: A Behavioral Science Approach*. New York: McGraw-Hill, 1961, 47.

21. Drucker, P. F., *op. cit.*

22. Levine, J. & Butler, J., *op. cit.* (See esp. the "lecture" condition in this study.)

23. Grace, H. A. Conformance and Performance. *Journal of Social*

Psychology, 40, 1954, 333-335; Asch, S. E. Studies of Independence and Conformity: I. A Minority of One Against a Unanimous Majority. *Psychological Monograph*, 70, (9), 1956; Brehm, J. & Festinger, L. Pressures Toward Uniformity of Performance in Groups. *Human Relations*, 10, 1957, 85-91; Merei, F., *op. cit.;* Jackson, J. M. & Saltzstein, H. D. The Effect of Person-Group Relations on Conformity Pressures. *Journal of Abnormal & Social Psychology*, 57, 1958, 17-24. The experimental and industrial literature provides many examples of group production standards and pressures against "rate busters" and deviants who attempt to violate group norms and standards. Ways of "beating" the supervisor and rules also are cited. See also, Blau, P. M., *op. cit.;* Blau, P. M. Co-operation and Competition in a Bureaucracy. *American Journal of Sociology*, 59, 1954, 530-535; Rice, A. K. The Use of Unrecognized Cultural Mechanisms in an Expanding Machine Shop; With a Contribution to the Theory of Leadership. *Human Relations*, 4, 1951, 143-160; Festinger, L., Gerard, H. B., Hymovitch, B., Kelley, H. H. & Raven, B. The Influence Process in the Presence of Extreme Deviates. *Human Relations*, 5, 1952, 327-346; Roethlisberger, F. J. & Dickson, W. J. *Management and the Worker*. Cambridge: Harvard University, 1939; Whyte, W. F. *Money and Motivation*. New York: Harper, 1955; Roy, D. Quota Restrictions and Goldbricking in a Machine Shop. *American Journal of Sociology*, 1952, 427-442.

24. Guest, R. H. *Organizational Change: The Effect of Successful Leadership*. Homewood, Ill.: Dorsey, 1962, 18.

25. Strauss, G. & Sayles, L. R., *op. cit.*

26. Green, E. S. The Nature and Use of the Committee. *Advanced Management*, 24, 1959, 24-28; Jennings, E. M., *op. cit.*, 1960, 28.

27. March, J. G. & Simon, H. A. *Organizations*. New York: Wiley, 1958, 54.

28. Smiddy, H. F., *op. cit.;* Koontz, H. & O'Donnell, C. *Principles of Management*. (2nd Ed.) New York: McGraw-Hill, 1959, 238-240; Jennings, E. M., *op. cit.*, 1962, 105-106.

29. Moser, G. V. Consultative Management. In K. Davis & W. Scott (Eds.), *op. cit.*, 249-252; Koontz, H. & O'Donnell, C., *op. cit.*, 226-234.

30. Riesman, D., *op. cit.*

31. Guion, R. M. Some Definitions of Morale. In E. A. Fleishman (Ed.), *op. cit.*, 301-304.

32. Barnard, C. I. *The Functions of the Executive*. Cambridge: Harvard University, 1938, 114-123; Koontz, H. & O'Donnell, C., *op. cit.*, 290-292.

33. Sherif, M. *The Psychology of Social Norms*. New York: Harper, 1936; Roethlisberger, F. J. & Dickson, W. J., *op. cit.;* Homans, G. C. *The Human Group*. New York: Harcourt, Brace, 1950; Sherif, M. Conformity-Deviation, Norms, and Group Relations. In I. A. Berg & B. M. Bass (Eds.), *Conformity and Deviation*. New York: Harper, 1961, 159-198.

34. Gulick, L. & Urwick, L. (Eds.), *Papers on the Science of Administration*. New York: Institute of Public Administration, 1927; Urwick, L. *The Elements of Administration*. New York: Harper, 1944; Mooney, J. D. *The Principles of Organization*. New York: Harper, 1947; Taylor, F. W. *Scientific Management*. New York: Harper, 1948; Fayol, H. *General and Industrial Management*. New York: Pitman,

1949; Holden, P. E., Fish, S. & Smith, H. L. *Top Management Organization and Control.* New York: McGraw-Hill, 1951; Koontz, H. & O'Donnell, C., *op. cit.*

35. Roethlisberger, F. J. & Dickson, W. J., *op. cit.*; Homans, G. C., *op. cit.*; Festinger, L., Schachter, S. & Back, K. *Social Pressures in Informal Groups.* New York: Harper, 1950; Festinger, L. Informal Communications in Small Groups. In H. Guetzkow (Ed.), *Groups, Leadership and Men: Research in Human Relations.* Pittsburgh: Carnegie, 1951, 28-43; Schachter, S. Deviation, Rejection and Communication. *Journal of Abnormal & Social Psychology,* 46, 1951, 190-207; Festinger, L., Gerard, H. B., *et al, op. cit.*, 1952; Seashore, S. E. *Group Cohesiveness in the Industrial Work Group.* Ann Arbor: University of Michigan, 1954; Sherif, M. & Sherif, C. *An Outline of Social Psychology.* (Rev. Ed.) New York: Harper, 1956, 146-177; Marrow, A. J. *Making Management Human.* New York: McGraw-Hill, 1957, 154-170; Zaleznik, A., Christensen, C. R. & Roethlisberger, F. J. *The Motivation, Productivity, and Satisfaction of Workers: A Prediction Study.* Boston: Harvard University, 1958, 121-135. Dalton, M. *Men Who Manage.* New York: Wiley, 1959. (See also studies cited in *f.* 23.)

36. Koontz, H. & O'Donnell, C., *op. cit.*, 291-292.

37. Doutt, J. T. Management Must Manage the Informal Groups Too. *Advanced Management,* 24, 1957, 26-28; Koontz, H. & O'Donnell, C., *op. cit.*, 291.

38. Davis, K. A Method of Studying Communication Patterns in Organizations. *Personnel Psychology,* 6, 1953, 301-312.

39. Whyte, W. F. An Interaction Approach to the Theory of Organization. In M. Haire (Ed.), *Modern Organization Theory.* New York: Wiley, 1959, 155-183.

40. Festinger, L., *op. cit.*, 1957; Osgood, C. E. Cognitive Dynamics in the Conduct of Human Affairs. *Public Opinion Quarterly,* 24, 1960, 341-365.

41. Koontz, H. & O'Donnell, C., *op. cit.*, 291.

42. Mills, C. W., *op. cit.*, 1953, 254-258.

43. Thibaut, J. W. & Kelley, H. H. *The Social Psychology of Groups.* New York: Wiley, 1959, 222-238.

44. Strauss, G. & Sayles, L. R., *op. cit.*, 68-74.

45. Mausner, B. Studies in Social Interaction: III. Effect of Variation in One Partner's Prestige on the Interaction of Observer Pairs. *Journal of Applied Psychology,* 37, 1953, 391-393; Cole, D. "Rational Argument" and "Prestige-Suggestion" as Factors Influencing Judgment. *Sociometry,* 17, 1954, 350-354; Sherif, M. & Sherif, C., *op. cit.*, 1956.

46. Stagner, R. *Psychology of Industrial Conflict.* New York: Wiley, 1956, 327.

47. Pitts, J. R. Introduction to Personality and the Social System. Part III. In T. Parsons, E. Shils, K. D. Naegele & J. R. Pitts (Eds.), *Theories of Society. Vol. II.* Glencoe, Ill.: Free Press, 1961, 711.

48. Allen, L. A., *op. cit.*, 327; March, J. G. & Simon, H. A., *op. cit.*, 129-130.

49. Koontz, H. & O'Donnell, C., *op. cit.*, 249-250.

50. Simmel, G. *Conflict* and *The Web of Group-Affiliations.* (Trans. by K. H. Wolff & R. Bendix.) Glencoe, Ill.: Free Press, 1955, 114-116.

51. Strauss, G. & Sayles, L. R. *op. cit.,* 178.

52. Danielson, L. E. & Maier, N. R. F. Supervisory Problems in Decision Making. In E. A. Fleishman (Ed.) *op. cit.,* 361-368; Maier, N. R. F. & Danielson, L. E. An Evaluation of Two Approaches to Discipline in Industry. In E. A. Fleishman (Ed.), *op. cit.,* 369-375.

53. March, J. G. & Simon, H. A., *op. cit.,* 54; Allen, L. A., *op. cit.,* 43.

54. Tannenbaum, R., *et al, op. cit.,* 1961, 108.

55. Brech, E. F. L. *Organization: The Framework of Management.* London: Pitman, 1956, Ch. 4; Koontz, H. & O'Donnell, C. *op. cit.,* 286, 288.

56. Blake, R. R., Shepard, H. A. & Mouton, J. S. *Managing Intergroup Conflict in Industry.* Houston: Gulf Publishing Company, 1964.

57. Mills, C. W., *op. cit.,* 1953, 53-54.

58. Dow, A. B. An Architect's View on Creativity. In H. H. Anderson (Ed.), *Creativity and Its Cultivation.* New York: Harper, 1959, 32-33.

59. Stoddard, G. D. Creativity in Education. In H. H. Anderson (Ed.), *op. cit.,* 181.

60. Hader, J. J. Role Perception in Management Training for Creativity. *Advanced Management,* 23, 1958, 18-31; Hilgard, E. R. Creativity and Problem-Solving. In H. H. Anderson (Ed.), *op. cit.,* 170-171; Bellows, R., Gilson, T. & Odiorne, G. S. *Executive Skills: Their Dynamics and Development.* Englewood Cliffs, N. J.: Prentice-Hall, 1962, 298-299.

61. Osborn, A. F. *Applied Imagination.* (Rev. Ed.) New York: Scribner's, 1957.

62. Stagner, R., *op. cit.,* 326; Bellows, R., et al, *op cit.,* 297.

63. Whyte, W. H., Jr. *The Organization Man.* New York: Simon & Schuster, 1956.

64. Koontz, H. & O'Donnell, C., *op. cit.,* 323.

65. Koontz, H. & O'Donnell, C., *op. cit.,* 343-344.

66. Maier, N. R. F. *The Appraisal Interview: Objectives, Methods, and Skills.* New York: Wiley, 1958, 4-9.

67. Stone, C. H. & Kendall, W. E. *Effective Personnel Selection Procedures.* Englewood Cliffs, N. J.: Prentice-Hall, 1956.

68. Koontz, H. & O'Donnell, C., *op. cit.,* 365-377; Marrow, A. J., *op. cit.,* 95-96.

69. Planty, E. G. & Efferson, C. E. Counseling Executives After Merit Rating or Evaluation. *Personnel,* March, 1951, 384-396; Koontz, H. & O'Donnell, C., *op. cit.,* 352.

70. Crutchfield, R. Conformity and Character. *American Psychologists,* 10, 1955, 191-198.

71. Riesman, D., *op. cit.*

72. Johnson, P. W. Human Relations in Modern Business. *Harvard Business Review,* 27, 1949, 521-541; McGregor, D. M., *op. cit.,* 1961, 241-251.

73. Lynd, H. M. *On Shame and the Search for Identity.* New York: Science Editions, 1961.

74. Riesman, D., *op. cit.* Fromm, E. *The Sane Society.* New York: Holt, Rinehart & Winston, 1955, 62-63.

75. Riesman, D., *op. cit.*, 11-12, 24, 38-40.

76. Lynd, H. M., *op. cit.*

77. Anderson, H. H. Creativity as Personality Development. In H. H. Anderson (Ed.), *op cit.*, 137-138. (Anderson makes an excellent distinction between socialization, 5,5, and social development, 9,9.)

78. Fromm, E., *op. cit.*, 196-197; Riesman, D., *op. cit.*, 24; Lynd, H. M., *op. cit.*; Gellerman, S. W., *Motivation and Productivity.* New York: American Management Association. 1963 151-159.

79. Riesman, D., *op. cit.*

80. Shull, F. A. *op. cit.*

81. Schoen, D. Human Relations: Boon or Bogle? *Harvard Business Review,* March-April, 1957, 15; Ohmann, O. A. Search for a Managerial Philosophy. *Harvard Business Review,* 35, 1957, 41-51; Lachman, M. S. The Supervisor Hasn't Had a Chance. *Advanced Management,* 23, 1958, 17-18; McGregor, D. *The Human Side of Enterprise.* New York: McGraw-Hill, 1960, 34.

82. Tannenbaum, R., *et al, op. cit.*, 67-71; Nelson, T. H. Mistakes of the '50's—Opportunities in the '60's for Management Development. *Advanced Management,* May, 1960, 5-7, 24-26; McGregor, D. M. *op. cit.*, 1961, 243-351.

83. Whyte, W. H., Jr., *op. cit.*, 1956.; Also see Randall, C. B., The Folklore of Management. New York: Mentor, 1961. (The 5,5 use of surveys, for example, is discussed on pages 52-53.)

84. McGregor, D. M., *op. cit.*, 1961, 243.

85. Riesman, D., *op. cit.*

CHAPTER SEVEN

The 9,9 Managerial Style

In the upper right hand corner is located 9,9, where a high concern for production, *9* is coupled with a *9* of high concern for people. Unlike the other basic approaches, it is assumed in the 9,9 managerial style that there is no necessary and inherent conflict between organization purpose of production requirements and the needs of people. Under 9,9 effective integration of people with production is possible by involving them and their ideas in determining the conditions and strategies of work.[1,2] Needs of people to think, to apply mental effort in productive work and to establish sound and mature relationships on an hierarchical plane and with one another are utilized to accomplish organizational requirements.[3] A basic aim of 9,9 management, then, is to promote the conditions that integrate creativity, high productivity, and high morale through concerted team action.[4]

The 9,9 orientation views the integration of people into work from a different perspective than other approaches. In contrast with 9,1, the solution for a given problem is not necessarily defined by the boss' authority.[5] Unlike 5,5, the 9,9 approach is oriented toward discovering the best and most effective solution in a given situation, not the one defined by tradition, etc.[6] By utilizing both the mental *and* execution skills of people, this approach aims at the highest attainable level of production. This highest level is only possible through work situations that meet mature needs of people.[7] Sociability for the sake of togetherness, status based on aspects unrelated to work, or power exercised for its own sake, or out of frustration, are not viewed as mature needs. Rather, *accomplishment* and *contribution* are seen as the critical aspect of organization performance and individual motivation.[8] When one is met, the other is gratified automatically.

Management Under 9,9

Mutual understanding and agreement as to what the organizational goals are and of the means by which they are to be attained is at the core of work direction.[9,10] In a real sense people and production *are* interconnected.[11] The manager with a 9,9 orientation views his responsibility as seeing to it (but not necessarily doing it by himself) that planning, directing and controlling *are* accomplished soundly. Who are best qualified to do it? Those with the most stake in the outcome, regardless of level.

As in the examples following, a boss with a 9,9 orientation still retains the responsibility for such aspects of work direction as planning. There is no abdication of the 1,1 variety, nor is there tolerance with "least common denominator" solutions of the kind that crop up under 1,9, nor of middle-road compromises of divergent interests as in 5,5. But in the 9,9 approach, others, where indicated, are drawn in on the actual planning of work activities. He might say that, "My job is not necessarily to *make* sound decisions, but it surely is my job to *see* to it that sound decisions are made." The 9,9 style is seen in the following:[12]

Planning. "I get the people who have relevant facts and/or stakes in the outcome to review the whole picture and to get their reaction and ideas. Then, I, with them, establish goals and flexible schedules as well as procedures and ground rules, and set up individual responsibilities."

Work Execution. "I keep familiar with major points of progress and exert influence on subordinates through identifying problems and revising goals and schedules *with* them as necessary. I lend assistance when needed by helping to remove road blocks."

Follow-up. "I conduct a 'wrap-up' with those responsible. We evaluate how a job went and probe what can be learned from it and how what we learned can be applied in future work. If appropriate, I give recognition on a team basis as well as recognizing outstanding individual contributions."

A general theme in the three excerpts above is that of *creating* conditions of work where people understand the problem, have stakes in the outcome, and where their ideas make a real contribution to the result obtained.[13] This concept of participation is based on the notion that when people can think, when they have influence on outcomes, they *support* rather than comply or resist. Furthermore, with effective leadership, which can arouse *sound* participation, the probability is increased that solutions achieved will be sound and fundamental, not needing constant review and revision.[14] People are able to give the best *of* themselves rather than seeking the best *for* themselves, as is often true when one's contributions are not sought.

9,9 DIRECTION AND CONTROL

How is correlating individual effort and organization purpose accomplished under 9,9 orientations? Under 9,9 direction and control are achieved, first, by working for understanding of and agreement by subordinates concerning organization purpose and how to contribute to it.

"Understanding and agreement by subordinates with organization purpose(s) . . ." cuts to the very heart of 9,9 management. What does this really mean?

Taken literally, as it is intended to be understood, this property of 9,9 requires a fundamental reorientation of managerial practices.[15] Far greater attention is required, through education, to the feelings and thoughts of people than has yet been considered except in a few experiments.[16] It can no longer be taken for granted, for example, that people accept profit as a legitimate organization purpose. Rather, it is inevitable that the concept of profit be "thought through," studied, and understood in depth. Where profit motivation is not the basis for organizing work, measuring performance, and motivating people, what replaces it? Or, has anything been found that can guide complex human effort in as sound a way? History is quite clear. The bureaucratically stiff companies that find change and innovation impossible, or the organizations that are chaotic, and more or less unable to respond to human needs to work, or of health, education and welfare, tell a dismal story of what happens when profit is eliminated as an organizing concept, as a measuring tool and as a source of motivation for individuals or organizations. This needs to be understood as a first step.

But profit in the abstract is only one aspect. Also needed, at all levels of management, is greater awareness of P/(L) circumstances within the specific organization, department, section, unit, in which one works.[17] To accomplish this requires that facts and figures be made available for discussion and understanding. Many section managements are unprepared to do this. They pay, in uninvolvement, in resistance, etc., for their closedness, because management and the worker alike have less stake in making the organization work.[18]

There are other aspects, but these are typical of the meaning of "understanding and agreement with organization purpose(s)."

Ordinary methods of education are relatively worthless for aiding understanding of concepts such as these, which are difficult to comprehend, and shrouded with emotions. Other educational methods, themselves consistent with 9,9, are available and have successfully been used, however.[19]

The 9,9 assumption is that when individuals who must coordinate their activities are aware of organization purpose and of their real stakes in the outcome, then it is no longer necessary for direction and control to be exercised by the boss in an authority-obedience way. Through the exercise of self-control and self-direction and with effective leadership, individuals can mesh their efforts in an interdependent way.[20] A sense of stakes and awareness of organization purpose(s) has been achieved in situations where approaches like the Scanlon Plan have been set into motion.[21] Under these conditions, each organization member feels keenly the stakes he and others share in the outcome of their efforts. Awareness of organization purpose(s) is possible because people interact directly or through their own representatives to influence decisions and to set organization direction.[22] Knowledge of one's stakes and of common purpose(s) set the conditions for releasing self-imposed control and direction.

Based on 9,9, it is clear that self-imposed direction and control cannot be achieved by edict, as in 9,1, nor through superficial loyalty or support as in 1,9. Neither can it be generated merely through a knowledge of procedures and practices as in 5,5.

Furthermore, self-guided actions with joint feelings of responsibility do not just happen naturally under 9,9 conditions. Rather, genuine understanding of organization economic health, of work goals, unity of effort and commitment arise out of discussion, deliberation and debate around major organization issues and by the mutual identification of sound objectives.[23] In other words, those who are involved in the overall effort participate in creating the conditions under which full production can be accomplished. Such action can result in self-control geared to organization goals and in the autonomous regulation of action.[24]

Certain distinctions for gaining an appreciation of 9,9 supervision can be made by drawing comparisons between 9,1 and 9,9 concepts. Supervision, as described here, is one area in which contrasts can be drawn.[25]

In the 9,1 situation, supervision tends to be centralized. The responsibility of those who execute the work consists of obedient compliance with the instructions. Here the attitude is that there is 100 per cent responsibility for getting the task done. To the degree one member of the pair feels responsible, the other person does not. Subordinates under a 9,1 system say, "That's my supervisor's responsibility. If he is responsible, then I'm not." Or, a subordinate may say, "I'm responsible for this part . . ." let us say 25 percent of the total effort, "they are responsible for the remainder." In this way 100 per cent responsibility is clearly and sharply subdivided. If one could sum individual feelings of responsibility, they would, in theory, total 100 per cent. Where this assumption undergirds organized effort, two or more persons can never share joint feelings of responsibility; that is, where *each* person involved feels 100 percent responsible and is committed to the *total* effort.

Areas of responsibility often are said to "fall into the cracks" because a manager has failed to plan and supervise adequately the efforts of those for whom he is responsible. However, under probing, it is often found that the pieces making up the 100 per cent area of responsibility are all accounted for, but that there is just enough air between the pieces to permit uninvolved people to say, "That's his problem (responsibility)," or "No one told *me* specifically to do that . . . if someone had asked me, I could have told them." Under conditions of involvement, on the other hand, individual responsibilities stand shoulder to shoulder. Responsibilities are laced together by a common bond—tensions and strains on one part are felt and adjusted for in other parts of the whole.[26]

The goal of 9,9 management, then, is to unleash participation and to exploit involvement in the *planning* of work so that *all* who shoulder concern for full production can find the opportunity to think through and to develop a basis of effort which reflects the best available thinking. In this way, all team members feel responsible for getting the job done in the best possible manner.[27] In other words, the 9,1 manager *directs* the job. The 9,9 manager works to establish *direction*, then, once that is accomplished, the job is self-directed by those doing it. Mutual advice, consultation, coaching and helping through removing road blocks serve to keep it meshed with a larger situation. In a real sense, the key to control is *commitment*.

Does the above regarding the 9,9 orientation imply that all aspects of work accomplishment are discussed and debated? This question merits closer examination.

It is true that many traditions, precedents and work practices that are recognized as useful derive their validity and appropriateness from social agreement rather than from logical inevitability. As with any mature adjustment, traditions, precedents and long-accepted practices guiding interaction often are established by a uniformly or a widely shared consensus as to what constitutes a sound base of action. The 9,9 approach recognizes the inevitability of socially-based consensus where other, more objective, criteria for interaction are lacking. What is being said here, however, is far different from ritualized acceptance of tradition and practices of the 5,5 character. Rather, guidance of interaction through explicit understanding and agreement, in the 9,9 context, means that organization traditions and precedents are critically and deliberately subjected to organizational examination.[28] Things are not done in a certain way "because that's the way they have always been done . . ." To be retained, they must make sense. In this way thoughtful and planned control over traditions is achieved rather than unwitting control of interaction being executed by traditions of the crabgrass variety. Again, educational methods are the means for studying and changing the culture of an organization.

Because the word, team, is likely to be used to refer to any set of individuals who cooperate in accomplishing a single overall result, the question can be asked whether team action of the kind being described leads to conformity pressures which dampen individuality and stifle independence of effort.[29] The answer is that the opposite is true. True team action is more like a football situation where division of effort is meshed into a single coordinated result; where the whole is more, and different, than the sum of its individual parts. Here, there is a common set of signals, based on understanding, which dictate action—a division of closely knitted individual activity combined with interdependent effort is the 9,9 pattern of integrating individual with organizational effort.[30]

Mistakes and Violations

Under 9,9, when mistakes do occur, the basic orientation of a manager is an educational one. He might say, for example, "Tough luck. It's embarrassing, but the thing is to study the problem and to learn from it. When can we get together?"

The first assumption is that mistakes occur because of misunderstandings, not because of deliberate intent. Thus, the issue is formulated as one in which it is the manager's responsibility to insure that the action is corrected. But, this is done in such a way that the *cause* is dealt with, and not just to point out the error in order to get the subordinate in line, as is true for 9,1.[31]

Mistakes frequently can be traced to misunderstandings, assumptions based on faulty information and facts or on differences in expectations between a boss and a subordinate.

Where either of the above or another situation is the cause of an error in action or judgment, it is likely the subordinate will be seen as ineffective unless the cause is uncovered by the boss and the subordinate talking through the circumstances surrounding the subordinate's actions.

A similar educational orientation is taken with respect to violation of policies and procedures. A manager operating under 9,9 is likely to say, "I discuss violations with those involved in order to diagnose what the problem is. If the procedure or policy producing the violation is unsound, steps are taken to change it. If it is misconduct, what motivated it needs understanding before corrective action is taken." In other words, the aim here is to discover the *cause* of the problem, not just to identify and punish the person associated with its occurrence. Through problem identification, critique and follow-up action, the work situation becomes a learning situation, *par excellence*.

A final point needs to be emphasized here. *Control* is no less and, indeed, may be more under 9,9 than under any other managerial system. The critical issue is not to reduce control. It is *how* control is best achieved. Self-control under 9,9 conditions means that an individual regulates his own performance in terms of understanding the purpose of and agreement with the organization's objectives of full production.[32] This degree of autonomy—under-integration—is far more rigorous than the kind of control that is exercised by close or tight supervision, when a person does not see the larger issues.[33] In the latter circumstance, the individual has to be guided and goaded to see distortions in his own performance which, from the standpoint of the organization, are detrimental to its goals. When a team member understands the signals, the play to be executed and its merits, he does not need the quarterback to run down the field with him to tell him what to do or why.

To follow the football analogy one step further, the team member, by knowing how his actions are a part but integrated into the whole play, is able to exercise sound autonomous judgment as to what to do should the situation change so that he is unable to carry out his initial assignment. For example, the man he is to block may be out of the play. He can then lend a hand to a teammate who may be encountering difficulty with his blocking assignment. Also, one does not hear of resistance to change when, after weeks of scrimmage and chalk talk, the quarterback finds it necessary to use his authority to shift assignment responsibilities in the midst of a game because the defensive situation has changed in an unexpected way.

THE CONCEPT OF GOALS UNDER 9,9

It is in a 9,9 context in which true goals orientation is the significant factor in accomplishing organizational purpose. Organization and individual purpose are seen as possible to mesh in such a way that each adds to and enhances the other in an interdependent fashion.[34] Then understanding with personal support of specific production goals in any concrete work situation is equivalent with organization purpose(s) at a more general level.

Much behavioral science experimentation, extensive study within ongoing industrial systems and observation across different cultures, as well, indicate that when people are oriented towards achieving concrete, specific goals that are understood and agreed with, their behavior becomes more orderly, meaningful and purposeful.[35] This general situation can be seen among children who engage in games under the goals orientation or purpose of winning. The game becomes an orderly and meaningful experience for the child engaged in such circumstances. The rules of the game make sense. The same is true with respect to completing college. Once a teenager has accepted the objective of getting a college education, the idea of completing the activity by getting a degree becomes dominant. At a broader level, it is said that Darwin formulated as the goal for himself, the idea of developing a general theory of development and change in biological phenomena. For years he strove single-mindedly in the direction of accomplishing that objective. The same is true for Einstein, who early in life saw the possibility of developing a general theory of relativity. The entire course of his career was dictated by the goal or objective of accomplishing that end.

The situation is similar in industrial application. When individuals are confronted to achieve production goals which they embrace because they understand and agree with them (as contrasted with quotas they are likely to resist), then effort is toward attaining the goal to which an individual is committed.[36] The managerial skills needed at this point are ones of communication, decision-making and other attributes which aid individuals to get with it and embrace personal accomplishment goals which are consistent with organizational objectives.[37] Then, an individual, in a certain sense, is not working for the corporation. Rather, he is working for himself. Individual and organizational purposes merge.[38]

There are many properties of goals that are rather well worked out and described within the behavioral sciences.[39] Several might be mentioned to give a sense of how the goals-oriented managerial approach gains many of the advantages of linking individuals together in total organizational effort.[40] One attribute of a goal is its *clarity*.[41] When a goal is unclear, then individuals are unable to strive toward it or join their efforts towards accomplishing it with others in a meaningful, sensible way. Though the goal may be clear to the supervisor and he is able to give adequate directions as to how work is to be accomplished, it may be resisted by subordinates because it makes no sense to them. But when subordinates are clear as to what the goal is, because they have thought it through, and have accepted the challenge of it, then they are likely to be fully committed to bend their efforts in the indicated direction.

Another property of a goal is related to its degree of *realism*.[42] A goal which is so small that it can be accomplished as easy as falling off a log has little motivating effect. Alternatively, a goal which is so difficult or complex as to be unrealistic also has very little motivating effect. In other words, for a goal actually to be motivating, it needs to be more difficult than can be easily accomplished, but not so difficult as to be near the impossible end of attainment. Setting before a new hourly-rated person the goal of becoming company president is likely to represent something which is not immediately attainable and which seems, except in an ideologistic mode, to be highly unrealistic. However, to confront the same person with a challenge of being elevated into a managerial position, faces him with a possibility of achieving something which is subject to his immediate effort.

Another characteristic of goals has been identified as the Zeigarnik effect.[43] The Zeigarnik effect is a statement that once an individual has accepted the idea of achieving a goal, then internal tensions arise towards successful completion. Under these circumstances, barriers that can block an individual from achieving the goals to which he has committed himself, run counter to the forces set in motion for goal achievement.[44] Rather than sitting back, and with resignation, saying, "I got blocked," the individual then increases his efforts to remove barriers to the goal. It is these tensions which constitute part of the motivating force toward goal attainment.[45]

It is for these reasons that the developing trend toward local profit centers is so important. A profit center within a larger corporation, for example, is the smallest unit of the organization which can be subjected to P/(L) accounting. Here is an example of taking organization purpose and translating it for application at the local level.

Under the profit center concept, each team member knows how his unit is doing. He can study what factors, and combination of factors, go into P/(L) arithmetic. He can see how local actions, over which he and others have some control, contribute to P/(L), in either a positive or negative way. It can be used as a basis for setting his present goals. Organization purpose, in other words, has been translated into a meaningful statement of local purpose. As with any management method, so too with profit-centering; it is subject to many uses. Given, for example, a 9,1 climate, a profit center P/(L) statement can become a "gun in your forehead." Equally, given a 9,9 climate, local P/(L) can become a:

1. Significant educational topic
2. Goal around which actions are integrated
3. Performance measure that motivates change, etc.

The way in which it is used is all important.

In summary then, the 9,9 managerial theory sees linking individual effort into organizational purpose(s) through goal-setting to be a significant force in organizing, measuring, motivating, coordinating and controlling people and their actions.[46]

BOSS-SUBORDINATE RELATIONSHIPS IN 9,9

Under a 9,9 orientation, the major work units are the teams, the supervisor-subordinate pairs and the individuals, considered singly.

A good analogy for boss-subordinate relationships under a 9,9 orientation can be had by reexamining the concept of the football team. A football team has hierarchy. The coach has overriding responsibility. The quarterback calls the plays within a generally prearranged plan which has flexibility to meet unforeseen difficulties. A football team has task specialization and division of labor. Each person shoulders a different part of the total job, with each having 100 per cent responsibility for success of the whole. The team is united in terms of a common purpose which defines direction—getting the ball across the goal line, while preventing the opponent from doing so. Furthermore, it has in common a set of strategies to fit a variety of situations and signals which are well understood, and which define the conditions of interdependent action.

Under these circumstances, attaining organization purpose—winning—includes:

1. Team action based on synchronized effort of all

2. Pair action, *i.e.*, based on meshing of effort between coach-quarterback, quarterback-center, halfback-end, etc.

3. Solo effort, *i.e.*, broken field running, pass interception, etc.

If the coach did as some industrial managers do, he would disregard, even prevent *1* from emerging; pay little attention to *2*; and hold each person responsible for his job as though there were no team effort and as though there were no pair relationships. The great likelihood is he would fail because coordination of effort, where needed, would be absent, and pair relationships, where required, would not be well enough worked out.

Good football coaches expend much effort in perfecting

those aspects needed for success which many managers disregard as "fol-de-rol."

Subordinates are viewed in terms of their capacities in attaining organization purpose. High concern for people is most likely to result in efforts to create conditions where people's ideas and feelings can be harnessed in a fully productive way. Most significant is the capacity of people to become involved in activities—to be committed to a purpose and to work autonomously once this condition has been achieved. 9,9, in a word, seeks to provide meaningfulness in work and to tap the creative resources of people and to mobilize their commitment under circumstances of cooperation and team play.

Three Conditions of Problem Solving

The manager uses his hierarchical position to insure that sound decisions are made. He can formulate the issue in at least three different ways.[47]

1. *One-Alone.* The first way in which problems can be considered and solutions evaluated is *one-alone.* The manager at any level is employed to meet problems that arise and subsequently to make the appropriate decisions for which he has adequate information. Those beneath him are to carry them into operation. The entire sequence from problem definition to decision making, then, may be *one-alone.*

2. *One-to-One.* Another possibility for problem solving is *one-to-one.* As seen by the boss, this is not "I alone," as one man who resolves dilemmas. It is *I,* a manager at some level, who works on a *one-to-one* basis in solving problems with each subordinate. Here there is a degree of cooperation as the boss discusses or interacts individually with each one under his span of control according to each person's specific area of responsibility. Little or no interaction takes place between people at the same level but rather, interaction takes place in different functional areas. Alternatively, when appropriate, the manager at any level seeks out his boss when higher levels need to be brought into the problem solving sequence.

3. *One-to-All.* A third possibility is *one-to-all* decision making. Under *one-to-all* conditions, the manager involves *all* of his subordinates when a decision needs to be made. He does not make it alone. Neither is the decision made with only one other person. Rather, the making of a decision involves all reporting to the manager or who are touched by or involved in the issue. Alternatively, he participates as a member in a *one-to-all* situation with his peers and common boss of the next higher level.

These, then, are the three problem-solving possibilities —*one alone, one-to-one,* and *one-to-all.* Realistically, they are not mutually exclusive in the sense that any organization can operate in the most adequate manner when managers employ any one of these kinds of decision making approaches and no other. There are circumstances under which one strategy is more appropriate and effective than the other two. However, it is not just a question of one being better than another. It is a question of when and what are the guidelines for one-alone, one-to-one, and one-to-all actions.[48]

The concept of *team action* of 9,9 is far more complicated than the physical presence of individuals interacting on all problems. This is just as ineffective and inappropriate as is the failure to involve people in problems where they do have a legitimate contribution to make. *However, it is not always easy to judge when the proper time is to involve and when not to involve others.* Table 1 presents some criteria for determining when action is most appropriately one-alone, one-to-one, or one-to-all. For a 9,9 manager, to operate most effectively under team action concepts means that he utilizes the most appropriate problem-solving strategies.

Several criteria for determining the appropriateness of action can be mentioned. When time is unavailable for debate, then discussion is inappropriate. If information that is needed for making a decision is in the possession of only one individual, then to involve others is a waste of time and a manipulatory practice. If two persons have the necessary information, then, it is obvious that *both* should be involved. When the pooling of information involves the intelligence of several people, then one-to-all action is necessary.

Another question to be asked is, *whose problem is it?* If it is the boss', and his alone, according to his job description and according to a previous common understanding, then his subordinates should not want to be involved. To do so would be to involve them in a responsibility that is not theirs. When a problem arises that is one subordinate's, then the one-to-one relationship applies, or when the problem is best described as belonging to the manager as well as to his subordinates, then there should be a one-to-all decision. When consequences for action are such that it is necessary or desirable to have commitment as to the outcome, then those whose commitment is needed should be involved. Another is that the more significant the issue, in terms of the stakes involved, the more the need to involve people.

In the area of coordination of effort, difficulties are created more frequently than in other areas. When coordination of effort is unnecessary, then clearly the action should be one-alone. If the only required coordination is vertical in the organization structure, then it should be one-to-one. Where the coordination need is both horizontal and vertical, then action most likely should be one-to-all. These are but several rules of thumb that can be applied in evaluating likely contributions of one-to-all problem solving. To summarize, the question discussed above then is, "When is one-to-all action, of a boss and subordinates interacting jointly for problem-solving reasons, under 9,9 required?"

Current myth to the contrary, large and complex organizations are rarely directed and guided by a given individual acting under solo circumstances. That is, the kind of decision-making and coordination of effort required in complex organizational situations of today is much more that of a jig-saw puzzle, with none having a sense of what the whole picture will look like once the various pieces are placed together. The challenge of leadership is to provide the conditions under which the pieces of the jig-saw puzzle are fitted together in such a way as to make a correct whole picture as the basis

TABLE 1

Three Strategies for Using Hierarchy

Action Indicated	One-Alone	One-to-One	One-to-All
Time	unavailable	available	available
Judgmental competence	full	insufficient	insufficient
Pooling of information	none needed	vertical only	needed
Whose problem is it?	mine	his	ours
Can others add anything?	no	yes	yes
Involvement-commitment	no signifi- cance	helpful-essen- tial	necessary- essential
Implications for others	none	present	present
Understanding by others of *purpose*	no problem or can be assumed	needed	needed
Coordination of effort	unnecessary	vertical necessary	horizontal and vertical
Followup	unnecessary	necessary	necessary
Teaching application	none	present	present

for organizational decision-making and direction. At either the policy, implementing, or executing levels, this is team action.[49]

Getting teamwork is not for the purpose of maintaining morale, as is likely to be true under 5,5. Nor does the team concept provide a hiding place for less than full excellence in performance, as frequently occurs under 1,9. Furthermore, it affords no resting time for 1,1. The key to team management is that sound interpersonal relations are seen as the best way to achieve and maintain production at peak levels.

9,9 *Attitude Toward His Boss*

Under a 9,9 orientation, a boss is not viewed in the controlling aspect. Rather, the subordinate sees himself as a contributing member within a network engaged in organizational problem solving. The boss is the key in the information flow from top to bottom. The subordinate is the gateway to those at higher levels concerning critical events occurring at lower levels, as well as being a link pin connecting higher with lower levels.[50] But, reviewed narrowly, this would be little more than 1,1 message-carrying.

The deeper boss attitude is that he—the boss—is seen as an advisor, consultant, coach, and helper regarding problems at the subordinate level.[51] He is an advisor primarily from the point of view of circumstances existing beyond the subordinate's situation but which are of relevance to his situation. In the advisor role he can offer perspective and sense of direction. He is a consultant in the sense of providing a sounding board and serving as a catalyst to aid the subordinate in seeing himself and his situation. As a sounding board, he can be used to test ideas regarding innovation and change to which, from his broader perspective, he often is able to contribute his own innovation and creativity. He can catalyze by challenging assumptions which, from his point of view, merit reexamination. As a coach he can review and critique past performance so as to achieve learning advantages from it. As a helper he can act at his own level to facilitate the subordinate performance efforts.[52]

Thus, the boss who is contributing to organization accomplishment in a 9,9 way is far more than an agent of authority in the 9,1 sense, a supporter or cheerleader in the 1,9 way,[53] a 1,1 message carrier, or a 5,5 go-between, a fixer. Rather, he is a source of perspective, a teacher, and an individual who enables performance improvement and personal organizational growth and development of those at lower levels to happen.

Creating and Maintaining Morale

There is a basic need of people that is met by the 9,9 theory but is not met by either 9,1 or 1,9. This need is the one to apply mental effort in meaningful and productive work; to have a stake in the outcome of things.[54] People are not machines, and their sole source of motivation is not security. Their jobs need to involve more than just mechanical or low-level mental effort. This basic need must also be considered in connection with another and equally important one of establishing sound and mature relations among individuals. By sound and mature relations is meant relations based on mutual trust, support and respect.[55] People can work together better in the solutions of problems and reach production goals as a team or as individuals when there is trust and mutual

support than when distrust, disrespect, and tensions surround their interactions.[56]

Thus, under 9,9, morale comes when successful work
performance is through team effort under conditions of
mutual trust, support and respect.

Communication Activities Under 9,9

A recent remark by a senior manager catches the
sense of communication attitudes in 9,9. His comment
was, "In the final analysis, words have no meanings, it is
only people that have meanings." In effect, this person was
saying that problems of communication actually are problems of *understanding* between people. Words are tools for
achieving effective exchanges of information, attitudes and
understandings.[57] There is no problem of communication,
per se. There are problems of people who work together in
trying to communicate with and understand one another.

One particularly important aspect of communication in
9,9 is with respect to its two-way character.[58] Communication, much like other properties of social systems, tends
toward an equilibrium between the amount which is
given and the amount which is received.[59] For example, if
an individual seeks a great deal of information but gives
only a very small amount, the system is unstable, and it is
not likely to retain the character long of one asking much
but giving little and of the other giving much but getting
little. Another way of putting it is: Openness, in a two-
way exchange of information, stimulates openness;
trust, trust; closedness stimulates closedness; hostility,
counter-hostility.[60] If an individual genuinely wants to
know what is going on, he needs to tell, in a forthright
and candid manner, what it is that he understands about
the situation. In a word, he *levels*. This two-way character
is rather seriously disregarded in a 9,1 managerial system
where communication is limited in the extreme to com-
manding-reporting back. Communication comes to have a
far different meaning within a 9,9 framework, based, as it
is, on the assumption that mutual understanding is the key
to agreement and control.[61] Furthermore, the 9,9 concept of
communication is little more than words unless the or-

ganization is seen as an integrated educational-production system.

The plea for openness which is so widely heard at the present time almost implies that openness of communication can be had by edict or an act of will. Rarely is such the case. Based on personal history, experience and the characteristics of an individual reared in the American culture and under its family and academic concepts of education of this century, a person is likely to listen through filters.[62] He tends to hear what he wants to hear and disregard what he considers irrevelant, trivial or unimportant.[63] However, what appears trivial to one man may seem earthshaking to another. Furthermore, unless he is very unusual, he listens defensively — explaining away or justifying what it is he most needs to comprehend and understand in order to increase his own capacity for being effective. This act of personal weighing of information is an obvious block to effective two-way communications.[64] If the person receiving the communication does listen, he finds many reasons for disregarding what he is being told as unimportant or incorrect. Rationalization, projection, compensation and other widely known mechanisms are immediately brought into play under such defensive conditions.[65] The goal is to be able to talk candidly—and negatively when necessary—and be heard. Educational methods to facilitate this result as between a boss and his immediate subordinates are now available and being applied in organizations that are stirring toward a 9,9 managerial system.[66]

Open and candid communication, which involves a transmission of both intellectual and emotional information, is subject to direct improvement, especially at the emotional level, through laboratory training of the kind that has become well known during the past fifteen years. On the other hand, the intellectual side of communication is subject to improvement through basic concepts that have been under development in general semantics for many years.[67]

Against this brief background, the goal of communication under 9,9, then, can be clearly stated. The goal is open, authentic and candid communication; that is, full disclosure.[68] Once the condition of full disclosure has been achieved, there are few reasons remaining for misunderstandings, or for withholding negative information, or for any of the many other communication pitfalls that are otherwise likely to arise as barriers to full effort.[69]

Since opinion polls and surveys are frequently used to gather information concerning facets of the organization which are unknown or unclear, in that information is not flowing freely, the question might be asked as to how these mechanisms are employed under 9,9. The general answer is that under a 9,9, as under other orientations, the poll provides easy access to information. However, as the basis for judgment and as a way of shunting resistances and avoiding clots within the functional communication system, polls and surveys are viewed as a patch — something to alleviate the symptom rather than to confront the cause — to a lack of openness within a wide spectrum of the total organization. The real problem is that opinion polls are needed in the first place.

The real problem to be solved then, is to eliminate the causes of poor communication that make the opinion poll a useful tool for assessing what goes on. With adequate understanding and acceptance of organization membership regarding goals of organization, with candid communication between levels, and with bosses at each level who see themselves as advisors, consultants, coaches and helpers, the need for opinion measurement disappears.[70] It disappears because it serves no useful function above and beyond the information already available through the live organization.

The 9,9 use of company publications is in the direction of a factual examination of significant developments and issues of interest to organizational members. An editorial column often is included; not of the preaching sort which might be found in the 9,1 newssheet, or of the encouragement and uplift of the 1,9 approach, but rather, of the sort that aids individuals to see the background of issues and the directions in which resolutions are being sought. It is newsworthy; it defines issues, emphasizes problems of performance being encountered, as well as describes accomplishments and future trends. The only constraints under which its editor is limited, as the policy is set in one corporate unit, are: "1) Information to be published should be accurate, 2) it should not give advantage to competition."

9,9 APPROACH TO MANAGING CONFLICT

The concept of 9,9 management emphasizes unity of effort of individuals in the team moving-in-concert and the interdependence among members on those matters that require joint effort, as well as acting independently on those which do not. Relationships of members to one another are dealt with as of core significance since all are embedded in a situation of common stakes where success for one and all comes from accomplishing the mission of the organization in the fullest way possible. In a real sense, *people and work are interconnected*.[71]

In the course of managing operations, tensions often arise among people in their interactions with one another, in deciding what should be done, how to do it, and in the actual execution of it.[72] Many underlying reasons for the development of disagreement and conflict are contained in the work situation where management takes place in this way. People with ideas about how to get things done seek to get them heard. But, when their ideas go against the grain of those who are responsible, conflict is a common result.

Conflict may be caused by rational, logical disagreement in points of view and ideas as to the best way of two or more directions to go.[73] It can range to the extreme of bitter antagonistic interpersonal friction. In the latter, real issues are minimized. Differences in basic values, differences in knowledge, status, the competition of two people for one available slot, procedural barriers to effective communication that result in misunderstanding, and "personality," all can be regarded as containing sources of disagreement and conflict.[74]

From a practical point of view, then, conflict might as well be accepted as inevitable. But this is far from saying that it is not resolvable. In areas where there is conflict, it must be dealt with in some way. On the one hand, conflict can delay or prevent the achievement of organization objectives and personal goals, and from that standpoint it is bad. But at the other extreme, conflict can promote innovation, creativity, and the development of new ideas which make organizational growth possible, and from that standpoint, conflict is good.[75] The issue, then, is not in whether conflict is present. It will be present. *The key is in how conflict is managed.*[76]

The 9,9 approach to managing conflict is clear. The solution to the problem is that of direct *confrontation.*[77] Direct confrontation means facing up to the conflict; getting it out on the table where it can be examined and evaluated by all who are a party to it.[78] In this way, the reasons for it can be examined and assessed. The conditions for its resolution then can be discussed by those who are involved.[79]

Though getting conflict into the open constitutes the most valid approach to its management, the thought of doing so meets strong resistance in our culture today. Such resistance springs from several considerations. 1,9 resistance stems from fear that in exploring the conflict situation, someone will be hurt. The resolution is to avoid open confrontation by the various ways of smoothing discussed earlier. The 5,5 resistance arises from the conviction that adequate conflict control can be had by oblique maneuvering. It is believed that such approaches, involving the various splitting mechanisms can get the job done in a quiet and sophisticated way without blood being spilt. The 9,1 resistance seems to come from the attitude that handling conflict is weak and that to deal with emotions directly is unmanly, soft and debilitating. Fear of personal inadequacy in coping with conflict directly leads to the strong solution — suppressing it and seeing to it that heads roll when suppression fails.

The question then is, with all these resistances, "Why is the position maintained here that direct confrontation does, in fact, contribute the most effective way of dealing with conflict?" The answer is that when people who work together are hampered from fully coordinated effort by tensions that produce closedness, or the necessity for maneuvering, or of avoiding tackling the problems that would cause tension, needed actions in terms of organization purpose are sacrificed or much personal energy is employed in applying patches that, at best, are detours around problems rather than resolutions of them.[80] These are the disadvantages of the failure to confront conflict when examined from the standpoint of the individual. Included are such commonly observed reactions as swallowing tensions to keep peace on the job, but kicking the dog in the driveway; excessive fatigue, accident proneness, and a host of other disturbed physiological and psychological reactions.

Many lines of evidence converge with one another and support the conclusion that the confrontation of conflict is, in fact, the most mature approach to its management and resolution. At the level of political systems, autocratic regimes tend towards the suppression of conflict and the elimination of disagreement by edict reinforced by naked power. Democratic institutions, in comparison, provide arrangements by which disagreement can be confronted and injustices redressed. The former kinds of systems have failed to persist over time; whereas, democratic institutions have been far more able to correct their own mistakes and simultaneously gain new directions through the clash of ideas.[81]

Evidence at the psychiatric level lends credence to the conclusion that much psychological illness has its roots in personal inability to relieve conflict through the talking out approaches that more healthy people seem able to employ.[82] Psychological experiments also support the conclusion that conflict is best managed when the individual who is in disagreement with another has the opportunity to express himself and be heard. A final line of evidence is one with which everyone is more or less familiar. It is pictured in the common language in the phrase, "Get it off your chest." People who have managed conflict in this way, whether in the family or on the job, are aware of the personal relief and the dissipation of tension that occurs when pent up emotions are released through uncorking the bottle.[83]

The implications for organizational life are far-reaching.

While some conflicts are limited to two people, it is relatively uncommon that only two are involved. Usually the situation of conflict spreads and touches the lives of several. When this happens, the several constitute the ones who must come to terms with one another, face-to-face, to talk through emotional feelings associated with operational disagreement.[84] Once these conditions are achieved, actions are possible with respect to many deeplying organization problems which, in some cases, have been unresolved for years.

From the Boss' Perspective

The implication is this: if conflict is best managed by directly confronting and correcting its causes, then it follows that those involved in the confrontation should be those who have a vested interest—a stake—in the outcome. The boss operating under a 9,9 orientation would automatically get with his own subordinates to talk through areas of friction that prevent them from working well together. In addition, he would purposely bring together subordinates who are tangled up with one another to work their differences through.[85]

From the Subordinate's Perspective

When conflict erupts between a manager and his boss, the 9,9 approach is based on the same concepts as those just discussed. The effective solution of conflict, even with one's boss, requires confrontation—openly working through the ideological and emotional components of the disagreement and identifying steps of resolution and followup. The obligation of the subordinate is not to withhold his convictions, but to exert influence upward on his boss.[86]

At this point, however, hierarchy appears to be a major stumbling block. The question frequently is asked, "How can I initiate direct confrontation with my boss?" However, the barrier may not be so great as imagined. As mentioned, openness provokes openness. A genuinely open and authentic approach often is enough to get one's boss to sit down and explore, in a problem-solving way, how his own actions may be frustrating the efforts of a subordinate. Bosses are of sufficient maturity to respond to such a confrontation when it has sincerity. The greater organization problem is that this approach is seldom tested with bosses. In order to escape bad consequences, *i.e.*, "getting in Dutch," the 5,5 fear, the common approach of most subordinates is to swallow resentments on a 9,1 manly basis or on the 1,1 basis of "I couldn't care less," even though such feelings can hamper their productive efforts.

IMPACT OF 9,9 ON CREATIVITY AND CHANGE

Creativity is high under a 9,9 managerial orientation. There are several reasons.

At the Boss Level

The manager with a 9,9 orientation is likely to be known as an experimenter and as an innovator due to his readiness to try out novel approaches.[87] He stimulates others and keeps a keen ear tuned for good ideas, no matter who possesses them. Because he listens for implications from a problem-solving point of view, the pick up and utilization of ideas is likely to be greater than for persons acting with other managerial assumptions.[88]

At the Subordinate Level

Because of the emphasis on participation and involvement of people in work activities, innovation in the work setting is more likely to arise. As conflict is seen as arising from the interplay of ideas, it too stimulates creativity and new ways of looking at production problems.[89] In other words, differences are not smothered or suppressed, but are challenged for potential and tested for contribution.

An attribute of 9,9 associated with creativity, which is not likely to be present under other managerial systems, is that of experimentation.[90] Looking for alternative ways of operating invites experimentation. This approach suggests moving forward into new terrain as contrasted with relying on tried and true methods of operating of the kind that frequently are relied upon in 9,1 or 5,5. But, the aim of 9,9 is not change for change sake. Rather, change is tested actively at decision-making points for the real possibility of doing things in different and better ways. What is being said, in other words, is that one of the critical ways of inducing change under a 9,9 system is by experimentation.[91]

COMMITMENT OF BOSS AND SUBORDINATE UNDER 9,9

Perspective on the matter of commitment can be had by reasoning what is meant by the word. First of all, the question can be asked, "What is it that commitment does not mean?" It does not mean going along because it is expected. It does not mean withholding disagreement to stay out of trouble. It does not mean acting under obligation without conviction.

Commitment does mean the opposite of all of the above, with the addition of an intangible but indispensable plus. The plus is a personal sense of desire to contribute to the organization success, through accomplishing the purposes of that component for which one has accepted responsibility. When an individual acts according to this sense of purpose in a spontaneous, self-generated and self-directing way, organization purpose and individual commitment are integrated.[92] They have become two sides of the same coin.

The kind of commitment pictured here is probably only possible under a 9,9 managerial system. The self-lessness of this kind of dedication is an essential condition of personal maturity. The consequence of 9,9 commitment is not that of a company man, *i.e.*, a man who respects the company, but rather is a company that respects men.

To the degree 9,9 managerial practices have been achieved, it means that organization goals and individual goals are in line with one another. The attainment of one means the achievement of the other.[93] Thus, personal commitment under 9,9 to organization achievement is high. Another way of saying this is that commitment, as experienced subjectively under 9,9, tends in two directions:

one, directly from the standpoint of task-oriented accomplishment; the other in terms of people-oriented contribution. The two mesh.

Commitment under the conditions described here cannot be accomplished by an individual operating in a vacuum. In other words, 9,9 is not achieved alone. Commitment, at its highest and most effective level, is generated in people who have been able to mesh their efforts with the boss and with one another toward the accomplishment of meaningful, productive goals.

MANAGEMENT DEVELOPMENT UNDER 9,9

Selection

Selection takes on interesting characteristics under 9,9. Involved in it is the idea that a searching examination both ways is the best way to aid an individual in a sound career decision. But it also is the best way to insure that corporate purpose can be contributed to in a sound manner through the employment of a given individual.

The chief issue is in the person having the information necessary for measuring his chances of being able to contribute effectively to the organization in a personally rewarding way. This means the organization has to provide a realistic assessment of its strengths and weaknesses, its growth trends, promotion practices, and the like. Avoided is holding out promises and hopes, or firing up aspirations, which against actuality lack realism, etc.

From the corporation's point of view the chief issue is in knowing the man, his capabilities and limitations, his drive to contribute, and, as important as any other, the managerial style to which he is predisposed.[94] Asking a person who is 5,5 by inclination, say, to join a 9,1 organization is as poor a match as it is to ask a 9,1 or 5,5 to pitch his tent in an organization striving toward 9,9.

In the latter connection, by ordinary interview it is very difficult for a new recruit to know toward which managerial style he leans. There are measurements that can aid the naked eye in such assessments.

Selection, then, involves a matching process where realistic attempts are made to insure a fit between individual characteristics and organization needs before employment.

As with 9,1, so too in 9,9, the idea of a trial or experimental period of on-the-job tryout is advantageous. It increases the chances that if the person continues, the fit will be a sound one.[95]

Induction

Induction of a new hire under 9,9 is a complicated and intricate process. Its basic feature, however, is that periods of on-the-job training in a number of sections are provided before a permanent assignment is made.

Another feature is in the organization education aspect. An example of an effective approach is where new hires, with technical help, organize and meet regularly 1) to review their experiences and 2) to formulate and define their own training needs with a curriculum of informal seminars available. Thus package courses are avoided and replaced by tailor made seminars.

In addition, technical subject matters not treated in adequate depth in earlier education, but needed to facilitate organization performance, are provided.

Management Training

The concept of management development is refocused in 9,9 by shifting attention away from the individual as the sole unit of development to the organization itself.[96] What is the significance of such a refocusing?

When a manager sees his responsibility as that of managing a culture rather than just managing people to get work out of them, the basic unit of development is no longer the individual considered separately and alone.[97] Rather, *the unit for development is the organization,* its goals, and its functioning. This means its people and how they work toward achieving organizational goals.[98]

The people of an organization are the carriers of its culture, traditions, and long established practices. It is they, obviously, who must change if the organization's practices are to be shifted and improved. Nonetheless, the primary focus is on the organization and on the kinds of barriers that prevent the effective promotion of work. Thus, management development is part and parcel of *organization development.*

A secondary facet is that under 9,9 the development of team action comes to replace the concept of improving individual action.[99] The idea here is that individuals are released, in terms of gaining new skills or employing those they already have, by virtue of increased organizational commitment through participation in teamwork. Thus, the problems of organization development at the team level are problems of reducing barriers to creative and productive work among those who are engaged in interdependent effort. The kinds of barriers involved are to be found in faulty decision-making, communication and control practices.

Four other facets of organization development under 9,9 need to be mentioned. One is that management development begins, when it is most successful, with the top team of the organization. It then moves down to lower echelons. The reason for this is that the top of an organization is, by all odds, the most important segment for organization development. If team and, thereby, individual improvement is good for the organization, it should be better for those at the top, whose influences are more deeply and widely felt than for those at any other level of the organization. This is in contrast to management development which emphasizes training primarily for those who are lower in the organization, or that picks one person out now, another then, and sends them off to school.

There is another reason for management development being concentrated initially at the top of an organization. It is that those at lower levels quickly sense that when the top is acting according to improved styles of managing, there are genuine convictions at lower levels that the organization means it. It can be put another way. What is the usual consequence when the top excludes itself from participation in organization development throughout management training? Then, automatically, what is being communicated is that these activities are good for subordinates, but top management's own behavior remains as a model of conduct and is not subject to improvement.[101]

The third factor of organization development and management improvement under 9,9 is with respect to its focus on organization problems. That is, an individual learns better management procedures, techniques and strategies in the process of searching for solutions to existing problems of organization. This is in contrast to studying hypothetical or abstract problems. The by-product is that organization problems get solved as people learn.

A fourth factor of organization development is with respect to *followup*. Another way of saying this is that if a management development effort is launched, it only is launched if its contribution to organization performance can be forecast. Its contribution to organization performance is unlikely to be predictable unless specific and concrete plans are arranged by which followup steps to implement what has been learned are taken *after* the formal training phase is completed. How is organization development of the kind being described undertaken?[102]

Such education contains many complex considerations, but a few will serve to give the gist of the approach.

Of greatest single importance is the learning, both from an abstract point of view and from the standpoint of personal application of management theories of the kind described in this book. *Indeed, this book is the basic text for several current organization development projects.*

Of equal significance, however, is the educational method that is employed. It involves laboratory learning, as contrasted with classroom instruction.[103] Briefly, this means learning by doing, as contrasted with learning by being told. Many experiments are employed as the basis for learning, in concrete terms, various aspects of the theory. Some of the experiments are standard, but others are tailor-made and use existing organization problems as their subject matter.

Followup includes using the 9,9 strategies to study organization traditions, precedents and practices, as well as a variety of specific problems that remain to be solved.

These remarks suggest how organization development takes place from a general point of view. However, because of the importance of organization development as the basis for achieving organization purpose(s) more fully, Chapter 12 is provided. It gives the problem fuller treatment.

Performance Review

The key to performance appraisal under 9,9 lies in the concept of *goal setting*.[104] The review setting offers an opportunity for supervisor and subordinates jointly to discuss the subordinate's present level of performance and to plot a future pathway toward eliminating barriers and toward achieving mutually agreed upon goals.[105] Barriers to the subordinate's development are identified, and may range all the way from technical considerations to highly personal ones. These also may include aspects of the supervisor's behavior and other features of the work setting, as well as factors over which the subordinate himself has direct control. These can only be alleviated through boss action in the helper sense as described earlier.

Although evaluation is not absent, it is not seen as the sole responsibility of the supervisor to judge the actions of the subordinate. Thus, the appraisal situation is extended far beyond assessment of past performance, to include diagnosing, planning, and followup for change.[106]

9,9 PERSONAL BEHAVIOR

What is the motivation of the person who manages according to a 9,9 orientation? His basic motivation is caught by the word *contribution;* a fulfillment of self through expression in work activities and in relationships with others which are characterized by respect and trust. 9,9 recognizes that human contacts are embedded in a situation of common fate, where success comes from accomplishing the purpose of the organization with others, whether it be in industrial, family, educational or religious settings.[107]

Outstanding Personal Characteristics

The person with a 9,9 predisposition places high value on getting sound and creative decisions.[108] He is not so interested in making a decision based on his own convictions, but rather his interest is in reaching out for solutions that represent best solutions. In doing so, he listens for and seeks out ideas, opinions, and attitudes different than his own. The 9,9 focus is on the quality of thinking and its essential validity, regardless of whether it represents his own or another person's view, or emerges from interaction. He is a real starter in the sense of initiating action, but he also follows through.[109] Others tend to pick up his sense of confidence in an enthusiastic way.

He is likely to have clear convictions of his own,[110] though he responds to sound ideas by changing his mind.[111] When conflict arises between himself and others, he tries to identify reasons for it and to resolve underlying causes by working them through. He rarely loses his temper, even when stirred up.[112] His humor fits the situation. Feelings, attitudes, and the more human elements of people, whether interpersonal or work related, are not regarded as barriers, but as capable of facilitating work effort. As such, they are seen to be significant elements of work situations, which should be managed.

Childhood Origins of 9,9

What constitutes the core of the person with a 9,9 orientation?

One attribute is respect. The 9,9 person both extends respect to others and has achieved respect for himself.

Many who have delved into the matter of respect are in agreement that a specific set of circumstances must be present before an individual can extend respect to others.[113] One seemingly valid conclusion is that for an individual to extend respect to others he must first have achieved respect for himself.

How is self-respect achieved? If the 9,1 orientation is examined from this point of view, it is reasonably clear that an individual who is driven to prove himself by guilt is not a person who fundamentally respects himself. He may hold to his own convictions, but it is more for the purpose of demonstrating his power and adequacy than out of self-respect. Such a person is unable to extend respect to others for they are adversaries whom he must defeat. A 1,9 person, on the other hand, is driven by anxiety and the fear of rejection. He overadjusts by accepting and promoting the ideas of others. He is not able to respect himself, but seeks his security in acceptance from others. Therefore, he is unable equally to extend respect to others in any genuine way. The same line of reasoning applies from the standpoint of the 5,5 person who is oriented toward the prestige and status that come from living with security by slavish adherence to entrenched codes of conduct. His values are placed on meeting the obligations and rules demanded of him, on conforming.[114]

The question remains, then, to identify what factors make it possible for a 9,9 individual to achieve self-respect.

Self-respect comes when an individual, having tested his judgment and emotions, is able to rely upon his own emotions and his own analysis of situations as an acceptable basis for personal guidance.[115] He can feel confident that his emotions are right and that his reasoning is sound. Now, as an individual, he is acting under conditions of respect for his own capacity to analyze situations, both productive and human, in mature, emotional and intellectual ways.[116]

An automatic feature of valuing one's own ideas and opinions, etc., is to extend respect to those held by others.[117] This has nothing to do with accepting or rejecting their ideas and opinions, however. It does have to do with listening to them, and understanding what they are. Such listening—with understanding—is, perhaps as much as any single factor, what is meant by respecting others.

Listening—with understanding—opens the possibility for two reactions to occur.[118] One is that it increases one's ability to exert influence, because, when one has earned respect, he *is* listened to. Thus, the execution of influence based on understanding, rather than on authority or by trading out, becomes a realistic possibility. Being influential on others in this way, where *they* change because they want to, results in a bonding of mutual respect, etc.

The other reaction is, if anything, even more important. It is this. When one listens—with understanding— he is opening himself up to the possibility others will exert influence on him. By hearing in this way, one is far more likely to recognize the limitations and inadequacies of his own ideas and opinions. Once having done so, he can change by revising, modifying or correcting his own position. To be accessible to influence by others—through understanding, rather than by submitting to their ideas and opinions—also results in the bonding of mutual respect.

Listening—with understanding—is a skill just as talking with clarity is a skill. It is learnable. Such a person has learned to be autonomous from others—to have his own opinions—yet to be interdependent—that is, open to change from influences acting on him.

When opportunity is afforded early in life to test judgment and to learn from realistic feedback the validity of one's position or how it needs to be shifted to be sound, it is likely that autonomy and self-respect is being developed.

Sense of Direction

An individual who has achieved this autonomous, yet interdependent, basis of adjustment can approach problem situations with others with confidence in their mutual ability to analyze and to solve them. He is much more likely to be open and spontaneous in his interaction with others; testing ideas with them and aiding others to test their ideas on him. In doing so, advantages are likely to be taken from the way in which different people view different problems, with an increase in respect for others because basic conditions of mutual respect are present.[119]

This kind of self-directed, yet socially-connected capacity is in the nature of autonomy.[120] The word *autonomy* contains *nom* of identity, also found in anomie, but with the *auto* placed in front of *nom*. It means self-identified, self-determined, self-directing. Autonomy, in other words, is the capacity to reason and to engage in deliberate choice of an action from among an existing range of alternatives, alone or in collaboration with others.

Where Does the Autonomous Self-Direction of 9,9 Come From?

Remaining to be considered is the question of how, in childhood, one learns to respect and to extend respect to others.

A first approach to answering this question is by reviewing the parental attitudes which lead a child away from self-respect. The 9,1 attitude, centering as it does on punishment, serves to promote guilt, and guilt is corrosive to self-respect. Though 9,9 child rearing exerts control on children, the method of doing so avoids punishment. 1,9, with its anxiety ridden fear of rejection, also fails to promote self-respect. It would be expected, then, that 9,9 child rearing would avoid exertion of control over children by provoking anxiety regarding their own acceptance. Parental rejection of children, which produces sulking and isolation, clearly tears down respect and, therefore, would not be expected in 9,9 child rearing.[121] The kind of child rearing that swaps out with the child by giving acceptance for his conformity with established practices and withholding it for non-conformity, also would be absent in 9,9 child rearing. Each, in one way or another, stunts the growth of self-respect and respect for others.

9,9 child rearing is in a different direction. It involves several features absent in the other approaches.[122]

First is the matter of *security*.[123] What makes a child feel secure? One answer is "he is loved." But love is communicated to a child when he is being controlled, not by punishment, but by parents helping him think through his own actions and the reasons for them.[124] He then understands why some actions produce good results for him and why others do not. By this approach the child is learning to listen—with understanding—an attribute of respect just mentioned. But for him to do so, parents have, in turn, to listen to the child with understanding. The cycle becomes reinforcing of itself. Respect brings respect.

A second facet is *experimentation*. 9,9 child rearing aids a child to experiment; it stimulates experimentation in a variety of ways. Of central importance in experimenting is learning how to test something but, as important, studying the results to learn from them; that is, critquing. There are innumerable ways adults aid children to experiment in the home and in school, with experiments graded to insure success as well as failure. They range from playing games, tests of memory, etc., to eating out, planning trips, etc. As a child learns to experiment under conditions of security, as mentioned above, he is learning to trust himself and his emotions and to trust those who help him—parents, teachers, etc.

A third facet has to do with how parents manage conflict between themselves and between themselves and children.[125] The appearance of conflict is used as a medium for education.

CONDITIONS AND CONSEQUENCES OF 9,9 ORGANIZATION STYLE

Conditions Prompting 9,9 as an Organization Style

There are a variety of circumstances and conditions that are promoting movement in the 9,9 direction.[126] Many relate to a desire of managements to avoid some of the negative consequences produced under the application of other theories of management. Some of these have been discussed already.

A primary condition is when a competitive advantage can be gained by an organization managed in this way. The combined efforts of committed people through better management is the only advantage still to be realized by organizations in certain industries. A reason is that capital investment, facilities and processes, technological knowledge and skills, all tend to be relatively equal across certain organizations. *Thus, the only way to gain a significant competitive advantage is through better man-*

agement—the kind of management that can tap its creative potential and achieve increased performance through having people who are involved in attaining organization goals. This indeed is motivation that pushes organizations in the 9,9 direction. Also, the kind of management that can confront conflict with a problem-solving orientation holds the promise of being able to establish more effective union-management relations.[127]

The growing appreciation and knowledge of behavioral science experimentation is also promoting a shift toward 9,9.[128] Attitudes and assumptions about how to effectively integrate people into production are coming under critical and systematic examination through the combined efforts of managements and behavioral scientists.[129] A result is that more and more management is becoming theory-based rather than being based on intuitions and common sense assumptions.

Other conditions promoting 9,9 include a gradual upward shift in the education of the general population. As this upward shift continues, the basic values of the culture shift. In addition, individual technical skills and knowledge are increasing, broadening and deepening. Highly capable people now begin their working careers at low levels of entry into the organization. People possessed of such skills, together with sound and mature judgment, no longer can be expected to work under unchallenging conditions, or under conditions of strict authority—obedience, or under a soft, slow-moving tempo where there is neither challenge nor the opportunity for accomplishment.[130] Improved economic conditions, which is another circumstance promoting 9,9, can be traced to education. So can technological innovation and the processes of automation. Here, for example, is another condition of 9,9—automation. The higher levels of skills required for the management and application of automated process means that more effective utilization of people is possible. They no longer must be assigned drudgery.

Needed also is a way of management that can stimulate the highest creativity among all organization members. More creative and innovative thinking is required when organizations move into new or unknown areas—such as that stimulated by the space and missile age—than is required when an organization is concerned only with producing and marketing an established product.

As mentioned, under 9,1, unionization and increased government control have moved managements away from old, ineffectual managerial approaches. Losing ground, yet not about to quit and move in a 1,1 direction, and no longer able to fight and finding compromise unacceptable, managements are moving toward problem-solving orientations, based on increasing managerial competence.

The real moving force through the years, though, has been education. And, as concepts and strategies of education improve, it is likely that education will play an even bigger part in the years ahead.

Long-Term Consequences of 9,9

In many respects, the really long-term consequences of 9,9 still remain to be seen. However, in organization improvement programs where the objective is that of moving in the 9,9 direction as an organizational style, there is every indication, after several years, that long-term, sustained growth for the organization and its members is the result.

Although many difficulties confront the objective evaluation of organization effort, conclusions drawn to date[131] indicate that among the gains attributable to a 9,9 change program are:

1. Contributions to organization profitability

2. The improvement of intergroup relations between the plant and the headquarters organization to which it reports, and between management and the unions with which it bargains

3. Strengthening of, awareness of, and making more effective the utilization of team action in various ways

4. Reduction of interpersonal frictions and increasing the degree of interpersonal understanding among individuals whose work requires close coordination of effort

5. Contribution toward increasing individual effort and creativity and toward heightening personal commitment to work.

As more organizations take deliberate steps to move in a 9,9 direction, the next decade should provide a more precise basis for evaluating the kinds of results possible from this organization style.

Summary

There is a basic need of people that is met by the 9,9 theory. This need is to be involved and committed to productive work. Thus, the situation is one in which the capacities of individuals to think creatively—to come up with new ideas—are utilized. One major difference between 9,9 and other managerial styles is in goal setting and its use as a basic management approach to a great variety of problems. The capability of people to be involved in organization purpose through commitment to goals is fundamental, etc.

The 9,9 orientation to the management of production and people aims at integrating these two aspects of work under conditions of high concern for both. The key is involvement and participation of those responsible for it in work planning and execution. This brings about the kind of team action that leads to high organization accomplishment.

The focus of 9,9 for improvement is the organization; that is, the unit of development is seen to be the organization, not individuals, one-by-one. True 9,9 conditions exist when individual goals are in line with those of the organization. Commitment comes from having a stake in the outcome of interdependent effort. And, high commitment is the basis of effective interdependent work effort. Under these circumstances, the needs of individuals to be engaged in meaningful interdependent effort mesh with the organization requirements for excellent performance.

References

1. Lawrence, P. R., Bailey, J. C., Katz, R. L., Seiler, J. A., Orth, C. D., Clark, J. V., Barnes, L. B. & Turner, A. N. *Organizational Behavior and Administration: Cases, Concepts, and Research Findings.* Homewood, Ill.: Dorsey, 1961, 185; Strauss, G. & Sayles, L. R. *Personnel: The Human Problems of Management.* Englewood Cliffs, N. J.: Prentice-Hall, 1960, 36-41.

2. The theory and concepts of 9,9 management find life in the pioneering work of Kurt Lewin and his associates, particularly the concepts of *participation, goal-setting, involvement* and *commitment, interpersonal relations,* and strategies for individual and organizational *change.* See especially, Lewin, K. *Field Theory in Social Science.* New York: Harper, 1951. Also, see Lewin, K. Forces Behind Food Habits and Methods of Change. *Bulletin of National Research Council,* 108, 1943, 35-65; Lewin, K. Frontiers in Group Dynamics: Concept, Method and Reality in Social Science: Social Equilibria and Social Change. *Human Relations,* 1, 1947, 5-41; Lewin, K. Group Decision and Social Change. In T. M. Newcomb & E. L. Hartley (Eds.), *Readings in Social Psychology.* New York: Holt, 1947, 330-344; Lewin, K. Frontiers in Group Dynamics: II. Channels of Group Life: Social Planning and Action Research. *Human Relations,* 1, 1947, 143-153; Lewin, K. *Resolving Social Conflicts: Selected Papers on Group Dynamics.* New York: Harper, 1948; Lewin, K. Behavior and Development as a Function of the Total Situation. In L. Carmichael (Ed.), *Manual of Child Psychology.* New York: Wiley, 1946, 791-844. (Also see references in Ch. 3.)

For a discussion of and additional relevant references to Lewin's work, see Deutsch, M. Field Theory in Social Psychology. In G. Lindzey (Ed.), *Handbook of Social Psychology. Vol. I.* Reading, Mass.: Addison-Wesley, 1954, 181-222.

3. Wolfe, D. M. Power and Authority in the Family. In D. Cartwright (Ed.), *Studies in Social Power.* Ann Arbor: Institute for Social Research, 1959, 100-101; Vroom, V. H. *Some Personality Determinants of the Effects of Participation.* Englewood Cliffs, N. J.: Prentice-Hall, 1960, 1-18.

4. Guest, R. H. *Organizational Change: The Effect of Successful Leadership.* Homewood, Ill.: Dorsey, 1962, 40-81. (This work of Guest is one of the best descriptions in the literature of the managerial actions of a 9,9 manager. See esp. "Plant Y," post-1953.)

5. See Ch. 3, this book. Also see Ch. 1 and 36-38 of Strauss, G. & Sayles, L. R., *op. cit.*

6. See Ch. 6, this book.

7. The work of Argyris and McGregor has crystallized and put into perspective the more mature needs of individuals in the work situation. See Argyris, C., *Personality and Organization,* Harper & Bros., New York, 1957, esp. pp. 20-53. McGregor, D. *The Human Side of Enterprise,* McGraw-Hill, New York, 1960, esp. pp. 45-58.

8. The work of Herzberg, *et al.,* demonstrates that motivation of a more fundamental and long-lasting character is embedded in the work itself *i.e.,* responsibility, achievement, advancement, and other factors that create a sense of significant accomplishment. Factors not directly

related to work, *i.e.* *hygienic*, take on more importance as work becomes less challenging and meaningful. See Herzberg, F., Mausner, B., and Snyderman, B. B., *The Motivation to Work*, New York: Wiley 1959, pp. 64, 70, 132, 144. Also see White, R. W., "Motivation Reconsidered: The Concept of Competence." *Psychological Review*, 66, 1959, 297-334.

9. Hare, A. P. Small Group Discussions with Participatory and Supervisory Leadership. *Journal of Abnormal & Social Psychology*, 48, 1953, 273-275.

10. Marrow, A. J. *Making Management Human*. New York: Mc-Graw-Hill, 1957, 29. (The work of Marrow, Bavelas and others at Harwood represents the successful attempt of one management group to apply 9,9 concepts in its organization improvement efforts.)

11. Roethlisberger, F. J. Human Relations: Rare, Medium, or Well-Done? *Harvard Business Review*, 26, 1948, 87-107; Guest, R. H., *op. cit.*, 50.

12. *The Managerial Grid: A Self-Examination of Managerial Styles*. Austin, Tex.: Scientific Methods, Inc., 1962.

13. In examining the great amount of literature and experimental work concerned with participation, it is important to distinguish between pseudo-participation and genuine participation as it is considered here. Attempts to make people *think* or *feel* their ideas are important, or manipulation of ego involvement, or artificial status raising are not seen to be *sound* participation. The important work of French and Coch and the insights of Levine and Butler make significant contributions to the concepts of 9,9. See, for example, Coch, L. & French, J. R. P., Jr. Overcoming Resistance to Change. *Human Relations*, 1, 1948, 512-532; and, Levine, J. & Butler, J. Lecture Versus Group Decision in Changing Behavior. *Journal of Applied Psychology*, 36, 1952, 29-33.

For additional representative experimental studies and discussions, see the work of Lewin, previously cited, and, Marrow, A. J. & French, J. R. P., Jr. Changing a Stereotype in Industry. *Journal of Social Issues*, 1, 1945, 33-37; Lewis, H. B. & Franklin, M. An Experimental Study of the Role of the Ego in Work; II. The Significance of Task Orientation in Work. *Journal of Experimental Psychology*. 34, 1944, 195-215; French, J. R. P., Jr. Group Productivity. In H. Guetzkow (Ed.), *Groups, Leadership and Men: Research in Human Relations*. Pittsburgh: Carnegie, 1951, 44-45; Gerard, H. B. The Anchorage of Opinions in Face-to-Face Groups. *Human Relations*, 7, 1954, 313-325; Kidd, J. S. & Campbell, D. T. Conformity to Groups as a Function of Group Success. *Journal of Abnormal & Social Psychology*, 51, 1955, 390-403; Berkowitz, L. & Levy, B. I. Pride in Group Performance and Group Task Motivation. *Journal of Abnormal & Social Psychology*, 53, 1956, 300-306; Cohen, E. The Effect of Members' Use of Formal Groups as a Reference Group Upon Group Effectiveness. *Journal of Social Psychology*, 46, 1957, 307-309; Marrow, A. J., *op. cit.*, 1957, 182-200; Juan, J. M. Improving the Relationship Between Line and Staff. In K. Davis and W. Scott (Eds.), *Readings in Human Relations*. New York: McGraw-Hill, 1959, 238-248; McGregor, D., *op. cit.*, 130; Vroom, V. H., *op. cit.*; French, J. R. P., Jr., Ross, I. C., Kirby, S., Nelson, J. R. & Smyth, P. Employee Participation in a Program of Industrial Change. In E. A. Fleishman (Ed.), *Studies in Personnel and Industrial Psychology.* Homewood, Ill.: Dorsey, 1961, 281-295.

14. Bradford, L. P. A Fundamental of Democracy. In G. Lippitt (Ed.), *Leadership in Action.* Washington, D.C.: National Training Laboratories, National Education Association, 1961, 51.

15. See Lewin, K., *op. cit.,* 1951, on his discussion on change and "unfreezing."

16. Mayo, E. *The Human Problems of an Industrial Civilization.* New York: Macmillan, 1933; Whitehead, T. N. *The Industrial worker.* Cambridge: Harvard University; Roethlisberger, F. J. & Dickson. *Management and the Worker.* Cambridge: Harvard University, 1933; Coch, L. & French, J. R. P., Jr., *op. cit.;* Marrow, A. J., *op. cit.,* 1957; Likert, R. *New Patterns of Management.* New York: McGraw-Hill, 1961; Blake, R. R. & Mouton, J. S. *Group Dynamics— Key to Decision Making.* Houston: Gulf, 1961; Blake, R. R. & Mouton, J. S. The Developing Revolution in Management. *Training Directors Journal,* 16, 1962; Blake, R. R., Mouton, J. S. & Sloma, R. *Designing the Managerial Operations of a Subsidiary Organization.* Dallas: Internal Revenue Service, 1963 (to appear).

For a review of additional experimental studies and investigations in this and related areas, see Wilensky, H. L. Human Relations in the Workplace: An Appraisal of Some Recent Research. *Research in Industrial Human Relations.* New York: Harper, 1957, 25-50; Cartwright D. & Zander A. (Eds.), *Group Dynamics—Research and Theory* (2nd Ed.) Evanston, Ill.: Row, Peterson, 1960; Hare, A. P., Borgatta, E. F. & Bales, R. F. (Eds.), *Small Groups: Studies in Social Interaction.* New York: Knopf, 1955; Fleishman, E. A. (Ed.), *Studies in Personnel and Industrial Psychology.* Homewood, Ill.: Dorsey, 1961; Lindzey, G. (Ed.), *Handbook of Social Psychology.* Vols. I & II. Reading, Mass.: Addison-Wesley, 1954; Maccoby, T. M., Newcomb, T. M. & Hartley, E. L. (Eds.), *Readings in Social Psychology.* (3rd Ed.) New York: Holt, 1958; Bass, B. M. *Leadership, Psychology and Organizational Behavior.* New York: Harper, 1960; Stoodley, B. H. (Ed.), *Society and Self.* Glencoe, Ill.: Rosenbaum, M. & Berger, M. (Eds.), *Group Psychotherapy and Group Function.* New York: Basic Books, 1963.

17. Guest, R. H., *op. cit.,* 77-81.

18. Opinion Research Corporation. *How to Develop More Profit-Minded Employees.* Princeton: Opinion Research, 1963.

19. Maier, N. R. F. An Experimental Test of the Effect of Training on Discussion Leadership. *Human Relations,* 6, 1953, 161-173; Bradford, L. P., *et al., Explorations in Human Relations Training.* Washington, D.C.: National Training Laboratory in Group Development, 1953; Blake, R. R. & Mouton, J. S. *Group Dynamics—Key to Decision Making, op. cit.;* Blake, R. R. & Mouton, J. S. Improving Organizational Problem Solving Through Increasing the Flow and Utilization of New Ideas. *Training Directors Journal,* 17, Oct.-Nov., 1963. Blake, R. R., Corsini, R. J. & Shaw, M. E. *Roleplaying in Business and Industry.* Glencoe, Ill.: Free Press, 1961.

20. Hemphill, J. K. Situational Factors in Leadership. *Ohio State University Educational Research Monograph,* 32, 1949.

21. Schutz, G. P. Worker Participation on Production Problems: A Discussion of Experience with the "Scanlon Plan." *Personnel*, 28, 1951, 201-210; Whyte, W. F. *Money and Motivation*. New York: Harper, 1955, 166-188; Lesieur, F. G. (Ed.) *The Scanlon Plan*. New York: Wiley, 1958; McGregor, D., *op. cit.*, 110-123; Strauss, G. & Sayles, L. R., *op. cit.*, 326, 662, 670-674.

22. Guest, R. H., *op. cit.*, 46-47.

23. Pages, M. The Sociotherapy of the Enterprise. In W. Bennis, K. Benne & R. Chin (Eds.), *The Planning of Change*. New York: Holt, Rinehart & Winston, 1961, 179.

24. Lewin, K., *op. cit.*, 1951, 229-236; Trow, D. B. Autonomy and Job Satisfaction in Task-Oriented Groups. *Journal of Abnormal & Social Psychology*, 54, 1957, 204-209; Bradford, L. P. & Lippitt, G. R. The Individual Counts . . . in Effective Group Relations. In L. Bradford (Ed.), *Group Development*. Washington, D.C.: National Training Laboratories, National Education Association, 1961, 28.

25. Fleishman, E. A. The Description of Supervisory Behavior. *Journal of Applied Psychology*, 37, 1953, 1-6.

26. Thomas, E. J. Effects of Facilitative Role Interdependence on Group Functioning. *Human Relations*, 10, 1957, 347-366; Shaw, D. M. Size and Share in Task and Motivation in Work Groups. *Sociometry*, 23, 1960, 203-208.

27. Levine, J. & Butler, J., *op. cit.*, 31-33; Marrow, A. J., *op. cit.*, 64.

28. Thomas, W. I. & Znaniecki, F. Three Types of Personality. In C. W. Mills (Ed.), *Images of Man*. New York: George Braziller, 1960, 406; Blake, R. R., Mouton, J. S. & Sloma, R., *op. cit.*

29. Asch, S. E. Effects of Group Pressure Upon the Modification and Distortion of Judgments. In H. Guetzkow (Ed.), *op. cit.*; Hochbaum, G. M. The Relation Between Group Members' Self-Confidence and Their Reactions to Group Pressures to Uniformity. *American Sociological Review*, 19, 1954, 678-687; Sherif, M. & Sherif, C. *An Outline of Social Psychology*. (Rev. Ed.) New York: Harper, 1956, 143-279; Berg, I. A. & Bass, B. M. (Eds.) *Conformity and Deviation*. New York: Harper, 1961. (The early work of Asch and Sherif have contributed fundamentally to present understandings of the formation, role and properties of group norms and their functioning.)

30. Deutsch, M. The Effects of Cooperation and Competition Upon Group Process. In D. Cartwright & A. Zander (Eds.), *op. cit.*, 414-448. Marrow, A. J., *op. cit.*, 57-58.

31. Guest, R. H., *op. cit.*, 62; Bellows, R., Gilson, T. Q. & Odiorne, G. S. *Executive Skills: Their Dynamics and Development*. Edgewood Cliffs, N. J.: Prentice-Hall, 1962, 239.

32. Selekman, B. M. Conflict and Cooperation in Labor Relations. *Harvard Business Review*, 25, 1949, 318-338; Goodacre, D. M. Group Characteristics of Good and Poor Performing Combat Units. *Sociometry*, 16, 1953, 168-178.

33. Maier, N. R. F. *Psychology in Industry*. Boston: Houghton, 1955, 172-173.

34. Stagner, R. Motivational Aspects of Industrial Morale. *Personnel Psychology*, 11, 1958, 64-70; Barnes, L. B. *Organizational Systems and Engineering Groups.* Boston: Harvard University, 1960, 152-156.

35. The early work of Lewin and others with groups of children, cited in Ch. 3, has led to increased understanding of the orientation of individuals around goals they help to create. The "Democratic" leadership described by Lewin, *et al.*, embraces a number of 9,9 managerial actions. See Lewin, K. & Lippitt, R. An Experimental Approach to the Study of Autocracy and Democracy. *Sociometry*, 1, 1938, 292-300; Lewin, K., Lippitt, R. & White, R. K. Patterns of Aggressive Behavior in Experimentally Created "Social Climates." *Journal of Social Psychology*, 10, 1939, 271-299; Lippitt, R. An Experimental Study of Authoritarian and Democratic Group Atmospheres. Studies in Topological and Vector Psychology. I. *University of Iowa Studies in Child Welfare*, 16, (3), 1940, 43-195; Lippitt, R. Field Theory and Experiment in Social Psychology: Autocratic and Democratic Atmospheres. *American Journal of Sociology*, 45, 1939, 26-49; Lippitt, R. & White, R. K. The "Social Climate" of Children's Groups. In R. G. Barker, J. S. Kounin & H. F. Wright (Eds.), *Child Behavior and Development.* New York: McGraw-Hill, 1943, 485-508; Lippitt, R., Lewin, Kurt, Adventures in the Exploration of Interdependence. *Sociometry Monograph*, 17, 1947, 22-28.

Bales, *et al.*, describes the observed and measured "phases" groups pass through as they move toward accomplishment of a task. The patterns of interactions becomes predictable. Parsons, T., Bales, R. F. & Shils, E. A. *Working Papers in the Theory of Action.* Glencoe, Ill.; Free Press, 1953, see esp. 111-161. See also, Kelley, H. H. & Thibaut, J. W. Experimental Studies of Group Problem Solving and Process. In G. Lindzey (Ed.), *op. cit.*, Vol. II, 735-785; Pepinsky, H. B. & Pepinsky, P. N. Organization, Management Strategy, and Team Productivity. In L. Petrullo & B. M. Bass (Eds.), *Leadership and Interpersonal Behavior.* New York: Holt, Rinehart & Winston, 1961; 229.

36. Coch, L. & French, J.R.P., Jr., *op. cit.*; Lewin, K., *op. cit.*, 1951, 229-236; Levine, J. & Butler, J., *op. cit.*; Horwitz, M. The Recall of Interrupted Group Tasks: An Experimental Study of Individual Motivation in Relation to Group Goals. *Human Relations*, 7, 1954, 3-38; Bass, B. M. Conformity, Deviation, and a General Theory of Interpersonal Behavior. In I. A. Berg & B. M. Bass (Eds.), *op. cit.*, 48-49.

37. Schein, E. H. Forces Which Undermine Management Development. *California Management Review*, Summer, 1963, 24.

38. Stagner, R., *op. cit.*, 1958.

39. Cartwright, D. & Zander, A. (Eds.), *op. cit.*, 345-484; Lindzey, G. (Ed.), Vol. II, *op. cit.*; Sherif, M. & Sherif, C., *op. cit.*, 1956, 152-156, 194, 230, 317-330; Bass, B. M., *op. cit.*, 1960, 63-70; Sherif, M., Harvey, O. J., White, B. J., Hood, W. R. & Sherif, C. *Intergroup Conflict and Cooperation: The Robbers Cave Experiment.* Norman, Okla.: Institute of Group Relations, 1961, 159-197; Krech, D., Crutchfield, R. S. & Ballachey, E. L. *Individual in Society.* New York: McGraw-Hill, 1962, 398-402.

40. Killian, L. M. The Significance of Multiple-Group Membership in Disaster. *American Journal of Sociology*, 57, 1952, 309-314; Sherif,

M. Superordinate Goals in the Reduction of Intergroup Conflict. *American Journal of Sociology,* 63, 1958, 349-356.

41. Lewin, K., *op. cit.,* 1951, 255; Raven, B. H. & Rietsema, J. The Effects of Varied Clarity of Group Goal and Group Path Upon the Individual and His Relation to His Group. *Human Relations,* 10, 1957, 29-44; Cohen, A. R. Situational Structure, Self-Esteem, and Threat-Oriented Reactions to Power. In D. Cartwright (Ed.), *Studies in Social Power.* Ann Arbor: Institute for Social Research, 1958, 35-52; Gerard, H. B. Some Effects of Status, Role Clarity, and Group Goal Clarity Upon the Individual's Relations to Group Process. *Journal of Personality,* 25, 1957, 475-488; Bass, B. M., *op. cit.,* 1960, 65-66.

42. Bass, B. M., *op. cit.,* 1960, 65.

43. Zeigarnik, B. Das Bekalten Erledigter Handlungen. *Psychologische Forschung,* 9, 1927, 1-85; Lewin, K., *op. cit.,* 1951.

44. Horwitz, M. The Recall of Interrupted Tasks: An Experimental Study of Individual Motivation in Relation to Group Goals. *Human Relations,* 7, 1954, 3-38. Also in D. Cartwright & A. Zander, (Eds.), *op. cit.,* 1960, 370-394.

45. Horwitz, M., *op. cit.;* Horwitz, M. & Lee, F. J. Effects of Decision Making by Group Members on Recall of Finished and Unfinished Tasks. *Journal of Abnormal & Social Psychology,* 49, 1954, 201-210; Smith, A. J., Madden, H. E. & Sobol, R. Productivity and Recall in Cooperative and Competitive Discussion Groups. *Journal of Psychology,* 43, 1957, 193-204.

46. French, J. R. P., Jr. The Disruption and Cohesion of Groups. *Journal of Abnormal & Social Psychology,* 36, 1941, 361-377; French, J. R. P., Jr., Group Productivity. In H. Guetzkow (Ed.), *op. cit.,* 44-45; Marrow, A. J., *op. cit.,* 1957, 108-122. For a discussion of organizational objectives, see Drucker, P. F. *The Practice of Management.* New York: Harper, 1954, 63.

47. Bavelas, A. Communication Patterns in Task-Oriented Groups. *Journal of the Acoustical Society of America,* 22, 1950, 725-730. Also in D. Cartwright & A. Zander (Eds.), *op. cit.,* 493-506; Leavitt, H. J. Some Effects of Certain Communication Patterns on Group Performance. *Journal of Abnormal & Social Psychology,* 46, 1951, 38-50; Kelley, H. H. Communication in Experimentally Created Hierarchies. *Human Relations,* 4, 1951, 39-56; Heise, G. A. & Miller, G. A. Problem Solving by Small Groups Using Various Communication Nets. *Journal of Abnormal & Social Psychology,* 46, 1951, 327-336. *(Note:* Experimental communication and problem solving networks typically studied represent, essentially, one-to-one interpersonal links, rather than one-to-all links as described here. However, in the "chain" of "circular" nets, an individual is able to interact with at least two people in a reciprocal fashion. The actual one-to-all pattern, where every person can interact with all others is usually not considered experimentally.)

48. Tannenbaum, R., Weschler, I. R. & Massarik, F. *Leadership and Organization: A Behavioral Science Approach.* New York: McGraw-Hill, 1961, 98-100.

49. Likert, R. A Motivational Approach to a Modified Theory of Organization and Management. In M. Haire (Ed.), *Modern Organi-*

zation Theory. New York: Wiley, 1959, 184-217. See also, *New Patterns of Management.* New York: McGraw-Hill, 1961. (The work of Likert in connection with "link-pinning" is relevant.)

50. Kelley, H. H. Communication in Experimentally Created Hierarchies. *Human Relations,* 4, 1951, 39-56; Likert, R., *op. cit.*

51. Lincoln, J. F. *Lincoln's Incentive System.* New York: McGraw-Hill, 1946, 170; McGregor, D., *op. cit.,* 1960, 28.

52. Pelz, D. C. Leadership Within a Hierarchical Organization. In G. Lippitt (Ed.), *Leadership in Action, op. cit.,* 43.

53. Fleishman, E. A. & Harris, E. F. Patterns of Leadership Behavior Related to Employee Grievances and Turnover. *Personnel Psychology,* 15, 1962, 43-56.

54. Herzberg, F., *et al., op. cit.,* 114, 117.

55. Maier, N. R. F., *op. cit.,* 1955, 139; Schein, E. H., *op. cit.,* 31-33.

56. Peterson, O. F. Leadership and Group Behavior. In G. Lippitt (Ed.), *op. cit.,* 27-30. Mellinger, G. D. Interpersonal Trust as a Factor in Communication. *Journal of Abnormal & Social Psychology,* 52, 1956, 304-309.

57. Marrow, A. J., *op. cit.,* 165-169.

58. Dymond, R. F. A Scale for the Measurement of Empathic Ability. In A. P. Hare, *et al.,* (Ed.), *op. cit.,* 244-245.

59. Newcomb, T. M. The Prediction of Interpersonal Attraction. *American Psychologist,* 11, 1956, 575-586; Gouldner, A. W. The Norm of Reciprocity: A Preliminary Statement. *American Sociological Review,* 25, 1960, 161-179.

60. Newcomb, T. M. Autistic Hostility and Social Reality. *Human Relations,* 1, 1947, 69-86; Festinger, L. Informal Social Communication. *Psychological Review,* 57, 1950, 271-282; Loomis, J. L. Communication, the Development of Trust and Cooperative Behavior. *Human Relations,* 1959, 305-315; Raush, H. L., Farbman, I. & Llewellyn, L. G. Person, Setting, and Change in Social Interaction. *Human Relations,* 13, 1960, 305-332; Deutsch, M. The Effect of Motivational Orientations upon Trust and Suspicion. *Human Relations,* 13, 1960, 123-139.

61. Leavitt, H. J. & Mueller, A. H. Some Effects of Feedback on Communication. *Human Relations,* 4, 1951, 401-410.

62. Krech, D., *et al., op. cit.,* 289-291.

63. Shibutani, T. *Society and Personality.* Englewood Cliffs, N.J.: Prentice-Hall, 1961, 351.

64. Rogers, C. R. Barriers and Gateways to Communication. In E. A. Fleishman (Ed.), *op. cit.,* 408-414.

65. Maier, N. R. F., *op. cit.,* 1955, 62; Harvey, O. J., Kelley, H. H. & Shapiro, M. M. Reactions to Unfavorable Evaluations of the Self Made by Other Persons. *Journal of Personality,* 25, 1957, 393-411.

66. Moreno, J. L. & Jennings, H. H. (Eds.), *Sociometry Reader.* Glencoe, Ill.: Free Press, 1960; Blake, R. R. & Mouton, J. S. *Group Dynamics, op. cit.,* 10-26; Bradford, L. P. & Gibb, J. R. Developments in Group Behavior in Adult Education. In L. P. Bradford (Ed.), *Group Development., op. cit.,* 1961, 94-106; Blake, R. R. &

Mouton, J. S. The Instrumented Training Laboratory. In I. Weschler & E. Schein (Eds.), *Issues in Human Relations Training.* Washington, D.C.: National Training Laboratories, National Education Association, 1962; *Business Week,* Managers Chart Their Way. October 20, 1962, 192.

67. Korzybski, A. *Science and Sanity* (Rev. Ed.) Lancaster, Pa.: Science Press, 1941; Hayakawa, S. I. *Language in Thought and Action.* New York: Harcourt, 1951.

68. Argyris, C. *Interpersonal Competence and Organizational Effectiveness.* Homewood, Ill.: Dorsey, 1962.

69. Leavitt, H. J. & Mueller, A. H., *op. cit.,* 409-410.

70. Thibaut, J. W. & Coules, J. The Role of Communication in the Reduction of Interpersonal Hostility. *Journal of Abnormal & Social Psychology,* 47, 1952, 770-777.

71. Barnard, C. I. *The Functions of the Executive.* Cambridge: Harvard University, 1938, 73-74; Roethlisberger, F. J., *op. cit.,* 1948, 87-107.

72. Pages, M., *op. cit.,* 176-177.

73. Simmel, G. *Conflict.* (Trans. by K. H. Wolff) Glencoe, Ill.: Free Press, 1955, 38-39. Tannenbaum, R., *et al., op. cit.,* 1961, 103.

74. Blake, R. R. Psychology and the Crisis of Statesmanship. *American Psychologist,* 14, 1959, 87-94. Also in W. G. Bennis, K. D. Benne & R. Chin (Eds.), *op. cit.,* 466-477; Blake, R. R. & Mouton, J. S. The Intergroup Dynamics of Win-Lose Conflict and Problem-Solving Collaboration in Union-Management Relations. In M. Sherif (Ed.), *Intergroup Relations and Leadership.* New York: Wiley, 1962, 94-140.

75. Pelz, D. C. Motivation of the Engineering and Research Specialist. *American Management Association, General Management Series,* 186, 1957, 25-46; Fromm, E. The Creative Attitude. In H. H. Anderson (Ed.), *Creativity and Its Cultivation.* New York: Harper, 1959, 51; Benne, K. D. Democratic Ethics and Human Engineering. In W. G. Bennis, *et al.,* (Eds.), *op. cit.,* 143.

76. Blake, R. R. & Bradford, L. P. Decisions . . . Decisions . . . Decisions. In L. P. Bradford (Ed.), *op. cit.,* 70; Likert, R. *op. cit.,* 1961, 117.

77. Anderson, H. H. Creativity as Personality Development. In H. H. Anderson Ed.), *op. cit.,* 124, 130. (This work by Anderson captures the essence of 9,9 attitudes toward creativity and conflict. A most penetrating concept is his concept of "social development" (9,9) versus "socialization (5,5).")

78. Blake, R. R., *op. cit.,* 1959, 87-94.

79. Kallejian, V. J., Weschler, I. R. & Tannenbaum, R. Managers in Transition. *Harvard Business Review,* 33, 1955, 55-64.

80. Eaton, J. W. Social Processes of Professional Teamwork. *American Sociological Review,* 16, 1951, 707-713; Selekman, B. M. Handling Shop Grievances. *Harvard Business Review,* 23, 1945, 469-483.

81. Anderson, H. H., *op. cit.;* Fromm, E., *op. cit.,* 1959, 51-52.

82. Rogers, C. *Counseling and Psychotherapy: Newer Concepts in Practice.* Boston: Houghton Mifflin, 1942.

83. Selekman, B. M., *op. cit.*

84. Gerard, H. B., *op. cit.*

85. Guest, R. H., *op. cit.*, 50-58.

86. Read, W. H. Upward Communication in Industrial Hierarchies. *Human Relations*, 15, 1962, 3-15.

87. Thomas, W. I. & Znaniecki, F., *op. cit.*, 409; Anderson, H. H. Creativity in Perspective. In H. H. Anderson (Ed.), *op. cit.*, 236-267.

88. Solem, A. R. An Evaluation of Two Attitudinal Approaches to Delegation. *Journal of Applied Psychology*, 42, 1958, 36-39; also, Hilgard, E. R. Creativity and Problem-Solving, 170-171; Dow, A. B. An Architect's View on Creativity, 41; Murray, H. A. Vicissitudes of Creativity, 110; and, Anderson, H. H., *op. cit.*, 130, 141; all in H. H. Anderson (Ed.), *op. cit.* Bass, B. M., *op. cit.*, 1960, 128-132; Ziller, R. C., Behringer, R. D. & Goodchilds, J. D. Group Creativity Under Conditions of Success or Failure and Variations in Group Stability. *Journal of Applied Psychology*, 46, 1962, 43-49.

89. Perlmutter, H. V. & De Montollin, G. Group Learning of Nonsense Syllables. *Journal of Abnormal & Social Psychology*, 47, 1952, 762-769; Hall, E. J., Mouton, J. S. & Blake, R. R. Group Problem-Solving Effectiveness Under Conditions of Pooling *vs.* Interaction. *Journal of Social Psychology*, 59, 1963, 147-157.

90. Marrow, A. J., *op. cit.*, 92-94.

91. Benne, K. D., *op. cit.*, 144.

92. Whyte, W. F. *Money and Motivation.* New York: Harper, 1955, 90-94.

93. Sherif, M. & Sherif, C., *op. cit.*

94. Strauss, G. & Sayles, L. R., *op. cit.*, 437-440; Tiffin, J. &. McCormick, E. J. *Industrial Psychology.* (4th Ed.) Englewood Cliffs, N.J.: Prentice-Hall, 1958, 11-15.

95. Strauss, G. & Sayles, L. R., *op. cit.*, 433.

96. Argyris, C. Organizational Health and Executive Development. *Advanced Management*, 12, 1959, 8-11. (More will be said in Ch. 12 concerning organization change and development.)

97. Shibutani, T. Reference Groups as Perspectives. *American Journal of Sociology*, 60, 1955, 562-570; White, L. A. The Concept of Culture. *American Anthropologist*, 61, 1959, 227-252.

98. Bennis, W. G. A New Role for the Behavioral Sciences: Effecting Organizational Change. *Administrative Science Quarterly*, 8, (2), 1963, 125-165.

99. Bidwell, A. C., Farrell, J. J. & Blake, R. R. Team Job Training—A New Strategy for Industry. *ASTD Journal*, 15, 1961; Blake, R. R., Mouton, J. S. & Blansfield, M. G. The Logic of Team Training. In I. Weschler & E. H. Schein (Eds.), *op. cit.*, 1962, 77-85; Blake, R. R. & Mouton, J. S. How Executive Team Action Can Help You and Your Organization. *A.S.T.D. Journal*, 16, 1962.

100. Blake, R. R. & Mouton, J. S. The Developing Revolution in Management Practices. *A.S.T.D. Journal*, 16, (7), 1962; Schein, E. H., *op. cit.*, 1963, 23-34.

101. Marrow, A. J., *op. cit.*, 87-88.

102. Blake, R. R. & Mouton, J. S. Improving Organizational Problem Solving through Increasing the Flow and Utilization of New Ideas. I. *Training Directors Journal*, 17, (9), 1963. 48-57 Part II in 17, (10), 1963, 38-54.

103. Shepard, H. A. & Bennis, W. G. A Theory of Training by Group Methods. *Human Relations*, 9, 1956, 403-414; Weschler, I. & Reisel, J. Inside a Sensitivity Training Group. *Industrial Relations Monograph, No. 4.* Los Angeles: Institute of Industrial Relations, University of California, 1959. Also in R. Tannenbaum, *et al.*, (Eds.), *op. cit.*, 1961, Ch. 10; Blake, R. R. & Mouton, J. S. *University Training in Human Relations Skills.* Austin, Tex.: University of Texas, 1960; Argyris, C., *op. cit.*, 1963, 137-152.

104. McGregor, D., *op. cit.*, 1960; Blake, R. R. & Mouton, J. S. *Group Dynamics, op. cit.*, 1961, 39-49.

105. Blake, R. R., Mouton, J. S. Re-examination of Performance Appraisal. *Advanced Management*, 23, (7), 1958, 19-20.

106. Blake, R. R. & Mouton, J. S. Power, People, and Performance Review. *Advanced Management*, 10, 1961.

107. Borgatta, E. F., Couch, A. S. & Bales, R. F. Some Findings Relevant to the Great Man Theory of Leadership. In A. P. Hare, *et al*, (Eds.), *op. cit.*, 1955, 568-574; Haythorn, W. The Influence of Individual Members on the Characteristics of Small Groups. *Journal of Abnormal & Social Psychology*, 48, 1953, 276-84.

108. Although confounded with certain aspects of 5,5 behavior, the "Stars" observed and described by Moment and Zaleznik exhibited behavior and actions like that characteristic of 9,9 managerial behavior. See Moment, D. & Zaleznik, A. *Role Development and Interpersonal Competence.* Boston: Harvard University, 1963, 17, 120-122.

109. Kipnis, D. & Lane, W. P. Self-Confidence and Leadership. *Journal of Applied Psychology*, 46, 1962, 291-295.

110. Cleveland, S. E. & Morton, R. B. Group Behavior and Body Image. *Human Relations*, 15, 1962, 77-85.

111. Crutchfield, R. Conformity and Character. *American Psychologist*, 10, 1955, 191-198. Anderson, H. H., *op. cit.*, 119.

112. Shibutani, T., *op. cit.*, 1961, 312.

113. Rogers, C. R. *Client-Centered Therapy: Its Current Practice, op. cit.* Also see, Hall, C. S. & Lindzey, G. Rogers' Self Theory. *Theories of Personality.* New York: Wiley, 1957, 467-502; Loomis, J. L., *op. cit.*; Deutsch, M., *op. cit.*, 1960; Shibutani, T., *op. cit.*, 1961, 291; Bowers, D. G. Self-Esteem and the Diffusion of Leadership Style. *Journal of Applied Psychology*, 47, 1963, 135-140.

114. Hochbaum, G. M. The Relation Between Group Members' Self-Confidence and Their Reactions to Group Uniformity. *American Sociological Review*, 19, 1954, 678-687.

115. Bowers, D. G., *op. cit.*

116. Fromm, E. *The Sane Society.* New York: Holt, Rinehart & Winston, 1955, 31-33; Shibutani, T., *op. cit.*, 1961, 291.

117. Fromm, E., *op. cit.*, 1959, 47; Steckle, L. C. *The Man in Management*. New York: Harper, 1958, 70-82.

118. Anderson, H. H., *op. cit.*, 1959, 130.

119. Anderson, H. H., *op. cit.*, 1959, 137-138.

120. Meier, R. L. & Bandfield, E. C. Review of "The Lonely Crowd." *Ethics*, January, 1952. See Riesman, D. *The Lonely Crowd*, for more on autonomy. New Haven; Yale University, 1961.

121. Bass, B. M., *op. cit.*, 1960, 197.

122. Bass, B. M., *op. cit.*, 1960, 197.

123. Maslow, A. H. Creativity in Self-Actualizing People. In H. H. Anderson, (Ed.), *op. cit.*, 85-86, 88. Sullivan, H. S. *The Interpersonal Theory of Psychiatry*. New York: Norton, 1953.

124. Baldwin, A. L. The Effects of Home Enviroment on Nursery School Behavior. *Psychological Monograph*, 63, 1949, 1-85. See esp. Dinkmeyer, D. & Dreikurs, R, *Encouraging Children to Learn*. Englewood Cliffs, N. J.: Prentice-Hall, 1963.

125. Rogers, C. R., *op. cit.*, 1951, 503.

126. Maier, N. R. F. & Hayes, J. J. *Creative Management*. New York: Wiley, 1962, 10-11.

127. Selekman, B. M. Conflict and Cooperation in Labor Relations. *Harvard Business Review*, 25, 1949, 318-338; Whyte, W. F., *op. cit.*, 1955; Blake, R. R. & Mouton, J. S. Union-Management Relations: From Conflict to Collaboration. *Personnel*, 38, 1961; Blake, R. R. & Mouton, J. S. The Intergroup Dynamics of Win-Lose Conflict and Problem-Solving Collaboration in Union-Management Relations. In M. Sherif (Ed.), *op. cit.*, 1962.

128. Bradford, L. P. A New Look at Management Development. *Advanced Management*, 23, 1958, 9-13.

129. Blake, R. R. & Mouton, J. S. The Developing Revolution in Management Practices, *op. cit.*; Clark, J. V. A Healthy Organization. *California Management Review*, Summer, 1962, 16-30. For a review of historical and background trends, see also, Gellerman, S.W., *Motivation and Productivity*, New York: American Management Association, 1963. Also see McDougall W., *An Introduction to Social Psychology*, p. 407-424. New York: Barnes & Noble, 1960, for a discussion of purposes and goals-oriented behavior.

130. Thompson, V. P. *Modern Organization*. New York: Knopf, 1961, 81-113.

131. See Chapter 13. Also see, Blake, R. R. & Mouton, J. S. Union Management Relations: *op. cit.*, 1961; Blake, R. R. & Mouton, J. S. Headquarters-Field Team Training for Organizational Improvement. *Training Directors Journal*, 16, 1962; Blake, R. R. & Mouton, J. S. Improving Organizational Problem Solving through Increasing the Flow and Utilization of New Ideas, *op. cit.*; Blake, R. R. & Mouton, J. S. The Intergroup Dynamics of Win-Lose Conflict and Problem-Solving Collaboration in Union-Management Relations, *op. cit.*

CHAPTER EIGHT

Managerial Facades

A variety of different attitudes toward the supervision of people in the setting of work have been examined in terms of five basic positions on the Managerial Grid. Features of managerial conduct that are deceptive or manipulative in character are explored in this chapter.

The concept of a *facade* is useful in this connection. It serves to distinguish manipulative managerial practices from ones presented earlier that have a more authentic quality. As used in architecture, the word *facade* refers to the face or front of a building, as distinguished from the parts lying behind it. Sometimes the front is *false*. It obscures what actually exists behind.

A managerial facade is similar. It refers to a front, a cover, for the real approach. The face obscures the true intentions behind it; they remain undercover. Hence, a managerial facade is deceptive.

DIFFERENCES BETWEEN AN AUTHENTIC STYLE AND A FACADE

The pure theories—9,9, 1,9, 9,1, 5,5 and 1,1, as well as the complex ones described in Chapter 9—all share a basic attribute in common. They all are well intended. They are authentic. None is dishonest.

A facade, on the other hand, is a cover for deception, intrigue, or trickery. In building a facade, the goal is to achieve, by indirect or by roundabout ways, something which otherwise is unavailable or believed to be unattainable if actual intent is revealed or issues confronted directly. The purpose does not appear on the surface. Thus, the approach is manipulative. Many authors, Machiavelli,[1] Carnegie,[2] Odiorne,[3] Jennings,[4] and Hoover,[5] have described ways and means of building and maintaining managerial facades.[6]

DISTINGUISHING FEATURES OF FACADES

The general feature of all facades is that the person avoids revealing the contents of his own mind, yet, he gives the impression of doing so. At a deeper level, then, he is closed and hidden, but to all appearances, he is open and above board. Why? If he were, in reality, open and above board, others could understand him. The deceptive facade would be apparent. But, neither can he afford to be seen as closed and hidden. The mystery is too challenging. It alerts curiosity. Others become inquiring as to his motivations and goal. His true goal is to remain closed and hidden concerning his intentions so that others do not really understand his motivation, but to throw people off by appearing to be open and well intended.

The facade maintained by a given individual may or may not be internally consistent. Stratagems may shift from time to time, depending upon what is workable or legitimate. The surface often appears as 9,9 or 5,5 and less frequently as 9,1, 1,9, or 1,1. Occasionally it is said of a person, "It's hard to tell exactly what his managerial style is. He can be fitted into several points on the Grid." It could be that, rather than being a statistical 5,5 (see Chapter 9) or having no consistent set of assumptions in terms of which to orient his actions, the person being described is, in fact, building or maintaining a facade.

The underlying aim beneath a facade varies in terms of specific personal intentions. However, there are at least two broad categories of motivation which serve as the underpinnings of a facade. The one most widely described, in terms of surface behavior, is the facade which covers some drive for control mastery and status over people.[7] An initial assumption regarding these people might be that a facade, in truth, covers a 9,1 personal orientation. However, the authentic 9,1 person's basic orientation is that of task mastery and achievement —toward proving himself through work or the validity of his position. He seeks to gain through winning his point to demonstrate his competence. He is open and honest with respect to his intentions. In comparison, the underpinnings of a person who builds and maintains a facade to cover his intentions are distorted. His goal is mastery and achievement in the control dimension. He seeks to control and influence people and events. In other words, striving for power and the capacity to exercise it, rather than productive accomplishment, distinguish the person who covers with a facade from those with well founded 9,1 managerial assumptions. Facade strategies of this character will be focused on here.

A second category of distortions is with respect to the aim of achieving acceptance and personal security in interpersonal relations. Here, the facade also covers the true intentions, so that, for example, 9,1 appearance of achievement and domination may, in truth, cover a deep sense of personal inadequacy. No matter what the true intention, however, the general features of all facade strategists are the clouded and hidden aspects of personal motivation.

Cloaking True Intentions

How can the facade builder hide his true aims? There are many simple ways of throwing a cloak over intentions. A few can be mentioned. One is that the facade builder simply avoids revealing his own intentions by not initiating discussions that invite probing. Then, there is no reason to be questioned regarding his motives. Another is that he withholds his own reactions to a problem by seeming not to notice it. The difference between 1,1 is that the facade builder does notice problems and seeks to actively use them, rather than remaining truly uninvolved as in the 1,1 approach. A third way is speaking so as to reflect others' opinions to them, without their noticing that personal opinions or attitudes are not being revealed. In a similar fashion, reacting to a question with a counter query may serve to deflect a probe. A fourth way does involve a reaction, but the reaction is in half-truths which invite favorable interpretation. Then, his motivation appears quite legitimate. Still another is outright lies. However, the most acceptable lie under a facade is the kind that can't be checked. For example, he might refer to a promise made by a dead associate, but not by a live one who can put the matter straight. When a facade is being built or maintained the goal is to avoid revealing actual intentions. But this is mere avoidance. Successful facades are based on a positive front.

Building and Maintaining a Reputation

Not only does the facade builder avoid revealing his intentions, but he also builds a positive reputation to aid in maintaining the deception. The reputation serves the purpose of actively causing intentions to appear quite different than they are. By throwing up a smoke screen, the likelihood is increased that true ambitions will not be recognized. In this way he can appear to have integrity as others are unable to see behind his outward appearances and to sense what he really is.

Pursuing a Good Cause. Writers since Machiavelli have suggested how a *reputation may be used to control, master and dominate.*[8] The reputation is built around virtue, good deeds, and subscribing to popular causes. Toward this end, for example, a person works to bestow honor on all who excel. By this means, he identifies himself with excellence. He also gains benefit from praising others, as noted below. Another cover up is to express lofty convictions and socially valued ideals; to be for the good, true and beautiful. On a more general plane, embracing and working for social movements and institutions, which are admired because they contribute to human dignity and to the reduction of human suffering, may, in fact, be a facade. Whether they are depends on the intent. The surface behavior frequently cannot be distinguished from that motivated by valid intentions.

In modern times, front organizations have been aptly described by Hoover,[9] where the surface intent of the organization hides an underground purpose which is different. A cover is deemed necessary because if the true intent were revealed, organization purpose might be thwarted. In a similar manner, using the names and ac-tivities of well respected persons to bolster one's own actions is a similar technique. If the facade builder can name drop or enlist the support of an opinion setter, then he can work undercover to further personal ambitions.

The Tough Guy Facade. The appearance of hardness or toughness, or of rejecting the more human or soft aspects of life may also be a facade. In this instance, the cover of aggressive intent or the exercise of arbitrary power may, in fact, hide an insecure person who wants liking and acceptance, but, fearing rejection by others, rejects first. The reputation of personal strength, in this instance, hides feelings of personal weakness.

Whatever the particular strategy, the goal in facade building is the same. It is to insure that aims are perceived quite differently than, in fact, they are. Then the facade builder may seize the opportunity to influence events. Influence or acceptance, then, can be attained far above (1) true contribution and (2) real capability.

There are many secondary ways of supporting a facade in addition to two basic ones of (1) obscuring (negative) intentions and (2) building a "reputation." For the most part they are practical procedures for achieving the above.

MOTIVATING AND CONTROLLING THE PERFORMANCE OF OTHERS

Interest in another person with praise on the positive side, and criticism and punishment on the negative, are central in motivating and controlling the performance of others. Facade strategists recognize this. They use these ways of extending their influence over and increasing their personal acceptance by others.[10]

Praise

A managerial facade involves building a positive rep-utation for oneself. Helpful in doing this is to build up the

other person. The clever use of praise is a key factor. In
the use of praise, then, the facade may give the flavor of
1,9 in that concern for another person may be read into
the recognition and emphasis given to the good points of
people. However, in 1,9, the concern is a genuine one.
The person with a 1,9 orientation, in truth, is interested
in people and wants to like and be liked by them. The
facade builder wants to use them. "You can catch more
flies with honey than with vinegar," is a well heeded
adage.[11]

The uniform recommendation, from Machiavelli to
Carnegie, has been to be "lavish with praise and approbation."[12] Praise and compliments make a person feel important and build up his pride. When given, the one who has
been made to feel praiseworthy also comes to like and to
admire the individual from whom the praise originated.
As a result, praise can buy influence and liking. There
is no indication that the praise should be earned or
merited.

But one should, in some degree, be discriminating.
Counsel is given regarding "going too far." The question
is, "How far is *too* far?"

Machiavelli,[13] Carnegie,[14] Odiorne,[15] all point to the dangers of flattery. In the present connection, flattery is
praise that can boomerang. The facade builder avoids the
falseness of flattering others so that his own illusions can
be maintained. He is careful not to be led astray by flattery
of others.

Concern for Other People

Showing concern for the other person's needs and
opinions is a more subtle form of influencing than praising
directly. The significance of demonstrating an interest
in people can hardly be overestimated, even to the point
of learning and using a name. Ways in which this is done
vary from being a good listener to others talking about
themselves, to never telling a person he is wrong, to
avoiding arguments. As one person said, "I make it a
point to find out what a person is most interested in so
that I can ask questions and get him to talk. In this

way, not only does he tend to be put in a positive frame of mind, but also it helps him to feel important. Because he is friendly toward me, he is more likely to buy what I want him to later on." The facade builder does not want to be disliked by those around him. He is sympathetic to their ideas and opinions.

When these actions are well founded, the behavior can appropriately be assessed as 9,9 or as 1,9. When the intent is that of gaining a private point of view or to achieve a personal advantage, which is unknown or misperceived, the facade-like characteristics are present.

Long Toes and the 1,9 Facade

Another pattern is the 1,9 face. This is the situation where an individual goes to no ends to create a purely social relationship, apparently for no other purpose than liking. On closer examination, however, the purpose is to achieve a hidden aim. On a social visit, for example, conversation is initially related to one's health, family, vacation plans, etc. Only after acceptance in the relationship is felt, does one approach his true purpose—asking a favor, borrowing something, requesting needed information, etc.

The 1,9 facade seems to derive its motivation from fear of offending which, in a deeper way, involves fear of being offensive. To reduce the latter fear, one takes out an insurance policy of personal acceptance by being nice, as a cover for real intentions. The reason the facade is labeled *long toes* is because of extreme sensitivity to feelings of rejection or being "stepped" on, which results in a person establishing a relationship of security as a background against which to get what he wants.

Criticism

Direct use of criticism carries many dangers. It is steered away from. As Carnegie says, ". . . even though one feels critical, and criticism is, in fact, justified, it should be avoided." Why? Carnegie explains in the following quotation:

"When dealing with people let us remember that we are not
dealing with creatures of logic. We are dealing with creatures
of emotions, creatures bristling with prejudices and motivated
by pride and vanity . . . And criticism is a dangerous spark—a
spark that is likely to cause an explosion in the powder keg
of pride . . ."[16]

Carnegie's suggestion, then, is that direct criticism is
much too dangerous for an individual to play with if
he wants to win friends and influence. By avoiding
criticism, the negative reactions often associated with it
are evaded. The act of deception itself is of no consequence.

What is manipulative here? The manipulative feature
is that negative information is withheld. In doing so, the
person to whom the negative information might prove
instructive is misled.

Punishment

When it comes to punishment, another somewhat
different aspect can be seen. If he can avoid it, the facade
strategist never is seen as the direct agent of punishment.
This is in contrast to the authentic 9,1 approach where
punishment is meted out directly. When punishment is
meted out, it can be done indirectly. One way is to
delegate the responsibility for dispensing it. If delegation
can be in such a way that one appears innocent or un-
knowing of the circumstances responsible, either for the
decision to punish or for its severity, then the facade
strategist is most successful. Henry Ford, for example, is
said to have been lavish in his praise of performance;
but, on the other hand, when punishments were meted
out, he employed a "hatchet man" to do his dirty work.[17]
A related technique here is that of "scapegoating"; finding a person or group on whom blame can be inappropri-
ately placed or towards whom hostility can be directed.
In this way negative tensions can be discharged in a harm-
less way to oneself.

In building and maintaining a managerial facade, a
person:

1. Is lavish with praise and approbation
2. Demonstrates a concern for people
3. Avoids direct criticism
4. Is not seen as the source of another's punishment.

In this way, dislike and resistance of others are less likely to be engendered and willingness to go along is enhanced.

DECISION MAKING AND PROBLEM SOLVING

Key features that serve to distinguish one managerial style from another are found in decision making and problem solving, particularly with respect to developing and maintaining convictions and to approaching and dealing with situations of conflict. Here, too, the facade builder is likely to react in a somewhat different manner than is characteristic of pure theories.

Convictions

A key feature of the 9,9 and 9,1 orientations has to do with being able to express strong convictions. Whereas the 9,1 person holds to his convictions, many times to win his position, the 9,9 person stands ready, when new evidence is presented, to change his position and to admit error where he is wrong.

In building a facade, a person expresses his convictions. But, this is done in a special way. Convictions are set forth so as to maintain maneuverability. He may use anonymous authorities or public opinion as sources of his beliefs. In this way, beliefs can be relinquished without his having to back down personally. He never presents his convictions so strongly that he can be proven wrong or stands so firmly that he is seen as obstinate or defiant. He remains tentative and keeps alternatives available toward which he can change. By expressing convictions while keeping other alternatives open, he is not demonstrated to be wrong if he needs to shift his course. Rather, he is proven wise. While gains (and contributions) from being deeply right may not be fully achieved, the losses from being deeply wrong are avoided. On the surface, then, the appearance of 5,5 may be given because of his apparent flexibility.

Intellectual Facades

A facade likely to be found in connection with lack of personal involvement in anything other than self goals is the intellectual facade. The approach is pseudo-intellectual in that there is no real involvement in ideas in the personal investment sense. Rather, the intellectual facade is adopted as a justification for open lack of concern for people. The pitch is that "People are victims of emotions. Emotions don't count. Only intelligence does." People, at best, are talking machines. Thus, people can be disregarded in the name of ideas.

Conflict

Dealing with conflict is also a critical area for orienting personal behavior. *The facade builder does not avoid conflict.* To do so can give the appearance of cowardliness. The goal is not to resolve it, as in 9,9, nor is it to suppress conflict, as in 9,1, etc., rather he *uses* conflict to gain his own purposes. Many ways in which this can be done are utilized by the skillful manipulator. For example, he avoids getting involved in direct conflict where he is vulnerable. Also, he wages only limited offensive battles. As one manager said, "It's better to ask for a smaller change and to go one step at a time, than to try to go the whole way at once and stir up resistance, resentment and open conflict."

Advantage is to be had by using conflict existing between others. He retains a neutral position only until factions in a conflict have become clear. *Once the issue is drawn, he enters the conflict and throws his weight to the stronger faction. If win-lose conflict between one's peers develops, he does not stand aside.* The reasons for avoiding neutrality are clear. They are based on "What happens afterwards?" What happens if one remains neutral while others fight it out? After the fight is over the victor well knows the support he might have been given during the fray which was not forthcoming. With the victor, then, one's stature is in jeopardy. Furthermore, if one has thrown his weight with the victor, the victor in turn is obligated for the help received. If neutrality is maintained, the vanquished is equally well aware that withheld support might have made the difference in his favor. He has no reason to be obligated to those who failed to support him, should fate again turn in his direction.

In building a successful facade, the significance of conflict and fighting to win one's own position is kept clearly in mind, while on the surface, the clever manager avoids the appearance of relishing a fight. In addition, he strives to avoid impatience, anger and temper while remaining calm and rational. It is winning in the long haul that counts, and then being able to persuade the loser to become an ally. In this respect, it is important to maintain and live by the rules of competition and to give the appearance of conformity so as not to attract attention to himself.

In taking a stance toward conflict, advantage can be taken of helpful alliances which aid in identifying situations of conflict. Not only can allies serve as reliable sources of information for what's going on, but their support can be counted on in times of trouble.

Attitudes toward conflict are different when conflict is between subordinates. Then, those in conflict are given the opportunity of direct accusation and confrontation of one another. In such disputes, the supervisor serves as the unbiased mediator, the fountainhead of justice. Then, subordinates are more fully aware of him as a fair administrator, a person to be respected.

Initiative and Perserverance

A characteristic of the facade builder is that he acts with initiative and continues to pursue his aim until success is insured. Although it might not appear on the surface, in his action he is tough-minded. He acts quickly when he sees an advantage is to be gained. Even though he feigns interest, he does not become sentimentally in-

volved with people. Rather he is able to use people and
to make alliances which are easily and quickly set aside
as the occasion demands. Because he is less likely to
have conflicting motives, he does not easily let obstacles
throw him. If one action does not succeed, he draws back
and then tries another tack, until his aim is assured.

In a like manner he is not daunted by difficulty of execution or external stress. However, he is responsive to new
facts and new opportunities which might provide additional leverage. He is inwardly much less likely to be
bound by authority and maintaining tradition, as these,
many times, provide obstacles to him. However, when it
is to his advantage, he upholds the *status quo*.

Compromise

Compromise, which is characteristic of 5,5 management,
is seen, under a managerial facade, to be a useful tool of
personal achievement. It is the appearance of compromise, however, which distinguishes the person with a
facade from one actually employing 5,5 assumptions. Even
if he has reservations, the facade builder feels no re-
luctance towards committing himself to a compromise solution or to an intermediate position. The 5,5 approach
believes the problem has been dealt with realistically.
The facade characteristic occurs when the person avoids
letting himself believe that the compromise solves the prob-
blem; that a half loaf is better than none. He recognizes
that compromise is a maneuver, a tactical accommodation. Compromise undercuts resistance because it presents the appearance of reasonableness. As one skillful
manager says, "I compromise at the time in order to be
able to go underground with my real purpose. Then, at a
later time, I come up again, and usually the second or
third time around, I win out."

ADVICE AND COUNSEL

Giving and receiving advice and counsel can be viewed
from several different perspectives. From one point of
view, it can be seen as an opportunity to take advantage

of experience and wisdom. On the other hand, involving others in problems connected with work may be seen as a sound way to release creativity as in 9,9.

For a person who is building a facade, however, advice and counsel are seen primarily in the perspective of his own personal gain or loss in influence over or acceptance by others.

Receiving Counsel and Advice

How a person receives advice and counsel is important in building a facade. There are several ways in which taking the advice of others is viewed.

While the aim of the facade builder is for others to feel important through praise and approbation, he avoids courting favors by asking unneeded advice from those above or below. Why? In doing so, he gives the appearance of being weak. Asking unneeded advice or seeking participation when he can make the decision himself, in other words, are dangerous things to do.

Another facet of equal importance is the acceptance of unsolicited advice. Unsolicited advice is undesirable because when received, it creates an obligation to the person who provided it. In addition, the smart manager knows what's going on, without having to be told. Through arranging for the acceptance of advice only when it is solicited, he avoids being obligated to the giver.[18] Furthermore, by this approach the information gleaned is likely to be more accurate because then the advice-giver can be kept uninformed of how much is really known.

To get candid and frank advice, it becomes important to choose trustworthy subordinates. They should know that honesty is expected and rewarded. How can the loyalty of subordinates be tested? The following has been commented upon favorably. To test the loyalty of a subordinate, he should be showered with power and authority. Then he should be observed for how he uses it. If he uses the power and authority extended him *in the supervisor's interest and not in his own*, his probable trustworthiness is increased. If he turns its use toward his own selfish gain, then it can be assured that he is not reliable.

Giving Advice and Counsel

Giving advice and counsel is equally fraught with danger. If a facade builder counsels action that fails, for example, the frustration associated with failure invites criticism, and possibly even punishment. Furthermore, his judgment is proven unreliable. On the other hand, if he counsels action that ends in success, he may receive commendation. The reward for counseling success, according to Machiavelli, rarely reaches the magnitude of the punishment associated with counseling an action that fails.[19] Over the long term, then, he is wary in giving advice.

In the area of giving advice and counsel, the goal is to act with moderation; to avoid acting out of zeal. Advice should be given calmly and modestly. If advice is given, the person who uses it should feel he is accepting it out of his own judgment and free will. In this way, it can be used to aid others to gain recognition without facing the risk associated with giving advice that ends in failure.

USING THE ORGANIZATIONAL FRAMEWORK

Anyone operating under a facade needs to maintain intimate knowledge of what is going on and to reserve key decisions to be made by himself only. Indeed, the making of the key decisions—alone—is indispensable in achieving control, mastery, and domination. The organizational framework is used by facade strategists to further their own purposes in many subtle ways. In this respect there is another point of similarity here to a person with a 1,1 approach. The 1,1 orientation is to personal goals of survival without regard for organization purpose. The facade strategist has a personal goal of control and domination which also has no regard for organization purpose as such.

Incomplete Delegation

Incomplete delegation is ideal for making it possible for the facade strategist to maintain control, while at the same time appearing to release subordinates to be independent. On the one hand, the goal is to be known as one who delegates authority—who uses people well. But, to protect himself, he insures that the delegation, though apparently full, is incomplete. Leaving jurisdictional boundaries fuzzy is one way to achieve incomplete delegation. It insures uncertainty as to who is free to act under authority. Another tactic is to arrange overlapping responsibilities. In both cases, subordinates act as counterweights on one another. No one has sufficient authority to decide an action by himself. Thirdly, it is imperative that information that would permit decisions to be made under conditions of delegating is not fully communicated, but enough is given so that people feel informed. Fuzzy boundaries, overlapping responsibilities, and partial information all lead in the same direction as far as decision making is concerned: upward. Then subordinates have to ask for help. In this way, control is increased and retained by the supervisor being able to make needed decisions by himself.

If these strategems are to be skillfully applied, the troubles people have in arriving at decisions should appear to be due to the system—not to the administration of it. Then, one accomplishes two indispensable conditions of a managerial facade: (1) a continuous flow of upward communication, and (2) the retention of power to make the decision.

One-to-One Supervision and Managing Cliques

Another significant way to insure retention of control is to operate on a one-by-one basis with one's subordinates or peers and to avoid situations of interaction where there is a free exchange of ideas and information. Two advantages can be gained. One is that needed information by subordinates to coordinate activities can only be had by their coming to the supervisor, who thus retains control. The other is that it becomes more difficult for peers or subordinates to track one's own actions.

Proper weight, however, is given by the facade builder to cliques and other features of the informal organization. By having a thorough knowledge of cliques and their membership, he can tap into the grapevine at strategic points and keep his finger on the pulse of the organization. Exerting influence on key members of cliques can usually result in a saving of effort in that others follow their lead. Consulting key clique members, before decisions that affect them are made, frequently can result in reducing or eliminating resistance points. Finally, by manipulating clique action, sanctions can be brought to bear on members who are running counter to his purposes.

Pseudo Team Action

Work teams, information groups and cliques, rather than individuals considered singly, are the building blocks of modern organizations. To a facade builder, a group is a significant unit to understand and to utilize to his own benefit. From one point of view, meetings enable him to exert influence on more than one person at a time. In this respect, then, a group is a convenient unit for the advancement of individual interests. Knowledge of power tactics and group dynamics are indispensable tools. However, the facade builder is not a team man, but leads and participates in group action for his individual interests.[20] Thus, in convening a group it is important for him to make known his noble intention.

Committee action serves several useful purposes for the facade strategist. Responsibilities for major changes or innovations that have high risk value are placed in a group. He sponsors the more minor changes that can be construed as tests of ability and which are most likely to succeed.

Tapping the resources of others can be facilitated through group interaction. Brainstorming, and other similar techniques in which ideas are elicited but not evaluated, make it relatively easy to take credit for ideas of others without either being forced to negatively discard a person's ideas or being committed to action by group problem solving. By clever hitch-hiking onto another's work or thoughts, they can be presented as if they are one's own.

These points demonstrate how the facade strategist can manipulate and maneuver in a more forceful way through group situations. On the other hand, team action in the sense of involvement of others in problem solving, interdependence of action, confrontation and working through of issues, and so on are fraught with pitfalls.

Interaction for the purpose of problem solving is viewed with distrust. In situations where team action is seen to be organizationally appropriate, the goal again is to give the appearance of team action. One way to avoid real interaction is to feel out positions and achieve commitment from those concerned, prior to assembling them. In this way, influence can be more easily exerted and uniformity of opinion quickly achieved, without the necessity for open debate and deliberation. Composing the unit from amongst one's allies, rather than convening those from whom divergent points of view are likely, is another. By intensely debating minor issues which make no real difference, the big ones can be reserved for unilateral decision making.

A useful way to keep control and to make certain that his own direction eventually is taken, under the guise of team action, has been described by one manager in this way. "In order to keep one part of the organization from achieving more influence than other parts (and thus to reduce my own power), I find it necessary to keep problems in a fluid state far beyond when a decision could be made. This can be done easily by keeping the situation open under the guise of not making a premature unworkable decision or by testing all possible alternatives before a step is taken. In this way, the stronger faction is weakened, the weaker faction is not hurt, and when I finally make a decision, everyone is relieved and ready to move my way in order to get some action." Because skills of team action are not highly developed by many persons, a group is an easy match for a clever facade builder.

WHY ARE MANAGERIAL FACADES EMPLOYED?

The common goal behind a facade seems to be to achieve personal goals, most likely in the areas of control and mastery over situations and people or through acceptance by others. People are brushed aside or used to advantage. The facade permits this fact to be obscured, however. Why? Because he feels that if his true intentions were visible to others, his efforts would be opposed. The facade permits a personal goal to be sought and prevents resistance from developing to reduce his own strength.

There are at least two reasons for building up and maintaining a managerial facade.

Disregard of Social Ethics

One deals with ethics. Mutual trust is not valued in its own right. Yet, the appearance of trustfulness is important. Through creating the impression of trust, confidence, and respect, as the basis for interpersonal relations, personal goals are achieved more easily. On the plane of social ethics, in consequence, short-cuts are taken to achieve an end. They are not governed by commonly accepted rules for maintaining social morality.

Attainment of Goals Beyond Capability

Another factor is when one strives to achieve a goal which is beyond his capability and skill. By employing a facade to hide trickery and deceit, objectives can be gained which cannot be achieved through honest, ability-based performance. The end sought justifies the means used for getting to it.

Both of these disregard commonly accepted rules of social morality. The disregard is in a calculated knowing way.

Self-Deception of Own Motivation

Facade-type behavior appears when the underlying motivation is hidden, even from the person himself. He literally doesn't know he is putting on a front. Not only are others deceived, he also deceives himself. Psychiatry and clinical psychology have described tricks of the mind. These are tricks by which a person's motivations are unclear to himself; they can't be identified by him or described to others. If directly confronted with his own self-deceptions, he would deny them. Rationalization, projection, justification, and compensation, are examples.

Facade-type behavior may be caused by any of these factors or by some mixture of them. To further complicate matters, the behavior may contain components of the pure theories as well. When the latter also are present it only adds to the subtlety of the deception (self and other) involved.

SUMMARY

A managerial facade may be adopted by a person who seeks to mask his pursuit of personal goals. As observable behavior appears well intentioned and true motivation is hidden, he is likely to be seen as 5,5, 9,9, 1,9, 9,1, or as a mixture of different Grid positions. Since his strategies vary to take advantage of the opportune situation and the weakness of people, it may be difficult to pinpoint the facade builder except by tracking his activities over a time span. The utilization of facades to cloak intentions constitutes a personal barrier to the achievement of 9,9 relationships.

References

1. Sforza, C. *The Living Thoughts of Machiavelli.* New York: Fawcett, 1958.

2. Carnegie, D. *How to Win Friends and Influence People.* New York: Pocket Books, 1958.

3. Odiorne, G. S. *How Managers Make Things Happen.* Englewood Cliffs, N. J.: Prentice-Hall, 1961.

4. Jennings, E. M. *An Anatomy of Leadership.* New York: Harper, 1960.

5. Hoover, J. E. *Masters of Deceit.* New York: Holt, 1958.

6. See also Potter, S. *The Theory and Practice of Gamemanship.* New York: Holt, 1948; Potter, S. *One-upmanship.* New York: Holt, 1951; and, Jennings, E. M. *The Executive: Autocrat, Bureaucrat, Democrat.* New York: Harper, 1962.

7. Shibutani, T. *Society and Personality.* Englewood Cliffs, N. J.: Prentice-Hall, 1961, 290.

8. Sforza, C., *op. cit.*

9. Hoover, J. E., *op. cit.*

10. Marrow, A. J. *Making Management Human.* New York: Mc-Graw-Hill, 1957, 73.

11. Carnegie, D., *op. cit.*, Maier, N. R. F. *Psychology in Industry.* (2nd Ed.) Boston: Houghton Mifflin, 1955, 3.

12. Sforza, C., *op. cit.;* Carnegie, D., *op. cit.*

13. Sforza, C., *op. cit.*

14. Carnegie, D., *op. cit.*

15. Odiorne, G. S., *op. cit.*

16. Carnegie, D., *op. cit.*, 28.

17. Jennings, E. M. *op. cit.*

18. Metcalf, H. C. & Urwick, L. (Eds.) *Dynamic Administration: The Collected Papers of Mary Parker Follett.* New York: Harper, 1940.

19. Sforza, C., *op. cit.*

20. Bradford, L. P. The Case of the Hidden Agenda. In L. P. Bradford, (Ed.), *Group Development.* Washington, D. C.: National Training Laboratories, National Education Association, 1961, 60-68.

CHAPTER NINE

Mixed Grid Theories

Beyond facades and in addition to the five basic managerial orientations already described, six additional ones that are complex or mixed theories of management can be identified in the operations of production and service organizations. It is perhaps better to think of these theories as compounds or combinations of theories, as contrasted with the simple or "pure" theories. The reason is that two or more of the basic approaches to management already discussed—9,9; 5,5; 9,1; 1,9; or 1,1— are used either simultaneously or successively in conjunction with one another. These are described below.

PATERNALISM

Paternalism, as the word implies, describes the relation between the organization and its members or between a supervisor and his subordinates.[1] This concept of management involves control on the one hand, but care on the other, similar to that which can exist under certain circumstances between a father and his children.[2]

Organizational Paternalism

In paternalistic organizations concern for people is expressed through taking care of them. Employees are given many fine things—good pay, excellent benefit programs, recreational facilities, retirement programs, even low cost housing. Because these contributions to the

welfare of people are not directly connected to their output or productivity, and also because such actions tend
to increase one's sense of economic and social security,
they appropriately are seen as carrying a 1,9 flavor or
overtone.[3]

The following example of paternalism emphasizes
some of the negative consequences associated with it.
In one manufacturing location during the depression,
a decision was made to uncover all pipes and conduits
underground, to wrap them with a protective material
and to re-embed them at a greater depth. The major
reason behind the decision to take these actions was
that the wage force would otherwise be laid off. When the
decision to do so was made, it also was concluded that
the rate of pay for this work be reduced by one-half.
Management's thinking at this point was that the work
was not necessary in order to maintain or to increase
productivity. Rather, the decision to do this work was
primarily based on keeping workers employed. Thus,
management felt quite justified in reducing the rate.
This action made it possible to employ twice the number of men in the project.

What was the result? At the time, the work was accepted by the wage ranks without criticism or com-
plaint. After a return of relative prosperity, however,
the example given above became a conspicuous indicator of management's paternalistic attitudes. Wage people said, "Not only did they—the management—call upon
us to do unnecessary work; they did so under conditions
where we were in no position to resist. When they had
us in that kind of a bind, what did they do? They cut
our pay in half."

Here, then, is an example where management's good
intentions to take care of people boomeranged. Management's actions failed to produce respect for their
good intentions. The opposite result was produced.
From management's point of view it was doing a good
thing; from the standpoint of wage personnel they were
victims of vicious exploitation.

Production in paternalistic organizations is demanded.

It is pushed for in a 9,1 manner. Little concern is demonstrated for involving the thinking and feelings of people in the conditions of productive effort. Good treatment by management is not for acknowledging contributions to production. Rather, it is to increase acceptance by organization members of the obedience requirements under which they are expected to produce. This approach to management is accurately referred to as paternalistic.

Individual Paternalism

Evaluated from the standpoint of individual supervision, then, a paternalistic manager tends to retain tight control in work matters. At the same time the boss is generous and kind in a personal way.[1] The spirit of paternalism is caught in the following quotation. A supervisor called one of his men over some 20 minutes before the end of his shift and said: "Joe, you've put in a good day's work and finished all your assignments. Go over to the pen and have a smoke."

At middle and higher levels, a paternalistic manager tries to treat his subordinates as part of his managerial family. On the one hand, he encourages them to take initiative and to be responsible. But, on the other hand, he is unable to truly delegate. Often he is heard to describe a subordinate in this way: "My assistant won't accept responsibility. He's bright and capable, with plenty of know-how, but he checks and double checks everything he does with me. He won't take the ball and run. It's difficult to see how he'll ever succeed."

In the paternalistic style, the work situation, in other words, approaches 9,1 conditions in terms of direction and control. But this is coupled with the 1,9 style of concern for the well-being of people. The reward for subordinates complying with directions, controls and push in work is security, happiness and being taken care of in terms of economic and social security.

The Price of Paternalism is Anti-Paternalistic Revolt

Over a long period of time, and with consistent application, paternalism can result in a highly stable organization where there is minimum turnover. Organization members tend to become compliantly obedient to the requirements of performance placed upon them. However, some of the worst upheavals and disruptions in organization performance have occurred in company locations where paternalism has been extensively practiced. Against a background of what appeared to have been a very stable and long enduring organization, waves of resentment and retaliation have arisen against the management which had for such long periods treated their people so well. Since such a gross shift from compliant acceptance to defiant retaliation appears contradictory, it needs explanation.

One way of explaining the contradiction—of people reacting with wrath against the hand that has fed them so well—is this: 9,1 work management, which tends to disregard the thinking and capabilities of people and to use them in a callous manner, tends to generate frustration and resistance and to produce feelings of alienation. But frustration and resistance are difficult to express directly. Even in more subtle ways, such as through unionization, frustration and resistance are difficult to express towards an employer who, at the same time, offers economic and social security. Reactions to indignities, as a result, tend to be swallowed and bottled up. This produces the appearance of compliant acceptance and dependence while, in fact, under the smooth surface of apparent cooperation there may be seething resentment and unrest.

Given these circumstances, even a minor irritation sometimes can serve as a trigger which causes an eruption of vitriolic and hateful reactions.[5] Another way of saying it is that *the formula for concocting hate consists of arousing frustrations under conditions of dependence.* One feels antagonized and aggressive. Yet one is prevented from responding in a counteracting manner which might have the effect of relieving the basic problem, due to his own fear of losing acceptance and security.

Although paternalism has failed repeatedly to solve problems of getting production through the involvement of people, it is still a rather widespread attitude underlying much organizational thinking.[6]

WIDE-ARC PENDULUM

The wide-arc pendulum is another way in which the 9,1 and 1,9 management positions are connected with one another. Under paternalism, aspects of these two approaches operate in juxtaposition. Under wide-arc pendulum management, either one or the other is operating, never both together.

Organization Wide-Arc Pendulum Swings

To understand how the wide-arc pendulum works, it is necessary to consider managerial shifts in the same organization over extended periods of time.[7] As often happens when profits fall off, there is a need to tighten up for increased output. Then, in order to get quick results, pressures are put on employees for production in a 9,1 way. The common consequence of such 9,1 pressures is that relationships can become so disturbed that production suffers. In due course, management feels compelled to ease off and to show increased concern for the thoughts, feelings and attitudes of people. In other words, management swings to a 1,9 approach to restore confidence that management cherishes human values.[8] This sequence results in a full pendulum swing by the organization into the 1,9 area. When a degree of confidence and peace has been restored, a tightening up takes place again in order to regain the losses in production which have been suffered during the previous swing toward 1,9.

At least two factors are responsible for the swing characteristics of the wide-arc pendulum.

One of the best times to see the wide-arc theory in actual practice is before and after a certification election in companies that want to keep an independent union which has been challenged by an international. Supervisors say, "The signal is out. Management wants to be sure that the independent will win the election coming up. For the next few months let up on the tough stuff.

Ease up on washup time and on the coveralls and gloves policies. Show an interest in people. Find out what's griping them. Take whatever actions are required to show employees that management is interested in them." When the election is over and the independent union has won the election, the same supervisors say, "Well, let's tighten up now. Get out production."

The other set of circumstances, which can set a wide-arc pendulum swing in motion, is related to cyclical movements of the economy from troughs of recession to peaks of prosperity. When recession conditions hit the economy as a whole or an individual production location, feverish activity intended to produce a P/(L) improvement can be seen. Included are such efforts as cost control, waste control, rolls readjustment, and so on. Such actions tend to be experienced by those whom they affect as cold and anti-personal because they result in an increase in the pressures exercised by supervision upon the conduct of work.

Sometimes the kind of production improvement decisions that are made do, in fact, result in an improved P/(L) position. But, as soon as economic health has been restored, attention turns away from the kinds of efficiency moves previously taken. The efficiency control programs tend to fade out and frequently uneconomical practices creep back in. Without the goad associated with economic threat, practices that are in fact "soft" tend to be overlooked or taken for granted and to come under organizational scrutiny only when unfavorable P/(L) circumstances return.

Randall, in *Folklore of Management,*[9] clearly depicts this situation, but he goes on to make a further point. Effective management rarely lets this kind of cyclical, wide-arc pendulum swing develop. It avoids these kinds of erratic fluctuations by keeping lean and hungry.

Wide-Arc Pendulum Swings in Personal Managerial Actions

The same kind of wide-arc pendulum swing can be seen in the managerial attitude underlying much individual thinking. Wide-arc pendulum swings can be observed in styles of individuals considered singly over a period of time. It comes about when a manager drives for production. However, in doing so, he arouses resentments and antagonisms among those whom he supervises. The manager comes to recognize that negative attitudes among those whom he supervises have been aroused. He then overcorrects, as if to ease feelings of guilt. He may become exaggeratedly solicitous for the thoughts, feelings and attitudes of those beneath him. Once relationships have been restored to a smooth basis, he may then become careless, and, as new pressures arise, to revert to a 9,1 manner of supervision. The effect is that the cycle repeats itself.

Cracking down to get efficiency, then easing off to get in the good graces of employees, and then pushing for increased production again is the pendulum swing from hard to soft, to hard, etc.

COUNTERBALANCING

Counterbalancing is a way of applying 9,1 and 1,9, not in succession with one another, but rather at the same time.

Organization Counterbalancing

Under counterbalancing, the line organization operates, more or less, on a 9,1 basis. The result is that negative reactions are produced. As a safeguard against feelings that can fester and smoulder and break out with disastrous effects, a staff organization is assigned the responsibility of keeping its finger on the pulse of the organization. If need be, a function of this staff is to provide disgruntled people the opportunity to blow off steam through ventilating their feelings.[10] The personnel department is an example. With a 1,9 orientation, its purpose may be to smooth over conflict generated from the 9,1 line production pressures.

This attitude of counterbalancing can be seen in a number of production centers today where a job description calls for an individual under the label field representative, personnel representative or employee relations coordinator, etc., to keep in touch with what is going on. In some settings, counterbalancing has taken an even more refined form. Psychiatrists, psychologists, ministers, and professional people skilled in listening, are employed for the purpose of relieving pent-up feelings.[11] The World War II theme which involved line management responding to gripes by saying, "Here's your card — take it to the chaplain and have it punched," also carries the counterbalancing concept.

An excellent example of the counterbalancing concept comes out of the Hawthorne experiment attributed to Mayo.[12] His advocacy of non-directive counseling took the following turn: In the course of the interviewing at Hawthorne the experimenters became clear as to the constructive effects the interviews had on the people who were working in the experiment. What they did then was to take another step. They made the interviews *a part* of the management approach to the maintenance of morale. The idea was to have counselors paid by management but not reporting to management. In this way, when people "spill their troubles" they would not need to worry about being reported. Workers could feel they were free to talk out their problems.

From the present point of view, the serious and obvious disadvantage of this kind of ventilating of hostility is that while tensions are reduced, the problems responsible for generating the tensions remain.

Although the way counterbalancing routinely appears is the "hard" line balanced by the "soft" personnel department, other forms also appear. For example in some organizations, the line organization has swung in the 1,9 direction. Under these circumstances, evaluation of managers for promotion may be the responsibility of the personnel department. The personnel department then, exercises critical evaluative judgments and functionally controls promotions. It serves to buck up line management where only a supportive consultative relationship exists between supervisor and subordinate.

As with other ways of dealing with the assumed conflict between production requirements and people needs, counterbalancing may serve to keep a problem under control, but it fails to offer a basic solution. The reason is that the style of management which is causing the problem is not corrected.[13] *Rather, counterbalancing is an approach which focuses on the relief of symptoms rather than digging in and eliminating the underlying causes.*

The critical feature to be understood in connection with counterbalancing is that responsibility for production and people is not seen as a singular obligation resting on the shoulders of those who manage. Rather, the responsibility is subdivided and separated into two aspects, production responsibility on the one hand and people responsibility on the other. Thus, one segment of the organization serves as a counterbalance intended to prevent the problems created by the first part from becoming fatally disruptive.

THE TWO-HAT APPROACH

The two-hat approach to management also occurs when concerns for production are viewed apart and separately from the concerns for people. However, both are held to be important. The responsibility for maintaining both rests on the shoulders of the same people. In other words, the split responsibility of counterbalancing is avoided. Two-hat retains the split between production requirements and people needs, but does so in a different manner.

Organization Two-Hat Approach

In a two-hat organization, it is likely, for example, that one day a week, say on Monday, the top group gets together to consider issues concerning P/(L) and problems of efficient operations. Then on another day, say Wednesday, the same group meets again. This time, however, its purpose is to discuss people problems. The actions taken on Monday to solve production problems, even though they may, in fact, be tied in with personnel problems, are not likely to be considered in light of the effects on people. They are considered mainly in terms of the production aspects of the problem. The same is true on Wednesday. The people problems considered at that time may bear significantly on production, but they are viewed mainly in the light of human relationships. In other words, on Monday, problems concerning people are tabled until Wednesday. On Wednesday, production problems are tabled until Monday. The two concerns are kept separate, but equal. The basic assumption again is that there are two sets of problems and frequently the connection between them is not adequately recognized.

Personal Two-Hat Approach

The two-hat approach also may be seen in supervisory practices of individuals, where management is applied in a 9,1 way in the course of daily work but where at six month or yearly intervals a man is counseled by his boss in a way which deals mainly with the man's attitudes— at large — and only incidentally with his work. Under these circumstances, job counseling is not seen as part and parcel of work activity and individual development. Rather, it is a scheduled activity which has a concentrated people orientation. Due to the character of job counseling, with its 1,9 aspect, many managers see these interviews as a farce. Line managers view counseling as an activity they must engage in, not because of a contribution of improving work, but because the personnel department has placed the obligation upon them to perform as a matter of company policy.

"STATISTICAL" 5,5

The "statistical" 5,5 manager employs all five styles in his daily supervision. The essential feature is that he manages according to what is most "acceptable"—whether or not it is appropriate. If a subordinate wants to be left alone, or if the supervisor doesn't know how to approach him, he is left to fend for himself, as in 1,1. If the subordinate seems to want warm, friendly relations and a supportive atmosphere he is given warmth, support, and friendship, as in 1,9. If the subordinate wants to knock heads and to fight with no holds barred, as in 9,1, the supervisor responds with a "tough" attitude. If the subordinate avoids conflict and wants to compromise, the supervisor responds in kind as in 5,5; and so on. In other words, the "statistical" 5,5 manager operates all over the grid. His managerial styles average out to 5,5. He behaves inconsistently, in other words, in the sense that he treats various people, each in a different manner. Yet, he sees little or no contradiction in his actions. His rationale is that each person is different than all the others and, therefore, you can't expect to treat them all alike.

THE 9,1 - 1,1 CYCLE

In order to round out the picture of how organizations accommodate to the apparently contradictory requirements for production on the one hand and people needs on the other, the issue of 1,1 needs examination in greater detail. While 1,1 has been described earlier as a "pure" adjustment, it nonetheless is an end result of the clash of different theories.

A variety of explanations can be given for what the circumstances are that produce a 1,1 adjustment. Among the more important are the following:

Management may behave in a 9,1 way in its effort to achieve organization production goals. The reaction from some is to resist 9,1 and to "fight back." In many instances such resistance is difficult to maintain with the result that individuals withdraw effort and abandon the attempt to counteract the situation.[15]

As the shift in behavior increases in a 1,1 direction, the accompanying low production, waste, and inefficiency tend to arouse the reaction of increased pressures — in a 9,1 direction.[16] That is, one level of management reacts to the 1,1 response of other levels by increasing the "9,1-ness" of its centralized work direction and tight control. This increase in 9,1 tactics causes those to whom it is applied to become even more 1,1, which, in turn, causes those above to become even more 9,1 in orientation. And so, the cycle runs its course. Like the dog that chases its tail, yet never catches it, management spends tremendous effort, time, and money in a futile effort to enforce obedience to its wishes through the exercise of authority.

SUMMARY

Each of six mixed theories, in one respect or another, recognizes the problems of people and production. Each tries in some way to handle them. However, mixed theories distort the basic issue as to how an integration of people into production can be accomplished effectively. The underlying limitation in them is that these approaches attempt to deal with the problem at the level of symptoms. They fail to recognize and deal with underlying causes.

The fundamental solution to the problem is not that of putting on a patch. Rather, the solution is in the direction of learning to apply principles of human behavior in the context of production in such a manner that individual goals and organizational needs are geared to one another. When an individual's stakes and the organization's fate are one and the same, then efforts to achieve production do not have to be pressured as under 9,1. Nor do the needs have to be compromised as under 5,5 or abandoned as in 1,1, or bought as in 1,9. Neither do they have to be managed as in paternalism, counterbalancing or two-hat. Rather, efforts to achieve production can result in high output through a maximum of involvement and commitment to organization objectives.

A final point needs to be emphasized. It is that realities being what they are in an industrial situation, the way a supervisor behaves is largely determined, not by what would constitute ideal management, but rather by what the existing constraints and pressures compel as realistic problem solving for that situation.

Organization development constitutes one way in which the performance of organizations can be improved. This can be done through making it possible for managerial personnel to come closer to applying managerial theory that results in the best integration of people in the achievement of production.

References

1. Marrow, A. J. *Making Management Human.* New York: McGraw-Hill, 1957, 75-76.

2. Maier, N. R. F. *Psychology in Industry.* (2nd Ed.) Boston: Houghton Mifflin, 1955, 1-2, 138; Gellerman, S. W. *People, Problems and Profits.* New York: McGraw-Hill, 1960, 164.

3. Stagner, R. *Psychology of Industrial Conflict.* New York: Wiley, 1956, 316-318.

4. Bradford, L. P. & Lippitt, R. Building a Democratic Work Group. In G. Lippitt (Ed.), *Leadership in Action.* Washington, D. C.: National Training Laboratories, National Education Association, 1961, 53-54.

5. Marrow, A. J., *op. cit.,* 76.

6. McMurry, R. N. The Case for Benevolent Autocracy. *Harvard Business Review,* 36, 1958, 82-90.

7. Guest, R. H. *Organizational Change: The Effect of Successful Leadership.* Homewood, Ill.: Dorsey, 1962, 17-38.

8. Stagner, R., *op. cit.,* 389-390.

9. Randall, C. B. *The Folklore of Management.* New York: Mentor, 1962, 66-71.

10. Stagner, R., *op. cit.,* 192-193, 316, 390-391.

11. Zimmerman, C. J. Management's Role in Mental Health. *Advanced Management,* Sept., 1960, 5-8.

12. Roethlisberger, F. J. & Dickson, W. J. *Management and the Worker.* Cambridge: Harvard University, 1939. Mayo, E. *The Human Problems of An Industrial Civilization.* Boston: Harvard Business School, 1946.

13. Stagner, R., *op. cit.,* 193.

14. Singer, H. A. The Management of Stress. *Advanced Management,* Sept., 1960, 11-13.

15. See Argyris, C. *Personality and Organization.* New York: Harper, 1957.

16. Argyris, C. Understanding Human Behavior in Organizations: One Viewpoint. In M. Haire (Ed.), *Modern Organization Theory.* New York: Wiley, 1959, 143; Argyris, C. *Understanding Organizational Behavior.* Homewood, Ill.: Dorsey, 1960, 17-18.

CHAPTER TEN

Career Accomplishment and Managerial Style

Men enter public corporations of today somewhere near the base of the organization pyramid. Most stay at the base, or shift little more than a step or two. Some move up, but only a third or half the way or so. Very few of those who start at the base progress to the top or even close to it.

WHAT ACCOUNTS FOR DIFFERENCES IN CAREER ACCOMPLISHMENT?

How are such differences in career development to be understood? The issue defines a basic query of modern industrial life. The question might be put this way. "What personal factors account for individual differences in career development? What characteristics of men distinguish their career lines from one another?"

Education

One answer given to explain this riddle is formal education.[1] True, education *is* an important factor. Those with it move along more swiftly than those without it. At best, however, it is only a partial answer. Indeed, even among those with college degrees, some move faster and farther than others. Since all have essentially the same education, schooling itself provides no easy key to account for differences in career development.

The same difficulty occurs among those without collegiate degrees. Some few move along. Most stand still.
Education *per se*, then, offers no complete answer. Factors other than education play central roles.

Motivation

Another factor is motivation.[2] "Those who succeed are
those who want to succeed, those who have a drive for
achievement," it is said.[3] Again, though it contains an
element of truth, this is no real answer. It merely repeats
an after-the-fact observation. Efforts to account for career outcomes by such coarse generalizations have not
yielded sound results.

Politics

A third is politics.[4] "It's not *what* you know, but *who*
you know that counts," or so the saying goes. And again,
the "right side of the street," and "boss' daughter" examples come to mind. As will be shown, however, performance factors are far more central.

Luck

"Being in the right place at the right time," is offered
as an explanation. Luck, or breaks, such as timing, surely
constitute tactical factors in certain critical promotions.[5]
To see the entire managerial system as the product of
Russian roulette, however, elevates chance to a position
of explanation that it has not been shown to merit.

Managerial Styles

This answer deals with human character. It relates to
how men use themselves; how they manage. Personal
orientations toward making decisions, standing by one's
own convictions, handling interpersonal conflict, coping
with personal tension, expressing humor, and exerting one's
own efforts, all are at the core of managing.

Among the several explanations, education and managerial styles offer the most promising basis for under-

standing individual differences in career development. They are evaluated here.

ASSESSMENT OF MANAGERIAL ACHIEVEMENT

Every organization is confronted with assessing its membership and identifying those most capable of moving higher in the organization structure. Because of the pyramid shape of organizational systems, there are far more people available to be selected than can be chosen and promoted. A selection process is inevitable.[6]

Promotional Policy

The process of grading individual capability is applied in various ways in different organizations. For the most part, however, man-to-man judgments as to those who are to be promoted rarely are based on a single individual acting alone. Rather, a number of persons, usually ones holding higher positions than the man being evaluated, contribute to the decision according to their knowledge of the man and his capabilities.

Granting the possibilities of human error in such judgments, this human basis of judgment has as yet to be seriously challenged by other more sophisticated methods, such as tests, etc., which might be thought more effective. Judgments are regarded here to be as adequate for calibration of managerial capability as any method currently available.[7]

Managerial Achievement Quotient

Direct comparison of managerial style with an individual's organization level is too simple, however. Age colors the picture.[8] Needed is a way of comparing managerial performance of many individuals in terms of each man's contribution to the firm, without regard for present age. Such a measure ought to reflect an individual's particular organizational level,[9] whether high in the hierarchy or low, as well as an individual's age, whether young or old. For example, in terms of promotion policy, the younger man who has advanced to the top is making a greater organizational contribution than another who, at the same age, is operating in a lower level position. The managerial achievement for the former person, who has been moved up, would be high, whereas for the latter person, who has been stalemated, it would be either average or low. In the same way, a younger man at any level in comparison with an older man at the same level, is seen by those exercising judgment as capable of making a contribution equal to the older man. In the selective grading for advancement, both men have come up side by side. Since capability increases with age, the younger man's achievement is higher.

The Managerial Achievement Quotient permits direct comparisons of individual contributions, independent of the level at which the contributions are made and with age eliminated as a consideration. This index, then, provides a measure of individual performance adequacy. It permits direct comparisons of higher level managers with lower level managers, and of older managerial members with those who are younger. By adjusting for level and age, a pure index of achievement is obtained.

MAQ Axioms

MAQ is based on four axioms. The discussion above is summarized below in axiomatic form.

Axiom	Statement
1	Managerial competence is evaluated validly.
2	The higher the level, the greater the managerial capability required.
3	Capability increases with age.
4	The greater the managerial capability, the greater the prospect of promotion.

To the degree that these axiomatic conditions prevail under actual operating circumstances, MAQ constitutes a valid basis for comparing one person's managerial capability with others in order to draw conclusions regarding factors that account for the differences among them.[10]

The Managerial Achievement Quotient (MAQ)

MAQ is computed in the following way:[11]

$$MAQ = \left[\frac{5(9\text{-}L)}{\text{Age to } 50\text{-}20} \right] \times 100$$

In the numerator, the term (9-L) is the actual managerial level subtracted from a constant (9), based on the fact that hierarchies of large corporations can be categorized according to eight levels. Level, in other words, can be any number from 1 to 8. One (1) is the highest level and 8 is the lowest. In other words, an individual at the lowest level would receive a score of (9-8) or 1, which indicates that he has achieved one managerial level, i.e., front-line supervision. Criteria for specifying levels based on job titles are in Appendix 1, (page 244).

Another value in the numerator is 5. It is a constant progression factor to indicate intervals of time in rank that would move an individual from the bottom to the top of an eight level organization in 40 years in the absence of other restraining or facilitating factors. With an entry age into the lowest level of supervision by the age of 20, and spending five years at each of the eight levels, an individual would retire at the age of 60.

The denominator provides an indicator of seniority—time in service an individual has had to advance from level-to-level, if advancement were purely mechanical, and based on the notion that individual differences in capability are only associated with age. Fifty is regarded as a ceiling beyond which age is no longer an influential factor. Twenty is taken as the more or less standard entry age. The number resulting from completing the arithmetical operations is multiplied by a constant of 100.

With an effective formula permitting comparisons in achievement among managerial members, it becomes possible to investigate factors responsible for individual differences in managerial achievement. In the next section is presented a new strategy for assessing key facets of managerial competence.

ASSESSMENT OF MANAGERIAL STYLES

Key Managerial Orientations Grid Booklet

The instrument used to assess managerial styles in this study is the Grid booklet, *An Exploration of Key Managerial Orientations,*[12] shown in this text as Chapter 1. The "Effort" element was not included.

It can be applied by a person to characterize the actions of others. Conditions of application are described more fully below.

Evaluation of Managerial Styles

During the one-week Managerial Grid Seminar, participants evaluated one another's styles of managing. To complete the procedure, 716 managers spent a total of forty hours each. The magnitude of the effort involved can be seen when this amount is converted into man years. Just under fifteen man years of work are involved.

The various conditions of interaction involved were such as to make it possible for each person to see how others reacted when decisions were required, when convictions and humor could be expressed, and when conflict and tensions arose.

After approximately 30 hours of such interaction, the team members assessed the Grid styles of one another in private. Each person rank-ordered the paragraph descriptions of Grid styles and selected the most characteristic style of each element. These assessments were made for each person on each 10-man team by every other member.

Next, the managerial styles of each participant, as they had been observed during the interaction period, were discussed, leading to a consensual ranking of the paragraphs. Rank 1 was used to identify that paragraph style most typical of the person's managerial behavior, with Rank 5 indicating the least typical managerial style. In addition, one element phrase of the five was selected that best pictured the individual's behavior with regard to Decisions, Convictions, Conflict, Temper and Humor.

These rankings and element selections serve as the basis for studying how MAQ and managerial style are related in the present investigation.

THE EXPERIMENT

Setting

Managerial members from one of America's largest industrial plants were studied. The plant is one of several P/(L) centers reporting to a major corporate headquarters. At the time the study was initiated, in excess of 3,000 personnel were employed in the plant. The managerial styles of 716 of those engaged in managerial assignments and having managerial rank were the subject of examination.

The results reported here also are found in the assessment of individuals representing many different publicly owned organizations. The study dealing with Managerial Grid validity for a variety of organizations is reported elsewhere.[13] Since results from both the intensive and the extended study support one another, findings can be accepted as being applicable in publicly owned American corporations of today.

RESULTS

General Observations Regarding MAQ—Progression Pyramid

Computed in the way described earlier, Table 1 and those following show that most individuals earned low MAQ's and only a few earned high scores. The ratio of frequency of scores is roughly 9 to 1 between those with MAQ's of 0-29, the lowest group, and those with MAQ's of 90 and above, the highest. These results parallel both the pyramid shape of the organization and its age structure. Furthermore, a larger number of younger people are found in the highest MAQ level than in the lowest. For each of these several reasons, MAQ appears to provide an excellent basis for picturing individual achievement as reflected in organizational contribution.

Ranking of Paragraph Selections and MAQ

Tables 1 through 4 summarize orderings of paragraphs by MAQ and by other variables related to MAQ. Results for the 716 participants are shown in Table 1. In Table 2, the results are broken down further to permit study of how MAQ is related to education; that is, whether an individual is a college graduate or not. It shows how paragraph selections are related to MAQ within each educational category. Table 3 subdivides the results by differentiating line from staff managers and studying the ordering of style paragraphs by MAQ for each. Table 4 completes the summary by a further subdivision. Here, the ordering of paragraph styles by MAQ is differentiated in both of the above two ways simultaneously. The line is separated from the staff and, within each, college graduates are distinguished from non-graduates.

When examining these Tables, bear in mind that Rank 1 was used to identify the most typical managerial behavior, and Rank 5 the least typical managerial style. Thus, the lowest number in the Table represents the most typical managerial style, the second lowest number the next most typical, and so on.

Average Rank Order of Paragraph Styles. As seen in Table 1, the most prominent managerial theory for the entire 716 cases is 5,5 and the second most, or the backup theory, is 9,9. The third, fourth and fifth theories are

TABLE 1

Grid Style Paragraph Rankings by MAQ Level
in One Organization

MAQ Level	Number of Cases	Managerial Grid Styles—Average Assigned Rank				
		1,1	1,9	9,1	5,5	9,9
0–29.............	323	4.8	3.1	3.1	1.5	2.5
30–59.............	224	4.9	3.7	2.8	1.8	1.8
60–89.............	133	5.0	3.8	2.7	2.1	1.4
90 and above.......	36	5.0	3.8	2.6	2.4	1.2
Average............	716	4.9	3.5	2.9	1.7	2.0

9,1, 1,9, and 1,1, in that order. From a statistical point of view, then, 5,5 represents the dominant managerial approach for integrating people into production in this organization.

Managerial Styles by MAQ. The degree of prominence of the various paragraphs is strikingly different when analyzed against MAQ, however. While the order for those with lowest MAQ's is 5,5, 9,9, 9,1, 1,9 and 1,1, the order for those in the highest MAQ group is 9,9, 5,5, 9,1, 1,9 and 1,1, with 9,1 almost as much as 5,5.

Reading down the 9,9 column of Table 1, it is to be seen that 9,9 becomes a progressively more prominent first theory as MAQ increases. *Indeed, among those whose MAQ's are in the 90 and above range, 9,9 is almost universally the dominant theory.* The inverse of these results can be seen reading down the 5,5 column of Table 1. Here the generalization is that the higher the MAQ, the less likely 5,5 is to be found as a first theory. Another way of saying it is that the higher the MAQ, the less characteristic is 5,5 of a manager's dominant style.

The 9,1 column repeats the trend of the 9,9 column; that is, 9,1 becomes progressively more characteristic of managers the higher the MAQ. The 1,9 column replicates the 5,5 column; 1,9 is more prominent at the lower MAQ levels and less prominent at the higher MAQ levels.

For all MAQ levels 1,1 is the most strongly rejected style, though strength of rejection is slightly less at the lowest MAQ levels.

Association Between Education, MAQ, and Grid Styles. Table 2 shows how education level and MAQ are related. It demonstrates that in this organization, members without college degrees are not found in the top two MAQ categories; that is with MAQ's of above 60. Slightly different results have been found in other large public corporations, but the trend is similar.[14]

Table 2 also demonstrates an important finding in that results obtained are essentially identical for those in Table 1. When the analysis is limited to those with college education, it remains true that the higher the MAQ, the

TABLE 2

Grid Style Paragraph Rankings by MAQ Level and
College/Non College in One Organization

MAQ Level	COLLEGE						NON COLLEGE					
	No. of Cases	Managerial Grid Styles					No. of Cases	Managerial Grid Styles				
		1,1	1,9	9,1	5,5	9,9		1,1	1,9	9,1	5,5	9,9
0–29	37	4.8	3.3	3.3	1.6	2.0	286	4.8	3.1	3.1	1.5	2.5
30–59	154	4.8	3.8	2.8	1.9	1.7	70	4.9	3.6	2.7	1.7	2.1
60–89	133	5.0	3.8	2.7	2.1	1.4	...	..	..	..	..	..
90 and above	36	5.0	3.8	2.6	2.4	1.2	...	..	..	..	..	..
Average	360	4.9	3.8	2.7	2.0	1.6	356	4.8	3.2	3.0	1.5	2.5

more prominent is a first choice of 9,9, the less prominent
5,5, etc. Furthermore, a trend is observed in the data
for non-college graduates. Differences are a matter of
degree. College graduates utilize 9,9 as a first theory
more and 5,5 less than non-college graduates.

MAQ Line/Staff Membership and Grid Style. Table
3 shows that while the number of people studied who
are in the line and with staff organizations are approximately the same, the preponderance of low MAQ's are
to be found in the line, with a large number of high
MAQ's found in the staff organization. Table 3 also
verifies that the trends present in Table 1 also hold in
both the line and staff organizations. But such trends
are accentuated at the extremes. 9,9 is a *more* prominent
first theory at the highest MAQ level for staff than line
managers.

*MAQ Grid Style, Line/Staff, and Education Cate-
gories.* When managerial styles are examined as a
function of MAQ for college graduates in a line organization only, and for college graduates in a staff organization only, the same trends are apparent. The
prominence of 9,9 and 9,1 increases with increases in MAQ;
the prominence of 5,5 and 1,9 decreases with increases of

MAQ. Each of these trends which is statistically significant is to be observed in Table 4 with minor fluctuations.

TABLE 3
Grid Style Paragraph Rankings by MAQ and
Line/Staff in One Organization

MAQ Level	LINE						STAFF					
	No. of Cases	Managerial Grid Styles					No. of Cases	Managerial Grid Styles				
		1,1	1,9	9,1	5,5	9,9		1,1	1,9	9,1	5,5	9,9
0–29	219	4.9	3.1	3.1	1.4	2.7	104	4.8	3.3	3.2	1.6	2.1
30–59	67	5.0	3.8	2.5	1.8	1.4	157	4.9	3.7	2.9	1.8	1.8
60–89	42	5.0	3.9	2.5	2.1	1.4	91	5.0	3.7	2.8	2.1	1.4
90 and above	20	5.0	3.8	2.5	2.4	1.4	16	5.0	3.9	2.6	2.4	1.1
Average	348	4.9	3.4	2.8	1.6	2.3	368	4.9	3.7	2.9	1.8	1.7

TABLE 4
Grid Style Paragraph Rankings by MAQ Level, College/
Non College, Line/Staff in One Organization

MAQ Level	LINE ORGANIZATION											
	No. of Cases	College					No. of Cases	Non College				
		1,1	1,9	9,1	5,5	9,9		1,1	1,9	9,1	5,5	9,9
0–29	5	5.0	3.6	2.6	1.4	2.4	214	4.9	3.0	3.1	1.4	2.6
30–59	27	5.0	3.8	2.4	1.9	1.5	40	5.0	3.6	2.5	1.7	2.1
60–89	42	5.0	3.9	2.5	2.1	1.4	...	..	..	..	..	..
90 and above	20	4.9	3.8	2.5	2.4	1.4	...	..	..	..	..	..

MAQ Level	STAFF ORGANIZATION											
	No. of Cases	College					No. of Cases	Non College				
		1,1	1,9	9,1	5,5	9,9		1,1	1,9	9,1	5,5	9,9
0–29	32	5.0	3.2	3.4	1.5	1.9	72	4.9	3.3	3.0	1.6	2.2
30–59	127	5.0	3.7	2.8	1.8	1.7	30	4.9	3.5	2.9	1.6	2.1
60–89	91	5.0	3.8	2.7	2.1	1.4	..	..	..	..	..	..
90 and above	16	5.0	3.9	2.6	2.4	1.1	..	..	..	..	..	..

SUMMARY

It is concluded that Grid styles vary with MAQ, independently of education and of the kind of work assignment in which an individual is engaged, whether line or staff. Three general trends are conspicuous. 9,9 and 9,1 become more prominent, whereas 5,5 and 1,9 become less prominent with increases in MAQ.

When evaluated quantitatively, the major trends noted here are all significant from a statistical point of view.

Grid Elements by MAQ, Education and Line/Staff Organization

Results with respect to each of the five Grid elements are presented in Tables 5 through 9. The order is *decisions, convictions, conflict, temper* and *humor*. Each table is organized so that the lower right hand corner represents the summary of data by MAQ for all participants. Other breakdowns and averages are presented in a form comparable to those in Tables 1 through 4.

The number of cases in these studies is 710, as element selections were not completed for six of the 716 participants.

A brief discussion of results with respect to each element follows:

Decisions. The 9,9 decision element is selected to picture individuals with greater frequency the larger the MAQ. Only 17 per cent of those in the 0-29 group were pictured as behaving according to the 9,9 decision element, whereas 86 per cent of those in the 90 and above MAQ group were so characterized (see Table 5).

The inverse of this trend is to be observed with respect to the 5,5 decision element. Reading up the four MAQ categories, a decrease in frequency is observed in the use of the 5,5 element to depict the decision-making approach. The per cents are 60, 45, 20 and 3.

The 9,1 decision element did not distinguish MAQ levels.

The statements above hold for both line and staff members considered separately of one another.

TABLE 5
Per Cent of Grid Style Choices for Element 1; *Decisions* by
MAQ Level, College/Non-College and Line/Staff in One Organization

	MAQ Level	College						Non-College						Averages for Line/Staff and Overall					
		N	1,1	1,9	9,1	5,5	9,9	N	1,1	1,9	9,1	5,5	9,9	N	1,1	1,9	9,1	5,5	9,9
Line	0–29	5	0	0	20	40	40	212	5	10	11	65	9	217	5	10	12	63	10
	30–59	27	0	0	15	33	52	40	3	0	21	61	15	67	1	0	19	50	30
	60–89	42	0	0	7	21	72	..	.	.	..	..	..	42	0	0	7	21	72
	90–up	20	0	0	15	5	80	..	.	.	..	..	..	20	0	0	15	5	80
	Avg.	94	0	0	12	22	66	252	5	8	13	63	11	346	3	6	13	52	26
Staff	0–29	32	0	6	9	54	31	72	1	3	10	54	32	104	1	4	10	53	32
	30–59	125	1	1	12	40	46	30	3	7	17	50	23	155	1	2	13	42	42
	60–89	88	0	1	7	19	73	..	.	.	..	..	..	88	0	2	7	20	71
	90–up	17	0	0	6	0	94	..	.	.	..	..	..	17	0	0	6	0	94
	Avg.	262	1	2	9	32	56	102	1	4	12	54	29	364	1	2	10	37	50
Averages for College/Non-College and Over-all	0–29	37	0	5	11	52	32	284	4	8	11	62	15	321	4	8	11	60	17
	30–59	152	1	1	13	39	46	70	3	3	20	55	19	222	1	1	15	45	38
	60–89	130	0	1	7	20	72	..	.	.	..	..	..	130	0	2	7	20	71
	90–up	37	0	0	11	3	86	..	.	.	..	..	..	37	0	0	11	3	86
	Avg.	356	1	1	10	29	59	354	4	7	13	60	16	710	2	4	11	46	37

Convictions. Results for convictions are shown in Table 6, where is to be seen that all but the 1,1 conviction element bear a systematic and consistent relationship with MAQ level. The higher the MAQ, the more frequently is the 9,9 conviction element selected to picture a person's most characteristic approach. The higher the MAQ, the less frequently is the 5,5 element selected, the more frequently is the 9,1 element selected, and the less frequently is the 1,9 element selected to picture the individual.

All of the trends are repeated when the data are subdivided by line and staff and by the education factor.

Conflict. Results for the conflict element are reported in Table 7. They are comparable with results for the conviction element shown in Table 6.

The higher the MAQ, the more frequently the 9,9 element is selected; the less frequently the 5,5 element is selected; the more frequently the 9,1 element is selected; and the less frequently the 1,9 element is selected to picture an individual's dominant style.

Results show little fluctuation from the above when the comparison is for line and staff.

While the trend is consistent among the college population, neither the 9,9 nor the 5,5 trends are to be observed among the non-college members. For non-college graduates, 9,9 does not increase with MAQ, nor does 5,5 decrease. However, 9,1 does increase with MAQ and the 1,9 conflict element is shown to decrease in frequency.

Temper and Humor. Results for the *temper* and *humor* elements are presented in Tables 8 and 9. These two elements seem quite similar to one another but they are different from the others. The 9,9 temper element does not vary in any consistent way with MAQ and, while the selection of the 5,5 element tends to increase with MAQ, the trend does not appear to be clearly consistent.

As a result, no clear trends are apparent for 9,9, 5,5 or 9,1 temper elements. Only the 1,9 temper element is selected less frequently as MAQ increases.

TABLE 6

Per Cent of Grid Style Choices for Element 2: *Convictions* by MAQ Level, College/Non-College and Line/Staff in One Organization

	MAQ Level	College						Non-College						Averages for Line/Staff and Overall					
		N	1,1	1,9	9,1	5,5	9,9	N	1,1	1,9	9,1	5,5	9,9	N	1,1	1,9	9,1	5,5	9,9
Line	0–29	5	0	0	40	40	20	212	0	25	16	42	17	217	0	24	17	42	17
	30–59	27	0	0	11	22	67	40	0	10	15	45	30	67	0	6	13	36	45
	60–89	42	2	0	24	14	60	..	..	..	..	..	..	42	2	0	24	14	60
	90–up	20	0	0	30	5	65	..	..	..	..	..	..	20	0	0	30	5	65
	Avg.	94	1	0	22	16	61	252	0	22	16	43	19	346	1	16	18	35	30
Staff	0–29	32	0	9	6	41	44	72	1	17	15	36	31	104	1	14	13	37	35
	30–59	125	0	5	19	19	57	30	0	13	20	23	44	155	0	6	19	20	55
	60–89	88	0	2	19	11	68	..	..	..	..	..	..	88	0	2	20	12	66
	90–up	17	0	0	24	6	70	..	..	..	..	..	..	17	0	0	24	6	70
	Avg.	262	0	4	18	18	60	102	1	16	17	32	34	364	0	7	18	22	53
Averages for College/Non-College and Over-all	0–29	37	0	8	11	40	41	284	1	23	16	40	20	321	1	21	15	40	23
	30–59	152	0	4	18	20	58	70	0	11	17	36	36	222	0	6	18	25	51
	60–89	130	1	2	21	12	64	..	..	..	..	..	..	130	1	2	21	13	63
	90–up	37	0	0	27	5	68	..	..	..	..	..	..	37	0	0	28	5	67
	Avg.	356	0	3	19	18	60	354	1	20	16	40	23	710	0	12	18	29	41

TABLE 7

Per Cent of Grid Style Choices for Element 3: *Conflict* by MAQ Level College/Non-College, and Line/Staff in One Organization

	MAQ Level	College						Non-College						Averages for Line/ Staff and Overall					
		N	1,1	1,9	9,1	5,5	9,9	N	1,1	1,9	9,1	5,5	9,9	N	1,1	1,9	9,1	5,5	9,9
Line	0–29	5	0	0	0	100	0	212	10	8	3	73	6	217	10	8	3	73	6
	30–59	27	0	0	4	59	37	40	0	3	15	74	8	67	0	1	10	70	19
	60–89	42	0	0	14	48	38	:	.	.	.	.	.	42	0	0	14	48	38
	90–up	20	0	0	20	35	45	:	.	.	.	.	.	20	0	0	20	35	45
	Avg.	94	0	0	12	51	37	252	8	8	5	73	6	346	6	5	7	67	15
Staff	0–29	32	6	6	3	63	22	72	3	8	4	67	18	104	4	8	4	65	19
	30–59	125	2	2	4	65	27	30	3	3	10	67	17	155	2	3	5	65	25
	60–89	88	2	0	6	47	45	:	.	.	.	.	.	88	2	0	6	48	44
	90–up	17	0	0	12	24	64	:	.	.	.	.	.	17	0	0	12	24	64
	Avg.	262	2	2	6	55	35	102	2	6	6	68	18	364	3	3	5	59	30
Averages for Non-College and Over-all	0–29	37	5	5	3	68	19	284	8	8	4	71	9	321	8	8	3	71	10
	30–59	152	1	2	4	64	29	70	1	3	13	72	11	222	1	2	7	67	23
	60–89	130	2	0	8	47	43	:	.	.	.	.	.	130	2	0	8	47	43
	90–up	37	0	0	16	30	54	:	.	.	.	.	.	37	0	0	16	30	54
	Avg.	356	2	2	7	52	37	354	7	7	5	72	9	710	4	4	6	63	23

TABLE 8

Per Cent of Grid Style Choices for Element 4: *Temper* by MAQ Level, College/Non-College and Line/Staff in One Organization

	MAQ Level	College						Non-College						Averages for Line/Staff and Overall					
		N	1,1	1,9	9,1	5,5	9,9	N	1,1	1,9	9,1	5,5	9,9	N	1,1	1,9	9,1	5,5	9,9
Line	0–29	5	0	0	0	80	20	212	5	13	2	38	42	217	5	13	2	39	41
	30–59	27	0	0	11	48	41	40	3	5	7	37	48	67	1	3	9	42	45
	60–89	42	0	0	0	69	31	.	.	.	.	.	.	42	0	0	0	69	31
	90–up	20	0	0	0	60	40	.	.	.	.	.	.	20	0	0	0	60	40
	Avg.	94	0	0	3	62	35	252	5	12	3	38	42	346	3	9	3	44	41
Staff	0–29	32	0	6	6	41	47	72	0	7	6	47	40	104	0	7	6	45	42
	30–59	125	1	2	3	52	42	30	3	7	0	57	33	155	1	3	3	52	41
	60–89	88	1	1	2	34	62	.	.	.	.	.	.	88	1	2	2	34	61
	90–up	17	0	0	0	76	24	.	.	.	.	.	.	17	0	0	0	76	24
	Avg.	262	1	2	3	46	48	102	1	7	4	50	38	364	1	4	3	47	45
Averages for College/Non-College Over-all	0–29	37	0	5	5	47	43	284	4	12	3	40	41	321	3	11	3	41	42
	30–59	152	1	2	5	50	42	70	3	6	4	46	41	222	1	3	5	49	42
	60–89	130	1	1	2	45	51	.	.	.	.	.	.	130	1	2	2	45	50
	90–up	37	0	0	0	68	32	.	.	.	.	.	.	37	0	0	0	68	32
	Avg.	356	1	2	3	49	45	354	4	10	3	42	41	710	2	6	3	46	43

TABLE 9

Per Cent of Grid Style Choices for Element 5: *Humor* by MAQ Level, College/Non-College and Line/Staff in One Organization

	MAQ Level	College						Non-College						Averages for Line/Staff and Overall					
		N	1,1	1,9	9,1	5,5	9,9	N	1,1	1,9	9,1	5,5	9,9	N	1,1	1,9	9,1	5,5	9,9
Line	0–29	5	0	0	20	20	60	212	3	25	6	25	41	217	3	24	6	24	43
	30–59	27	4	7	11	22	56	40	33	8	5	27	57	67	3	7	7	25	58
	60–89	42	5	0	5	24	66	..	..	..	..	..	..	42	5	0	5	24	66
	90–up	20	0	0	20	25	55	..	..	..	..	..	..	20	0	0	20	25	55
	Avg.	94	3	2	11	23	61	252	3	23	6	25	43	346	3	17	7	24	49
Staff	·····	32	0	16	0	6	78	72	0	14	6	21	60	104	0	14	4	16	66
	30–59	125	0	10	6	14	70	30	0	13	3	23	60	155	0	10	5	15	70
	60–89	88	0	7	5	10	78	..	..	..	..	..	..	88	0	8	4	10	78
	90–up	17	0	0	12	41	47	..	..	..	..	..	..	17	0	0	12	41	47
	Avg.	262	0	9	6	13	72	102	0	13	5	21	61	364	0	10	5	15	70
Averages for College/Non-College and Over-all	0–29	37	0	14	3	8	75	284	2	22	6	24	46	321	2	21	5	22	50
	30–59	152	1	9	7	15	68	70	1	10	4	26	59	222	1	9	6	18	66
	60–89	130	1	5	5	15	74	..	..	..	..	..	..	130	2	5	5	15	73
	90–up	37	0	0	16	32	52	..	..	..	..	..	..	37	0	0	16	32	52
	Avg.	356	1	7	6	16	70	354	2	20	5	24	49	710	2	13	6	20	59

As far as the humor element is concerned, the decrease in frequency of selection for the 1,9 element with increases in MAQ is the most conspicuous result. No other trends that merit comment are to be observed.

Summary

The selection of Grid elements for conflict, convictions, and decisions bear out the findings reported earlier for paragraph selections. In each of these cases, the 9,9 element is selected with increased frequency for increases in MAQ. The same is true for the 9,1 element. The 5,5 element is selected with decreased frequency, as is the 1,9 element as MAQ increases.

With respect to temper and humor, only the 1,9 element in each case shifts uniformly with MAQ. The higher the MAQ the less frequently are the 1,9 elements for temper and humor used to typify the individual.

CONCLUSIONS

This chapter reports an investigation of the manner in which career development, as measured by the MAQ, is related to education and managerial styles.

Based upon a 40-hour period of interaction taking place in ten man teams, 716 members of one organization depicted how they saw each person responding to problem-solving situations. The method of assessment involved a technique of measurement of individual styles of approach which is based on the Managerial Grid.

Results demonstrate that career accomplishment is consistently related to managerial style.

The generalization which is supported in many different ways is that the greater an individual's career accomplishment, the more likely his style of approach is 9,9 and 9,1 and the less likely his approach is 5,5 or 1,9. The 1,1 style does not offer a way of distinguishing among levels of managerial accomplishment, except that it appears occasionally at the lowest MAQ level.[15]

These statements hold whether the individual's present

work assignment is in a line or staff organization and without regard for whether he holds a collegiate degree.

Appendix to Chapter 10

Criteria for Assessing Organization Level (L) in Determining MAQ: The Managerial Achievement Quotient (MAQ) depends, in part, on the attained organizational level (L) of the manager being assessed. The criteria below are intended to serve as guide lines for determining equivalent levels *across* organizational systems. One organization level may include two layers of supervisor-subordinate reporting relationships.

Level 1: Chairman of the Board, persons with supra-organization responsibilities.

Level 2: President and vice presidents to whom more than one major organization segment report.

Level 3: Vice presidents and department managers responsible for the operation of a single major function with multiple units.

Level 4: General manager responsible for a region or for a large operating unit, *i.e.*, a factory, a sales division, overall responsibility for an R&D facility, and those reporting directly to the general manager or regional executive. Typical supervisory titles included might be Regional Sales Manager, General Manager, Assistant General Manager, Products Manager, Coordination Manager, Administrative Manager, Technical Manager.

Level 5: Department and assistant department heads in headquarters locations (staff or line) and department and assistant heads in field locations (staff or line) generally fall into Level 5. Typical supervisory titles are Area Sales Manager, Operating Superintendent, M&C Superintendent, Technical Superintendent, Department Head-Technical, Service Laboratory Head, Division Engineer, Chief Accountant, Head of Business Services, Employee Relations Manager, Purchasing Agent, Department Head R&D. Typical professional titles are Engineering Associate, Research Associate, Assistant to Administrative Manager.

Level 6: Section and unit heads and other senior supervisory personnel reporting to department level in either headquarters or field. Typical supervisory titles include Head of Section, General Foreman, Assistant Chief Accountant, Section Head—Employee Relations, Section Head—Purchasing, Zone Supervisor-M&C, Section Head—Technical, Section Head-R&D, Senior Supervisor Engineer; typical professional titles include Senior Staff Engineer, Senior Research Specialist, Physician.

Level 7: Second line supervisors, those to whom more than one direct work supervisor reports and who, in turn, report to a section head or his equivalent in either headquarters or field installations. Typical supervisory titles include Foreman or Assistant Foreman-Operations, Section Head-Accounting, Head of Plant Services, Craft Foreman-M&C, Assistant Zone Supervisor-M&C, Foreman-M&C, Technical, R&D. Typical professional titles include Senior Professional, Senior Engineer, Assistant Cost Engineer, Coordination Specialist, Senior Research Chemist.

Level 8: Those responsible for the direct supervision of work. Typical supervisory titles include Group Head-Accounting, (Group) (Section) Supervisor, Area Supervisor-M&C, Supervisor-Technical. Typical professional titles include Engineer, Assistant Engineer, Senior P/R Assistant.

In applying the formula, determination of the level of an individual's position is by using the appropriate *category description*. (Actual job titles may shift from organization to organization.) The numbers representing the actual organization categories defined by these criteria are used even if one or more of the levels described here is absent. For example, if levels 6 and 4 are present but level 5 is absent, then in applying the formula, level 5 would be omitted, but 6 remains 6 and is *not* shifted to 5.

References

1. Tiffin, J. & McCormick, E. J. *Industrial Psychology*. (4th Ed.) Englewood Cliffs, N. J.: Prentice-Hall, 1958, 31.

2. Maier, N. R. F. *Psychology in Industry*. (2nd Ed.) Boston: Houghton Mifflin, 1955, 203-204.

3. McClelland, D., Atkinson, J. W., Clark, R. A. & Lowell, E. L. *The Achievement Motive*. New York: Appleton-Century-Crofts, 1953; Atkinson, J. W. (Ed.) *Motives in Fantasy, Action, and Society*. Princeton: D. van Nostrand, 1958.

4. Hardwick, C. T. & Landuyt, B. F. *Administrative Strategy*. New York: Simmons-Boardman, 1961, 337-341.

5. Hardwick, C. T. & Landuyt, B. F., *op. cit.*, 117.

6. McGehee, W. & Thayer, P. W. *Training in Business and Industry*. New York: Wiley, 1961, 5-7.

7. Bass, B. M. & White, O. L. Situational Tests: III. Observers' Rating of Leaderless Group Discussion Participants as Indicators of External Leadership Status. *Educational Psychological Measurement*, 11, 1951, 355-361; Bass, B. M. & Coates, C. H. Forecasting Officer Potential Using the Leaderless Group Discussion. *Journal of Abnormal & Social Psychology*, 47, 1952, 321-325; Blake, R. R., Mouton, J. S. & Fruchter, B. The Consistency of Interpersonal Behavior Judgments Made on the Basis of Short-Term Interaction in Three-Man Groups. *Journal of Abnormal & Social Psychology*, 49, 1954, 573-578; Hollander, E. P. The Reliability of Peer Nominations Under Various Conditions of Administration. *Journal of Applied Psychology*, 41, 1957, 85-90; Ghiselli, E. E. Managerial Talent. *American Psychologist*, 18, (10), 1963, 631-642.

8. Ghiselli, E. E., *op. cit.*

9. Hulin, C. L. The Measurement of Executive Success. *Journal of Applied Psychology*, 46, 1962, 303-306; Ghiselli, E. E., *op. cit.*

10. Factors undoubtedly intrude themselves to limit the validity of these axioms. Physical appearance, one's wife, etc., are examples of secondary factors that may be present to influence selections. Those who judge managerial competence, in fact, may not be using a fully valid basis for judgment, and so on.

11. Dr. Benjamin Rhodes, R&D, Humble Oil & Refining Company, Baytown, Texas, formulated the conceptual and structural aspects of this equation.

12. *The Managerial Grid: An Exploration of Key Managerial Orientations*. Austin, Tex: Scientific Methods, Inc., 1962.

13. Blake, R. R. & Mouton, J. S. *Validity Studies of the Managerial Grid: II. Managerial Achievement and Style in American Corporations*. To be published.

14. Blake, R. R. & Mouton, J. S. *op. cit.*, 1963.

15. Blake, R. R. & Mouton, J. S. "The Managerial Grid in Three Dimensions." *Training and Development Journal*, 21(1), January 1967.

CHAPTER ELEVEN

Analyzing Personal Managerial Styles

Before you started reading about the Managerial Grid, you were invited to evaluate your own managerial styles. Chapter 1 provided a brief description of each managerial style. The five paragraphs were to be ranked from 1, the most characteristic of your actions, to 5, the least like you. In addition, you were requested to select one phrase in each of the five elements of decisions, convictions, conflict, temper, and humor.

IDENTIFYING THE MANAGERIAL STYLES

The first paragraph (*a*) in Chapter 1 is the 1,1 paragraph. It is followed, in order, by (*b*)—1,9; (*c*)—5,5; (*d*)—9,1; and (*e*)—the 9,9 paragraph. The same order applies for each element. The first phrase under *Decisions* (a1) describes the 1,1 attitude. It is followed by (b1), 1,9; (c1), 5,5; (d1), 9,1; and (e1), the 9,9 phrase. The same order applies for each of the other elements.

RANKING THE GRID PARAGRAPHS

Now it is possible for you to return to Chapter 1 and to interpret your selection of managerial styles to depict your own behavior. That is, by which paragraph did you place a 1 to indicate how you viewed your dominant style? What paragraph did you select as 2 or your backup style, and so on?

This provides one basis for you to evaluate how you were thinking about managing before reading this book. In addition, it gives an opportunity for you to think through whether you wish to change your managerial behavior, and if so, in what direction.

Data presented in Chapter 10 lead to the conclusion that overall, the typical sequence in which managerial styles are ranked is 5,5; 9,9; 9,1; 1,9; and 1,1. Those managers who are judged by their supervisors as most promotable (the better managers), however, have the pattern of 9,9 as a dominant style, followed by either 5,5 or 9,1 about equally as often as a backup; and then followed by 1,9 and 1,1. The less successful the manager in getting promoted, the greater the likelihood his first theory is 5,5; followed by 9,9; and then 9,1; 1,9 and 1,1.

Other evidence, based partly on measurements and partly on detailed observation, suggests the best managers—those who get to the very top in terms of career progress—tend toward a pattern of 9,9; 9,1; 5,5; 1,9; and finally 1,1. In other words, 5,5 which seems to be the backup theory for those who achieve average success, is replaced by 9,1 as the backup for those who achieve the most success, with 5,5 appearing in third place. Available evidence does not lend support to the notion that 9,1 is the dominant theory for the most successful, even though it may be their strongest backup theory.

Now, how do your rankings compare? How did you order the paragraphs to picture yourself?

If your order was 9,9; 5,5; 9,1; 1,9; and 1,1, and you found no difficulty in choosing, then your responses fit those typical of managers who are generally successful. If 9.9 was your first theory but you had difficulty choosing between 9,1 and 5,5 as your backup, or if you placed 9,1 in the backup position and pushed 5,5 into third place, then your responses were more like the better managers. If you chose 5,5 as your first theory and it was followed by 9,9 or 9,1, then your reactions were more like those of managers who have not been promoted so rapidly. If your first theory was 1,9 or 1,1, your way of managing is quite different from the average manager and still more different from those who are best.

Three words of caution in interpreting your answers need to be mentioned. One is that you are comparing yourself with statistical trends only. A margin of error is always possible in such comparisons. The second caution is that you may have misjudged yourself. Having read this text, you may now see yourself differently. Only you can judge that.

A third caution is worthwhile to mention. It can be pointed out in the following way. If you asked those with whom you work and who know you well to rank the paragraphs for how they see you, would it be the same as you describe yourself?

The major difference is likely to be this. Persons who select the 9,9 paragraph as their dominant theory before studying the Grid are less often depicted in this manner by their associates. Their associates are more likely to use 5,5 as the first paragraph and to use 9,9 as the backup theory. The error of self judgment, then, turns out to be that people picture themselves as 9,9 with a 5,5 backup whereas their associates are more likely to see them as 5,5 with a 9,9 backup. If you selected 9,9 as your first theory, you will have to decide whether you described yourself accurately. Alternatively, you might ask those who know you well which way they see you.

Choosing Grid Elements

Next, the Grid elements you selected in Chapter 1 to picture your most characteristic approach to Decisions, Convictions, Conflict, Temper, and Humor, can be examined. The same basis of interpretation can be followed here as was done in connection with the paragraphs.

In the study presented in Chapter 10, you will recall that the managers who had been promoted the most rapidly were more likely to select the 9,9 element on Decisions, Convictions, and Conflict in comparison with those who were being promoted less rapidly. The slower the promotion rate, the greater the likelihood that 5,5 elements depict the person's managerial style. The Temper and Humor elements are subject to more variation. They do not shed too much light on helping you see how you manage.

Now then, do your elements fit together, *i.e.*, do they all come from the same Grid style or are they picked from different positions? Again you will have to judge the meaning of consistency or discrepancy. Then you can decide whether you want to change and how, if you do.

TYPICAL INDIVIDUAL VARIATIONS IN MANAGERIAL STYLE DESCRIPTIONS

Some additional assistance can be given to help you see how much consistency is typical of people when tailor-made descriptions of managerial behavior have been formulated.

A number of these word pictures of people are presented below. As you study them, you can see the way people shift the element statements around to picture one another more precisely.

"His conclusions are based upon philosophical and creative reasoning. His decisions are oriented toward perfection, and he finds it difficult to convince the group the quality he is seeking is justified. If he finds it necessary to compromise, it is foreign to his basic make-up, creating an emotional disturbance which he attempts to relieve through injecting humor."

"He continually tests new ideas but backs off under group pressure. He places high value on human relations and works actively to maintain harmonious group atmosphere by his friendly tongue-in-check humor and even temper. He has an earnest desire to learn, as evidenced by being a good listener, and frequently rephrases the group's position for clarification."

"He drives aggressively towards making decisions, using the contributions of others if possible, but not if delay is involved in obtaining them. His standards are high, and although he recognizes the high value of decisions based on understandings and agreement, he will rely on confidence in his own judgment under pressure. He is deliberate, precise, determined, and self-confident. In the face of conflict, he will try to win his own position immediately unless the opposing point of view has strong merit. His temper and impatience are well controlled. His humor fits the situation and he retains it under pressure."

"He places high value on reaching agreement towards sound decisions. He looks for and seeks out opinions from others to thoroughly explore a point. He responds to sound ideas by changing his mind. His manner creates an open and stabilizing effect on the group and he displays an evenness of temper. His humor is used to give perspective. He is aggressive and if continually opposed, will hold out for his ideas at the expense of good feelings."

"He is a very methodical person who works by himself as much as possible. He makes 'alone' decisions only when it is a must. He never expresses his opinions, but remains silent when in the midst of conflict. When he becomes disturbed, he 'flights' from the situation in order to avoid losing his temper. He is completely humorless."

"He seeks sound, creative decisions that will give understanding and agreement. He seeks out ideas, opinions, and attitudes of others which may be used to support his own views and opinions. He does not yield easily in conflict but seeks to identify ideas and opinions of others. Being emotionally sound, his temper is well controlled even under provocation. Humor is well balanced and characterizes a pleasant personality."

"He has strong convictions that actively prevail in decision making. He actively seeks out the ideas of others and when convinced, is likely to respond to them. When conflict arises, he tries to resolve differences but failing to obtain quick resolution, moves forcefully toward the objective. Generally, his temper is under good control, but he becomes impatient when progress toward the goal lags. His humor is genuine and fits the situation."

"He is very active in promoting and seeking out ideas from others that result in agreement, understanding, and sound decisions. He does not avoid conflict even if it results in stepping on toes, but tries to resolve conflict when it does occur. He tends at times to fall back on precedent and established procedures. His temper is well controlled but he evidences impatience at times. He retains a sense of humor even under stress."

"He works very hard to keep everything harmonious. Even though he expresses his opinions, he does it in a way to avoid being 'pushy.' He is the first to soothe feelings when conflict arises, by injecting humor which shifts the controversy. He never allows himself to lose his temper, but expresses a philosophy of 'turning the other cheek.' "

"One of his characteristics is empathy. He listens for ideas, opinions, and attitudes different from his own. He has clear convictions based on competence and confidence, but these may be modified by views of others. He is fair and firm in identifying reasons and in arriving at an equitable solution. He has a good sense of humor. Tolerance and patience are characteristic of his personality."

"He has a basic 9,1 orientation with respect to decision making, but in an effort to establish and maintain good relations, he tends to give a little ground in order to arrive at a workable solution. He places high value on creative decisions but does not always aggressively pursue acceptance of his own. He has strong opinions but will move to middle ground under majority pressure. He does not avoid conflict but tries to get an equitable solution through a fair but firm approach. He keeps his temper under control in the interest of friendly relations and a productive atmosphere. His humor fits the situation and gives perspective."

"He seeks ideal solutions and compromises only for group action. He is intellectually honest and has perfectionist tendencies. He will delay group action to speak further on his ideas, opinions, and attitudes. He attempts to identify reasons for conflict and probes for underlying reasons. He becomes impatient eventually, but strives for unemotional consideration and deliberations. He takes himself quite seriously and does not use humor in discussion and meeting situations. He is inclined to a theoretical approach and has limits beyond which further discussion accomplishes little."

"He usually accepts opinions and attitudes of others, especially if he feels that to express his own opinion might create conflict. If conflict does arise, however, he tries to remain neutral. Even though a situation tends to disturb him, he pouts or withdraws instead of openly losing his temper. He is either humorless or aims at maintaining friendly relations."

"He demonstrates impatience or curtness as a chairman in his determination to get the job done, yet when functioning as a group member, he is less driving, more passive. He is either black or white in his convictions. When the group has difficulty in solving conflicts, he uses a statistical approach to solve problems, although it is not necessarily best for the group. He is interested in the initial contribution of a group participant but is not inclined to probe for more."

"He frequently is ineffective in getting sound decisions. This results in frequent compromise. If others wait, he starts to seek out ideas and opinions. There is a slowness between will and execution. When he has time to firm up ideas, he is firm in his convictions. When pressed, he has a tendency to compromise his position to keep the meeting effective and congenial. When faced with conflict, he enters into it only when he has a firm contribution to make—he does not like conflict, but does not avoid it. He rarely loses temper but tends to be impatient when things are not moving—he might lose his temper when provoked. He has a natural sense of humor but does not use it often enough."

"He has high regard for maintaining good relations, and to avoid conflict, he tends to take the easy way out. He places high value on making an individual decision as opposed to group determination. He foregoes convictions to avoid conflict. He prefers to accept others' ideas, but will deal in compromise; he tends to remain neutral, but as a practical matter tries to maintain good relations. He rarely loses his temper but might when situational pressures demand. When faced with conflict, he becomes impatient with a tendency to contain temper inside. His humor aims at selling himself or his position with a secondary aim of maintaining friendly relations."

"He participates in discussions in a procedural way by asking others for their opinions and summarizing their viewpoints. When pinned to the wall for an opinion, he always balances a positive statement with a negative one. Where tension arises he suggests ways in which action can be tabled until things 'cool off.' He does not appear to respond to pressure but always remains calm and optimistic."

"He places high value on getting sound decisions that are understood and agreed upon. He knows he can make good decisions, and is occasionally too aggressive and too quick to allow the group to develop to its full potential. He is very dedicated to his convictions, but willing to change when presented with sound ideas. He occasionally can tend to go too fast, anticipating others' viewpoints and tending to suppress them in this manner. When faced with conflict, he tries to identify reasons for it and to resolve it. He uses conflict to gain understanding; can be stimulated by conflict, causing occasional trend towards suppressive tendencies. He rarely loses his temper, even when stirred up, but tends to be impatient when things are not moving. His humor tends to be hard hitting—could be used more often to good advantage."

"He enjoys competition inherent in decision making, taking a determined stand toward making decisions which stick. He strongly defends convictions and manipulates the group to prove a point, but operates in a searching, probing manner to arrive at a sound decision. He enjoys conflict which he can stimulate and manipulate; his baiting approach is generally used to control unproductive conflict, but frequently acts to the detriment of discussion progress. Occasionally he is impatient to the point of detracting from listening ability. However, his obvious impatience sometimes brings the group back to the central idea. He uses a generally hard hitting humor to sell himself."

"He prides himself on being known as the 'peacemaker,' and strives to create a jovial atmosphere in the work situation at all times. Before making a decision, he gets the opinions of all his group. If conflict arises, he is immediately on top of things, soothing feelings—his motto—a 'joke for every occasion.' He never loses his temper, but has a way of shifting the topic of conversation when he is confronted with a controversial issue."

"Relative to decisions, he operates as a statistical 5, 5—willingly resorting to concern for people, high concern for production, etc., to accomplish the team purpose—when he feels the situation is appropriate, he will use a 9,9 approach—convictions are carefully derived and stoutly defended. He uses a questioning approach to seek out opinions. When confronted with conflict, he appropriately questions to determine causes, and tries to capitalize on the conflict when it is defined. He rarely loses his temper, but tends to be impatient when things lag. He retains his humor under pressure.

You may now want to stop reading and, using the elements listed in Chapter 1, write a single paragraph that really fits you. This you can compare with those just given and draw your own conclusions as to whether or not changes in any of the picture would enable you to become a more effective manager.

CHAPTER TWELVE

A 9,9 Approach to Organization Development

Improvements in individual managerial competence are almost inevitable when men understand more fully how to utilize themselves in getting work done with and through others. Yet, only so much organization improvement is possible through individual management development. To attain the fullest possible organization achievement requires educational steps beyond individual or team study—that is, organization development.

PURPOSES OF ORGANIZATION DEVELOPMENT

Several purposes of organization development should be mentioned.[1] Included are to eliminate:

1. Common sense-based management assumptions and to replace them with systematic management concepts that increase individual involvement, commitment, and creativity towards sound problem-solving and production.

2. Unproductive thought patterns within each individual and to replace them with mental attitudes that result in a better identification of problems and novel solutions.

3. Interpersonal and intergroup blockages which prevent effective discussions and to replace them with interpersonal openness and candid communication that can

255

sustain sound deliberation and insure effective problem-solving between individuals and groups.

4. Organization traditions, precedents, and past practices which stifle productive effort and creative thinking and to replace them with standards and values which promote efforts of excellence and innovation.

5. Unresolved problems preventing attainment of organization competence by (a) defining what they are, (b) designing solutions to them, and (c) insuring their elimination by executing the plan(s).

ORGANIZATION DEVELOPMENT THROUGH THE USE OF EDUCATIONAL STRATEGIES

The idea of applying educational methods under 9,9 concepts to bring an entire organization to a higher level of development and functioning is a new one.[2] It should not be confused with more conventional approaches[3] which include changing organization structure, leadership replacement, tightening controls to catch poor performers, or simply pressuring for more output.[4]

The general strategy of organization development is simple, though its execution is quite complex. In a broad way, the approach is one in which the entire organization studies itself and the workings of its various parts. Diagnosis of all the major organization problem areas such as long-range planning, profit, union-management relations, promotional policy and incentive awards, new product development, absenteeism, utilities conservation, safety, and a seemingly endless variety of other matters as well, is also a part of organization development.[5] Concrete arrangements for executing agreed upon changes are implemented under a carefully designed execution and auditing program. Organization development is self-administered by the organization membership, except for broad consultation regarding major issues of strategy and tactics.

The broad-based educational strategy to be described here has been tested through a series of experiments in management education. In addition, specialized problems of organization development such as spinoffs,[6] mergers,[7] and integration of headquarters and field installations,[8] have been experimented with in the same manner. Each application of the basic strategy has improved it. Thus the model presented here is a well tested one. Near term changes are likely to be ones of degree rather than of the basic approach.

THEORY OF ORGANIZATION DEVELOPMENT

One way to penetrate the theory surrounding organization development is through answering a number of questions.[9] Answers to these questions provide a broad framework for viewing any specific development activity.[10] Concrete answers, tailored to fit an existing situation, sketch the outlines for any particular organization development effort.

Identifying the Problem(s)

Organization development is based on the notion that some present circumstances are less than fully acceptable. The troubles, so to speak, are ones that people have potential control over. Thus, by utilizing an effective approach, they are subject to correction. Another way of saying it is that the authority, energy and ability needed to solve problems are available within the organization's membership, but are not being fully applied. The development aspect also implies that it would be desirable to correct, replace, shift, remove or to improve some existing features.[11]

Diagnosing the problems as problems is a first step. Before dealing with a disturbance in an intelligent manner, it must be recognized in systematic terms. This is in contrast with a common sense description or intuitive account of what is wrong. A significant issue underlying planned development efforts then is, "When described from a systematic point of view, what existing conditions is a development effort intended to correct?"

Identifying the Unit of Development

A second and related question is, "What unit of behavior needs changing?" Is an individual the target of
development; is it a given group's performance, or is it
the organization as a whole?[12] The answer is linked closely
with the systematic framework used in diagnosing the
problem. But, here, too, the issue itself appears deceptively
simple. For example, it is convenient to see a group as
a number of separate individuals with a culture of attitudes and codes of conduct that no single member would
deviate from or relinquish on a one-by-one basis.[13] The
same may be said for an organization which may be
seen as many separate individuals or groups with no interplay in terms of interpersonal, group, or intergroup influences. Yet, as is now well known, the concept of organization as an aggregate of individuals is far too simple.[14]
Yet, in spite of this, the generalization that the unit of
change must be accurately identified is violated in efforts
of many managers to bring about organization improvement. Differences between a common sense evaluation
and a systematic view of the same problem or of the appropriate unit for change can be critical to the success of an
effort for planned development.[15]

Establishing the Goals and Directions of Development

Another consideration in designing organization development involves identifying the direction of the change.
It is not enough merely to diagnose the problem and define the unit of change. Frequently it is necessary first to
identify a number of alternatives and then select from
among them the ones to pursue. Therefore, a third issue
is, "What goals does a given organization development effort want to achieve?" When this can be fully answered,
then the major concepts of the planned development have
been outlined. These should be classified as:

1. What things within the organization should be
   changed?
2. Which undesirable present conditions should the organization move away from?

3. Which desirable aims should the organization move toward?

These three questions identify the basic issues of organization development. These will be dealt with later in this chapter.

Systematic vs. Common Sense Formulation of the Problem of Organization Development

Recognition that something is less than fully acceptable is the first step to organization development. Those who have such a problem may not recognize it as symptomatic of organization malfunctioning at a more basic level. Such naive acceptance as contrasted to the actual problem when it is diagnosed in systematic terms, may be one of the strongest barriers to organization development. Common sense descriptions frequently are grossly different from the true, *i.e.*, systematic, problem diagnosis.

At the present level of its development, the Managerial Grid (and more broadly the behavioral sciences) constitutes a framework of ideas for understanding concrete behavior situations in much the same manner (though not to the same degree) that the physical and biological sciences undergird diagnosis of physical conditions.[16] Thus, to build a sound planned development program it is necessary to utilize a systematic framework as the basis for change.

What Is the Behavioral Unit of Planned Development?

Given the necessity of applying a systematic framework for diagnosis, the next choice point has been reached. The question is, "What is the behavioral unit of development?" There are several possibilities.[17]

The Individual-in-Isolation. Much common sense precedent identifies the individual, *i.e.*, "inside the skin," as the fundamental behavioral unit of change.[18] In addition, examination of the current status of psychiatry, clinical psychology, formal education and management development leads to the conclusion that present practices emphasize the individual-in-isolation, and more or less totally disregard the individual's environment as a relevant consideration.[19] This definition places the variables responsible for an individual's present actions within him, and potentially or actually subject to his autonomous control.

With the definition of the individual-in-isolation as the unit of change, it is seen as possible, with educational or professional aid, for the individual to improve through his own initiative. In many applications, however, such an overgeneralized common sense concept has resulted in needless and wasteful effort. Convenient though it may be and accessible though he is, the individual-in-isolation is, rarely, a valid definition of a change unit because too many critical influences outside his control determine his behavior. Needed, in other words, is a more overall concept of the total situation.

The Whole Situation. An alternative to the too quick acceptance of the individual-in-isolation definition is the Lewinian treatment.[20] Lewin's formula was $B = F(P,E)$, indicating that Behavior (B) is a function of the interdependence between a Person (P) *and* his Environment (E). *Behavior, in other words, is a function of the total situation.* Accordingly, a condition for organization development involves the situation as a whole, that is, the *culture* of the organization, with all that the word *culture* implies. Anything less is likely to be ineffective or piecemeal, or may even stimulate active resistance. Thus, a first answer for the question, "What is the unit of development?" then, is *the whole situation.*

It follows from Lewin's formula that the unit of change is rarely restricted to a given individual.[21] A worker, for example, may be thought of as a behavioral unit-in-isolation. Efforts to change the individual which disregard his connections to the situation including attitudes of others toward him, the reward system, the quality of supervision being administered, etc., are likely to be less effective than if these interrelated factors are regarded.[22]

In a similar manner, efforts of a group of individuals to change-in-concert are equally likely to meet environmental counterpressures to maintaining accustomed ways of behavior and conduct if change is contrary to the group environment. Experience to date suggests that most groups, particularly work groups in organizations, are too intimately linked into an organization network to be considered in isolation.[23] Groups, then, frequently are too narrow in definition to constitute effective units of change.[24]

The Organization as a Unit of Development. What, then, is left? Starting from the same conceptual framework, a realistic behavioral unit of development is found in the organization. The behavioral unit *becomes the organization membership* including all the significant variables such as policies, rules, regulations, reward and punishment systems, production controls, informal social systems, etc. The organization, then, is the environment within which individuals and groups perform and interrelate toward accomplishing organizational aims.[25] In this sense, the organization is the critical behavioral unit of development.

The answer for one of the questions, "Development of what behavioral unit?" is, then, "Planned change of the *whole* organization, (whether the definition is the entire company or where relevant, a decentralized unit such as a division or a plant)."

Change from What to What?

The next two questions are, "Change from what?" and "Development to accomplish what purpose, what aim?" In any actual situation, these two questions may appear distinct and separate. From the standpoint of planned development, however, they must be considered together. When answered, they define the framework for organization development.

The variables that define an existing situation or any desired one are, for the most part, the same. Differences between what exists and what is desired are matters of degree or relative weighing of interaction among these factors. Therefore, the first issue is, "What variables affect the total situation when the unit of development is an organization as a whole?"

Variables in Industrial Organizations. The purpose of industrial organizations is to make an acceptable profit by manufacturing a needed product or providing a desired service. Only with an adequate profit is continuity insured. Output or production, then, is one variable.

Production often is not the result of individuals working one-by-one, in isolation, with output attributable to factors "within the skin" of each employee. Rather, if an organization is of any size, its output is accomplished through the coordinated efforts of many individuals.[26] The various individual contributions are interdependent and are organized so as to build one upon another, often in a quite complex manner. The relationship between those engaged in production (people) viewed against the organization as a whole constitutes another significant variable in any industrial organization.

For analytical purposes, these two variables—production and people—can be treated as though they were independent of one another. In any concrete situation, however, they are truly interdependent. That is, production conditions influence people relationships and, in turn, these relationships facilitate or hinder productive effort. These are, then, two important and interdependent variables of industrial organization.

The next points have to do with the psychological aspects of production and people and the interdependence of one with the other.

Psychological Aspects of Production. Production, of course, does not happen in a haphazard manner. Rather, it requires intelligent mental effort of responsible persons. It is in the planning and execution of production where human capacity for mental effort finds expression.

What are the relevant characteristics of mental effort that are associated with production? From the person's point of view, it is the nature of mental effort to search for and to create conditions that are meaningful and purposeful.[27] Thinking cannot be based on a sheer randomness, nor can it be adequately understood if regarded as a mechanical process of trial and error. If entire situations of production, not just the parts concerned with the mechanics of work, disregard or violate this human mental effort, then production problems are likely to appear. The task, or the work itself, must provide organization members the challenge to think toward psychologically purposeful goals.[28] If it does not, then thinking is likely to take directions which detract from production. Thinking, in other words, moves in an anti-organizational direction, and even works actively against it. Organization members then ask, "How can we strike back at the company?" rather than, "How can we contribute more fully to its success?"

If the work activity fails to meet or even violates needs for meaningfulness, it can generate feelings of boredom, apathy, fatigue, dissatisfaction, resentment, and active resistance.[29] On the other hand, if the total situation of production involves a purpose to which members are committed, then their reactions are likely to be ones of satisfaction, interest, excitement, challenge, gratification, and so on. Among the more meaningful and gratifying efforts are those which promote deliberate effort to solve underlying organization problems which have been disturbing or irritating for years.

One goal of organization development, then, is to increase the degree of meaningfulness in production. In this respect, the question, "Away from what condition?" might be answered as, "Away from situations which are repetitious, mechanical, arbitrary, or senseless and toward ones which are meaningful, purposeful, problem-solving and goal-oriented."

People. The other variable in an organization's culture involves relations among those engaged in production. Again, from the psychological point of view, feelings of acceptance and rejection are a product of human interaction. Under circumstances of production, they can range from full acceptance (positive feelings toward people) to complete rejection (negative, hostile, or antagonistic feelings toward others). Rejection tends to provoke distrust, tension, a sense of uneasiness and withdrawal.[30] Acceptance, on the other hand, is associated with trust, mutual support, involvement and a sense of personal worth. Thus, the direction of the change effort is, "Change *away from* interactions that arouse distrust and disrespect and *toward* interpersonal relations which are based on problem-solving that promotes mutual trust, support and feelings of personal worth."

The Interaction of Production and People. While productive effort may occur in social isolation, that is, independently of other people, and while relations among people may occur in purely social terms without any connection to production, these pure conditions—pure production and pure relationships—certainly are exceptions rather than the rule. The logical conclusion, therefore, is that a theory of organization development must take into consideration the interaction of these variables.

Production which involves mental effort based on mutual support and trust is seen as representing the best interaction between these two factors. An observer might describe such a situation with phrases like, "People are talking through decisions about next steps," or "They are trying to break the production run record." Then, goals embraced by organization members are the same as the goals of the organization itself. Then, people are not applying effort to defeat the organization; they are striving for its success; they are working with it; an integration between production and relationships among people has been achieved. Members are described as participating, involved, and committed—it is a 9,9 situation.

The operation of an industrial organization, then, is an expression of how the variables of production and human relationships interact in actual practice. Each of the points of interaction of these two variables described earlier in Chapters 2 through 9 can be called a theory. Thus, it will be possible to provide an answer to the question, "Change away from what?" by describing any given organization in terms of how these variables interact. The goal, "Change to what?" will also be indicated by specifying the desired interaction between production and human relationships. Where organization members have studied the Managerial Grid, and where there has been an organization development project, the broadest goal has been that of becoming a 9,9 organization.

Using these two descriptions as a basis, it becomes possible to design action strategies for achieving organization development.

A Six-Phase Approach to Organization Development

The six-phase approach to organization development[31] considers within a single long term effort, the achievement of production through mature interpersonal relationships which are integrated with the purposes of the organization. While the six phases are not applied in a step-by-step sequence, but rather are intertwined, the sequence is in the *direction* described.

We will discuss each of these phases in complete detail, but here is how the six-phase approach breaks down.

Part I. Management development within an organization.
> Phase 1. Managerial Grid Seminar training.
> Phase 2. Teamwork development.

Part II. Organization development.
> Phase 3. Horizontal and vertical intergroup linking.
> Phase 4. Setting organizational improvement goals.
> Phase 5. Implementing planned change by attaining established goals.
> Phase 6. Stabilization.

As mentioned in the chapter introduction, the entire organization development effort is self-administered by the membership itself, except for broad consultation on major issues of organization development strategy and tactics. The self-administering aspect is a key element. Rather than handing itself over to an outside specialist who gives consultation and guidance,[32] the line organization retains full responsibility for planning, designing and executing the effort. In this way, many sources of resistance are not encountered. Rather, because the organization membership has a stake in the outcome of its own efforts, heightened improvement motivation is achieved.

The feasibility of line management undertaking responsibility for such development efforts is based upon two considerations. The first is that key members of the line organization, through public seminars currently available, learn the concepts and strategies involved as well as how to develop skills in implementing them.[33] In turn, they take responsibility for teaching the members with line assignments. The second consideration is that training designs and learning instruments, which are utilized within the Managerial Grid Seminar of Phase 1, are administered, evaluated, and interpreted by participants themselves.[34]

Expert consultation is limited to testing the appropriateness of approaches and broad strategies and to the technical features of designs and learning instruments developed to meet specific local circumstances of the kind that reoccur in Phases 3, 4, and 5.

In an organization of a substantial size, say as many as 2,000 or more, these phases may require from 3 to 5 years or even longer to complete. The length depends on the intensity of the effort, the seriousness of the problems confronting the organization, and the amount of development sought.

PART I: MANAGEMENT DEVELOPMENT WITHIN THE ORGANIZATION

Phases 1 and 2 are concerned with aiding individuals and teams to increase their performance capability within the existing framework. The primary goal of these two phases is management development, not of increasing organization competence except as individual performance contributes to that end.

Phase 1: Managerial Grid Seminar Training

Organization development begins with learning sessions built on focusing attention of organization members on the interdependence between production and people.

Theoretical Considerations. Phase 1 is designed around two theoretical considerations. The first is that intelligent managerial choice of the best manner of achieving production through people is possible where managers understand and employ a systematic framework for diagnosing organization, team, interpersonal, intergroup and individual problems, and, at each level as appropriate, choosing actions from among several alternatives. The second consideration is based on Lewin's theoretical position that behavior is a function of the total situation.[35] Since the total situation is the organization, common understanding of theories of management across the entire organization membership aids communication, control and decision making.[36] Thus, the aim is for managers to study and to understand the Managerial Grid in a concrete and personal way so that they can replace intuitive assumptions and habits with sound thinking for getting work done in a manner that generates mutual confidence and respect.

Activities. All members of the managerial organization, from 8 to 48 per session, participate in an intensive 50-hour Seminar session conducted by line management.[37] Core activities include studying the Managerial Grid, participating in structured experiments dealing with how interpersonal relations affect task accomplishment. They also engage in face-to-face feedback regarding each member's managerial styles. Continuing attention also is placed on factors affecting team effectiveness.[38]

Participation in any one Seminar is on a "diagonal slice" basis, so that as many levels as possible within the organization are represented, but no person participates at the same time as his boss or his work group peers. In this way a range of personal managerial assumptions, interdepartmental issues and problems of the hierarchical organization as a whole are represented in the experiences of those studying together.[39] This is the first step for becoming better acquainted with the organization as a whole and with the problems that confront others on a daily basis. In addition, the learning of Managerial Grid concepts is enhanced because many of the ordinary strictures that surround openness under conditions of formal hierarchy are reduced or eliminated. Thus, a beginning is made toward developing new standards of openness and candid communication. Such standards reinforce the readiness of people to talk more openly with their bosses and immediate work group members in Phase 2.

Phase 2: Teamwork Development

After Phase 1, organization members appear to develop greater awareness of barriers *to* and possibilities *for* improving production-people interactions. However, general principles and concepts and direct personal learning of the kind emphasized in Phase 1 are unlikely to find concrete application in daily work without additional development phases explicitly designed to facilitate such application.

The second phase involves using the background knowledge from the Seminar sessions on a tailor-made basis for aiding members to apply it directly in their work group operations. The rationale for doing so includes the following considerations.

Theoretical Considerations. The fundamental building block of an organization is the team composed of individuals who work together to discharge that part of the work of the total organization for which they carry individual as well as overriding responsibilities.[40] Such teams are typified by the basic properties of all groups, including hierarchy, norms that depict traditions, precedents, and established practices, cohesion and purpose. In addition, groups have relations with other groups beyond themselves but within the organization environment. The main purpose of Phase 2 is to achieve concerted effort where individual responsibilities are effectively discharged and where sound coordination with efforts of other members can be accomplished.

The teams under study may or may not be family groups as defined by organization structure. They usually are not when the family group is composed of individuals who are assembled as an entity for housekeeping and bookkeeping purposes only.

Activities. A sound way to accomplish team development is to start with the top team consisting of the most senior manager and his immediate subordinates. The development activity begins with members exploring their individual managerial styles; a step which frequently serves to identify and relieve interpersonal blockages. In addition, members examine their operating practices as a work team. When indicated, they next set goals for improving their own interpersonal relationships and for eliminating team difficulties which are reducing the quality or quantity of their problem-solving and production efforts. Through these steps of team development, members can evaluate actual difficulties existing among themselves which appear on the surface as problems of communication, control and decision making. The significant point here is that the content of team development is concerned with the problems of hierarchy,[41] interpersonal conflict, traditions and norms, cohesion and goals considered from an intrateam point of view.

Emphasis here is placed on study by the top team of its own problems of operation first and of lower level teams later. When team development is initiated at the top and continued downward through the organization, vertical linking, which can improve control, communication, and decision making between levels also is facilitated. The critical role of the vertical linkpin has been cited frequently.[42] Since a subordinate in the top group is the supervisor of the next level down, one by-product is likely to be improved integration between hierarchical levels in the organization.

In summary, the second phase involves the individuals, segregated into the various working teams of the organization, coming to terms with themselves and their work problems as a group of people with common work goals. The following are examples of the character of changes likely to occur in connection with Phases 1 and 2 of an organization development activity:[43]

1. Heightened self-reappraisal of personal characteristics in one's own performance.

2. Changes in one's own managerial effectiveness, including (a) improved listening, (b) greater readiness to face conflict, (c) reduction of interpersonal frictions and blockages, and (d) increased rejection of compromise as the basis for decision making.

3. Improved relationships between region and division, within levels, and between bosses and subordinates.

4. Awareness of and some control over outworn traditions, precedents, and past practices.

5. A better comprehension of where the problems of management are and a greater variety of alternatives for developing solutions to these problems.

But individual and team development are only the first two phases which in themselves are limited to examining problems, not of the organization as a whole, but only from a working team point of view. Additional significant phases need to be taken if conditions under which total organizational effort is to be integrated toward a higher level of proficiency and sense of individual contribution are to be achieved.

Part II: ORGANIZATION DEVELOPMENT

Contribution to organization development of Part I, Phases 1 and 2 is primarily in terms of increased individual competence in and commitment to problem solving and interpersonal skills of supervision. Problems posed and subject to resolution in Phases 3, 4, and 5 are in the realm of operations effectiveness. These are the kinds of problems that are subject to resolution only through the committed and concerted efforts of several, many, or all.

Phase 3: Horizontal and Vertical Intergroup Linking

Many production problems of communication, control and decision making extend beyond primary work team boundaries in both horizontal and vertical directions.[44] Another way of saying it is that coordination is as indispensable between working teams which must mesh efforts as it is between individuals if a job is to be effectively carried out. Yet, except for solving intergroup problems through formal hierarchy, the standard table of organization makes no explicit arrangements for problem solving between groups.[45]

Theoretical Considerations. Behavioral science studies of intergroup relations demonstrate that groups in parallel are prone to drawing of invidious distinctions which in turn often lead to win-lose competitiveness between groups.[46] Under these circumstances group representatives frequently interact from a win-lose point of view. These circumstances can result in a representative being so loyal to his group's position that the desire to win can overwhelm the logical requirements of intergroup problem solving. These phenomena, in turn, can lead to withholding needed information, reducing intergroup contacts with mutual recrimination, attack and counterattack. These phenomena have been observed repeatedly between organization subunits such as sales and manufacturing; headquarters and field locations or plants; union and management; manufacturing and R&D; purchasing and technical; employee relations and the mechanical services division, etc.

Activities. Activities in Phase 3 are specifically designed to achieve better intergroup problem solving through a closer integration between those units of organization that have working interrelationships. The units of organization may have hierarchical relations such that one group is responsible to another or they may be horizontal in that each has an equal degree of formal authority relative to the other, as is often the case in union-management relations, etc.

The initial focus during Phase 3 activities is on studying and planning for change in the existing relations between any two groups that have working relationships. The reason is that operational problems lend themselves to more ready solution once difficulties of a relational character have been identified and talked through to resolution.

A procedure involves each team, usually two at a time but working independently of the other, developing an image of itself and of the other group.[47] The character of the relationships between them also is described in sufficient detail to insure understanding. Performance problems between groups are identified and reasons for them are evaluated.

In the second step, each group represents its own image and its image of the other, usually through representatives, but with all members of both groups present. Then, through interaction and discussion between the two groups, areas of misunderstandings, tensions, conflict and so on can be brought into the open and talked through. Once negative feelings have been relieved, the way is then open for discussion, debate and resolution of concrete operational problems. The strategies involved in the removal of intergroup blockages are quite complex and have been outlined in substantial detail elsewhere.[48]

Another variety of horizontal linking involves relationship-building within a total level of hierarchy, such as foremen. Under these conditions, personnel are at the same level but have membership in different work teams. Yet they have similar problems of supervision and responsibility. As a level of supervision, they constitute a reference group in the sociological meaning of the phrase, yet in terms of job responsibility they may not constitute a membership group. As intergroup team members, they often are placed in situations of invidious intergroup comparison, which can make for difficulties in the cooperation of effort. As reference group members, they shoulder common responsibilities which place a premium on mutual understanding and support.

Because such a horizontal reference group may involve people from different work groups, different departments, and even different regions, it is likely that they have no explicit procedure for solving common difficulties encountered in their work. The goal of horizontal linking is to create a stronger normative culture which will link personnel at the same level together as an effective unit. When this is done, many problems of work supervision which are *not* subject to change or correction through edict or command decision can be solved by people who are at the same hierarchical level, but who have many different bosses.

The development procedure first works through feelings and attitudes and then deals with operational issues. Here it is necessary to work through representatives from each family work team. One procedure is for the representatives to meet and to talk through problems of mutual concern on a face-to-face basis. Representatives then return to their own work teams and report face-to-face discussions, again on a "talk-through" basis which can lead to understanding and agreement. Thereafter, representatives review discussions that took place in their groups with other representatives, who in turn talk through other problems and so on. Such a cycle may occur many times in the problem-solving activities of a horizontal reference group.

Phase 4: Developing a Long Range Organization Blueprint

At the beginning of Phase 4, organization members are investing much energy in solving problems of the organization as a result of the activities of the earlier phases. Many steps taken increase organization effectiveness by correcting deficiencies in ways of operating. Though Phases 1 to 3 provide excellent moves toward "bottleneck removal," they are based on an assumption that the way the organization is constituted is the sound way to run a business, that if the organization is made to work more efficiently, total effectiveness will be achieved.

Theoretical Considerations. Developing a long range organization blueprint as a Phase 4 activity starts with the fundamentals. Its overall aim is to insure that the basic strategies of the organization are "right," that they provide a durable foundation for a sound and profitable organization that can endure for many years under the most severe requirements. The immediate objective of Phase 4 is to set up a model for an obtainable organization system for the future. The basic model may resemble the existing system in varying degrees, or it may differ radically from it. In either event, it is not viewed as fixed and unchanging but is subject to modification or redefinition as changes occur. Major unforeseen influences are likely to come from the external environment. As development takes place, condi-

tions within the organization may also allow for a reformulation of objectives. Future events may provide
opportunities for critique and reformulation. Therefore,
provision must be made for modification as circumstances
and situations require. The top team is the key unit for
accomplishing this objective. Their task is to provide the
organization with a plan of growth and development for
the future.

Activities. The development of a future organization
blueprint involves five steps, (1) testing the concepts on
which the organization is based through a searching examination of existing policies, (2) developing convictions about
ideal management practices by testing existing ones against
it, (3) creating a future organization blueprint, (4) developing the organization through understanding the organization blueprint, and (5) setting practical attainable
objectives within a time framework. This latter activity
is participated in by all members of management. In this
way, the total organization can set a new direction or shift
an old one, rather than one part of the organization's at-
tempting to pull or coerce other parts to move.[51]

Through the use of the blueprint, goals at each level are
linked. Individual and team development, as well as organizational development, take place in an integrated manner.
In fact, they are often mutually reinforcing.

The major contribution of Phase 4 is in terms of making a start on the fifth purpose: defining unresolved problems preventing attainment of organization competence
and designing solutions to them. Some steps of progress
toward their elimination also occur in the fourth phase,
but concentrated effort on the problem-solving plane
takes place in Phase 5.

Phase 5: *Implementing Planned Change by Attaining
Established Goals*

Depending upon organization size, the severity, magnitude and number of problems, and amount of effort applied in the induction of planned change, the phases in-

volving Managerial Grid Seminars (Phase 1); teamwork development (Phase 2); vertical and horizontal intergroup linking (Phase 3); and the setting of organizational goals (Phase 4) may require two years or longer to complete. Implementing the changes initiated by Phase 1, given increased significance in Phases 2 and 3, and given final definition with plans for solutions designed in Phase 4 may take as much as an additional two or even more years to bring to realization in a concrete manner in Phase 5 which concentrates on the execution effort.

Table 1 presents typical problem areas which have been defined and improved or successfully resolved in Phases 3 thru 5 of organization development work. Tactics used to bring about organization development in Phase 5 include all of the regular organization mechanisms of problem solving and execution. There are also overriding assignments by a task force or by specific individuals for problems which are not effectively carried out through routine supervisory practices.

In addition, continuing intervention in the improvement effort is made by an organization development specialist who is specifically accountable for auditing the entire effort from an achievement point of view. Also, a new educational strategy is employed.[52] This educational approach, which uses the task paragraphs and the team effectiveness design, involves the application of the learning theory and methods of inquiry of Phase 1 to resolve operational and organization problems. Because of the wide use of the task force approach and individual assignments, further comment on this approach is unnecessary.

Integrating Supervisory Problem-Solving Through Organization Education.

The idea that organization problems can be solved by diligent supervision alone is a limited one. In some forms of problem solving, some feel all that is necessary is to tell those responsible what the solution is in order for them to implement it. Alternately, the assumption is that people have the "facts" and that a discussion of the problem is, therefore, wasteful. In other

TABLE 1

Typical Problem Areas Which Have Been Defined and Improved or Successfully Resolved in Phases 3, 4 and 5 of Organization Development

Growth and new product development	Integration of headquarter-region; headquarters-field
Long range planning	Reduction of friction between departments such as accounting and technical; employee relations and mechanical, etc.
Improving corporate reputation and image	
Profit centering	Relations with government regulatory body
Increasing product outlets	
Increasing cost consciousness	Working with city fathers on property taxation
Rolls readjustment	
Burden reduction	Improved utilities management
Shifting R & D values from pure experimentation to business oriented research	Introduction of running maintenance
	Shifting to craft flexibility
Revision of organization structure	Improved warehouse utilization
Reducing age structure	Defining and gaining understanding of job descriptions
Revision of promotion policy	
Improvement in the organization reward system	Allocation of space and facilities
	Vacation scheduling
Management development	Absenteeism
Improved performance appraisal and review	Early quitting
Revision of philosophy of the company organ	Safety
	Pollution control
Improved union-management relations through contract bargaining, etc.	Waste control
	Tool control

cases, the assumption is made that, if the facts available are insufficient, verbal communication or written memoranda suffice to acquaint organization members with the issue at hand.

That these assumptions are insufficient as the basis for bringing about resolution of problems of organization effectiveness has been demonstrated in innumerable ways. This demonstration continues every day in the untold

number of efforts which fail to solve the basic problem
when the approach is limited to these methods.

The conclusion is that the basic problem of organization development in Phases 3, 4, and 5 needs reorientation. The direction of reorientation is one of supplementing supervisory approaches with education methods. Such
methods should enable individuals to engage in a study
of problems of the organization as the subject matter of
learning. When this educational step is taken, organization
members are aided, through educational methods to comprehend the organization problems in a fundamental and
systematic way.[53]

An aspect of organization development, particularly
in Phase 5, involves study by all organization members
who have a stake in the outcome of basic problems as
the subject matter. The educational methods to be pictured suggest how organization problems as the subject-
matter of learning can be facilitated.

Team Effectiveness Task Paragraph Discussions. One
of the key learning activities of Phase 1 deals with team
effectiveness. The team effectiveness design employed
is integrated around a paragraph written to define a task
in which each member in the beginning has only partial
information. The learning goal of the activity is to pool
individual resources and to coordinate their efforts to
develop a final team answer. The final team answer can
be scored objectively, and team performances can be
compared. During a critique session, team members
conduct a detailed review of the problems of pooling their
resources to a final answer. They also plan how to solve
problems faced in the previous exercise during the next
problem, which also involves team performance.

This training design is also employed, with certain
modifications, when the topic of study is an organization problem of the kind defined in Phase 4. A typical
picture of such a learning sequence which extends over a
10-hour period in Phase 5 is pictured below.

1. *Assessment of Individual Knowledge.* At 3 o'clock
in the afternoon, a segment of the organization member-

ship convenes. Its first activity is to complete a true-false (multiple choice, etc.) test regarding the facts of some management problem.

2. *Individual Study of Facts.* As a second step, each member receives a packet of background reading which contains a technical study of the problem at hand. The true-false test is constructed from the facts contained in this packet. The instructions request that each member study the materials contained in the packet before the next morning. All participants in any given class reconvene the next morning in self-guided groups (similar to the Grid study groups of phase 1).

3. *Definition of the Study Topic through Task Paragraph Instructions.* At this time, the study group receives a task paragraph which usually formulates the dilemma of solving the problem which is defined by the materials being studied. It might ask, for example, "Based on the facts studied in the packet of materials received yesterday, does this organization have a problem in the area of safety which it can do something about? If there is a safety problem, what are the factors causing it? Finally, what steps might be taken to improve the quality of performance in the realm of safety?"

This example is only one of many employed for studying organization subject matter. Within the educational strategy, it defines the issue to which organization members are to react.

4. *Team Agreement Regarding Facts.* Before reacting directly to the questions in the task paragraph, however, participants interact with one another based on the previous night's study material. Their purpose is to develop a single team answer to the true-false or multiple choice test. Such discussions clarify many points of misunderstanding that remain in spite of diligent study efforts. On completing the team true-false test the answers are made available. Each team evaluates how well it was able to pool individual resources of understanding to coordinate its efforts relative to a full comprehension of the issues as reflected in an accurate team performance score. Questions

which remain incorrectly answered are discussed until there is full comprehension of the facts. Depending on the complexity of the problem, the learning sequence may take from two to four hours to complete. In terms of the understanding and agreement objectives of a 9,9 approach to organization development, these steps meet the purpose of increasing understanding of what the problem is.

5. *Agreement With and Commitment to Problem Solution.* The next step is concerned with agreement and commitment in defining the basic problem and steps to be considered for its solution. This sequence starts after lunch and continues through the day. Its purpose is to aid participants, with facts in hand as developed in a study and discussion period, to react to the basic question. As appropriate, participants develop in their own thinking, commitment to acting under personal responsibility in such a way as to contribute to the solution of the problem.

The cycle, starting as it does on one day at three and continuing through to the end of the next day may be repeated until the entire organization membership has had an opportunity to study and discuss the problem and to develop agreement concerning approaches to it and concrete steps toward its solution.

In a 1,000-man managerial organization, an administrative arrangement which has been found practical is for each class, which consists of 40 people, to discuss in teams of 10. In a sequence where a new class comes every day, this means that 100 per cent coverage of the organization can be completed in 25 days. Alternatively, with classes of 100, a complete total organization study can be made in two weeks. An advantage of massing education effort within a short time space is that family group members who are in different classes can then take step two shortly after completion of the first step. In step two, the problem is brought back into the work group domain where decision-making steps between a boss and his subordinates can be discussed and agreed upon as to concrete action for problem solution. If higher level decisions are required before action is taken, the organization development specialist, who also audits the entire effort, assigns responsibilities for seeing the sequence through to completion.

The educational model as described is basic but an infinite variety of modifications are possible. It has been used to study a wide range of organization subject matter (see Table 1). The reason that this kind of educational effort is contained in a 9,9 approach to organization development is that *it insures understanding, rather than presuming it.* It supplements supervision with organization education. Under these circumstances, agreement on desired courses of action and commitment to their execution is greatly facilitated.

Organization Development Specialist. In Phases 3, 4, and 5 a development specialist takes part in organization activities which deal with day-by-day operational problems. He interacts with individuals and subunits of the organization in Phases 3, 4 and 5. The organization development specialist *intervenes*—steps into an ongoing activity to stop it, to "freeze" the action for a sufficient time to insure that the projected action has been evaluated from the standpoint of theory, and that it is consistent with operational goals set in Phase 4 before being taken. He intervenes not on the basis of hierarchy, but in terms of the authority of ideas. His goal is to get action through understanding and agreement, not through his "authority."

Interventions are needed in the development effort because of the pull from cultural aspects of traditions, precedents, and past practices. An ever present tendency exists to accept old and recurring problems as inevitable, rather than as being subject to resolution through deliberate effort. His primary goal is to further progress toward the achievement of organization goals set in Phase 4. His secondary purpose is to identify problems not previously recognized and defined and to initiate action that could contribute toward their solution.

The Job Description of the Development Specialist(s). The development specialist may be either an outsider, who is retained by the organization during Phases 3, 4 and 5, or one of its permanent members. In either case, his work is not defined by hierarchical position but rather in terms of his particular relationship to the organization.

Without going into detail, several criteria governing this relationship can be stated. The organization development specialist *has neither line nor staff responsibility* in the conventional sense. The situation is somewhat similar to that of an industrial medical officer whose assignment makes it difficult for line or staff management to give professional direction to or to exercise performance control over his efforts. Rather, as is true for medical specialists who deal with personal health in an industrial setting, it is the organization development specialist's responsibility to define from his own professional viewpoint within broad and agreed upon general limits, the way in which he will apply his efforts toward the development and maintenance of organization health. He remains the specialist responsible for the sound application of his technical knowledge.

An organization development specialist can exert many influences on individual, team and organization behavior to bring about the kinds of actions required to achieve the goals of Phase 4. From a most general point of view, he gains access for diagnostic and training purposes to a variety of work situations within the organization to aid members to solve their own problems rather than to make specific recommendations regarding operational details. Access is achieved not by edict from the top, but rather by discussion and agreement within each of the working teams. This procedure, though much more difficult than access through authority, reduces resistance and increases the quality of the joint effort between the organization development specialist and the individuals and various components of the organization.

Kinds of Intervention. With arrangements enabling him to work freely with various individuals and teams and yet without being a part of the power structure of the organization in the ordinary sense, the question is,

"What does an organization development specialist do?"
"How does he work?"

He intervenes in organization, intergroup, team and individual development problems at critical points of here-and-now problem solving where actual difficulties are being experienced.[54] There are at least nine major kinds of interventions which can unblock indecision and relieve impasses of the kind that frequently arise and that prevent the achievement of development objectives. With such interventions available, developmental aims are more likely to be realized. These kinds of interventions include the following:

(a). *Discrepancy.* This intervention calls attention to a contradiction in action or attitudes. This kind of confrontation is useful for keeping the organization on a new course defined in Phase 4, rather than allowing it to shift unwittingly into old and less satisfactory behavior patterns, due to momentary pressures.

(b). *Theory.* A second kind of intervention is where a confrontation draws on behavioral science concepts and theory to throw into bold relief the connection between underlying assumptions and present behavior. In addition, theory sometimes can be useful in predicting the consequences likely to follow from embarking on any specialized course of action.

(c). *Procedural.* A critique of how various steps of effort in organization development activities may or may not aid problem solving.

(d). *Relationship.* This kind of intervention focuses attention of participants on issues which arise between people as they work together. It is needed to reduce or to eliminate interpersonal frictions. With this focus of attention on personal feelings, particularly strong negative tensions which hinder coordinated effort, emotions can be examined and resolved.

(e). *Experimentation.* Another intervention involves experimentation which permits testing and comparing two or more courses of action *before* a final decision is taken, particularly when the way to proceed has become institutionalized or tradition-bound.

(f). *Dilemma.* A dilemma intervention, which aids in accurately identifying a choice point in managerial actions, often can help members re-examine outworn assumptions and search for alternatives other than those under consideration.

(g). *Perspective.* Many times in the intensity of the effort applied in production settings, it seems almost inevitable that individuals or teams will lose their sense of direction. Thereafter, it is increasingly difficult to reestablish a course of action which can move the situation away from momentary problem-solving toward larger issues. A perspective intervention permits present actions to be evaluated by providing a background of broader historical orientation.

(h). *Organization Structure.* It is possible to think of many organization development efforts which leave the very structure of the organization unevaluated and unexamined. Students of organization change are correct in pointing out that many causes of organizational effectiveness are not found in procedures or team effectiveness or even in the absence of performance goals. Rather, the fabric of the organization itself can prevent communication, decision making and the application of effort from being as effective as it might be under different organizational arrangements. An organizational intervention focuses on issues which confront the total organization membership or its various sub-components.

(i). *Cultural.* A "cultural" intervention examines traditions, precedents and established practices which constitute properties of the organizational fabric itself. Challenging the appropriateness of organization culture is difficult, because it permeates actions in such a silent way. Yet, the great challenge is to bring organization culture under deliberate management. The intervention which lifts up culture for examination may indeed be one of the most critical of all.

The work of the organization development specialist is not to suggest specific solutions to problems identified in Phases 3, 4 and 5. His purpose is to monitor and to audit progress to solve such problems, to keep attention of relevant groups focused on objectives they have set for themselves, and to aid in releasing and mobilizing efforts in problem-solving directions. Where his interventions shift away from the process of problem solving toward content solutions, his effectiveness is likely to markedly decrease. The reason is that, by taking content positions, he is likely to be in the position of countering alternative positions which in the final analysis are ones over which the line organization has final responsibility. Rather, his purpose is that of enabling the line organization to discover for themselves valid and acceptable positions on problems which, as solutions, they can support.

Summary. A variety of organization-wide problem areas which have been improved or successfully resolved in organization development work are presented in Table 1. Some of these problems are ones which, in other settings have been subject to correction by administrative methods alone. Given the same magnitude of problems, in no case have we seen the degree of improvement or correction achieved by administrative practices that has been accomplished through the more systematic organization development approach described here.

Phase 6: Stabilization

The final phase is a period of stabilizing the changes brought about in prior phases.

Almost without regard to the effectiveness of the previous phases, the tendency is for the organization as a whole to slip back into patterns and traditional ways of the old culture, which require less skill and less effort to apply and which afford more comfort because they are second nature. A period of time, perhaps as long as a year or so, is necessary after the completion of the first five phases to identify throwback tendencies and to take corrective action. As throwback effects are noticed and deliberately assessed, continuous practice of newer kinds of performance over a period of time can lead to the newer patterns becoming habitual such that confidence in acting according to improved ways of operating also becomes second nature.

From the standpoint of a change program, therefore, Phase 6 is a more passive period on the part of the organization development specialist whose interventions are limited primarily to those of identifying discrepancies and developing and maintaining perspective. The character of the interventions in other words is that of reestablishing a sound relationship between the goals and actions previously set in motion and current activities. The aim here is not to increase organizational effectiveness by setting new goals or by interventions which emphasize new directions of change. Rather, the effort is limited to insuring that the changes of earlier phases actually are able to withstand the pressures toward regression that seem to be present in an operational setting where quick decisions are needed and where crises are a daily occurrence.

Since organization development efforts of the kind pictured here extend over several years, there has been insufficient time available as yet to picture the kinds of developments that are likely to occur after the conclusion of Phase 6. However, in the oldest organization development project based on this phase strategy, Phase 6 has drawn to a conclusion and another entire sequence of organization development, commencing with a new educational Phase 1, has been started.

References

1. Blake, R. R. & Mouton, J. S. Improving Organizational Problem Solving Through Increasing The Flow and Utilization of New Ideas. I. *Training Directors Journal*, 17, (9) 1963, 48-57. Part II in 17, (10), 1963, 39-54.

For a review of the focus and direction of present-day organization change efforts, see Bennis, W. G. A New Role for the Behavioral Sciences: Effecting Organizational Change. *Administrative Science Quarterly*, 8, (2) 1963, 125-165.

2. Blake, R. R., Mouton, J. S. & Sloma, R. *Designing the Managerial Operations of a Subsidiary Organization.* Dallas: (to appear); Also, see Blake, R. R. & Mouton, J. S. The Developing Revolution in Management Practices. *ASTD Journal*, 16, 1962, 29-50; Bennis, W. G., *op. cit.*

3. Appley, L. A. *Management in Action.* New York: American Management Association, 1956, 355-363.

4. Miner, J. B. *The Management of Ineffective Performance.* New York: McGraw-Hill, 1963, 334.

5. *The Managerial Grid: An Investigation of Organization Health.* Austin, Tex.: Scientific Methods, Inc., 1963.

6. Blake, R. R., Mouton, J. S. & Sloma, R., *op. cit.*

7. Blansfield, M. G., Blake, R. R. & Mouton, J. S. The Merger Laboratory: A New Strategy for Bringing One Corporation into Another. *ASTD Journal*, to appear (1964).

For a discussion of the concepts and strategies underlying the training approach to these and similar efforts, see Blake, R. R. & Mouton, J. S. The Instrumented Training Laboratory. In I. Weschler & E. Schein (Eds.), *Issues in Human Relations Training.* Washington, D. C.: National Training Laboratories, National Education Association, 1962, 61-76.

8. Blake, R. R. & Mouton, J. S. Headquarters-Field Team Training for Organizational Improvement. *ASTD Journal*, 16, 1962, 3-11.

9. Blake, R. R. & Mouton, J. S. The Managerial Grid as a Framework

for Inducing Change in Industrial Organizations. In P. Worchel & D. Byrne (Eds.), *Personality Change.* New York: Wiley, 1964, (in press).

10. Bennis, W. G., *op. cit.*

11. Lippitt, R., Watson, J. & Westley, B. *The Dynamics of Planned Change.* New York: Harcourt, Brace, 1958.

12. Lippitt, R., *et al, op. cit.*

13. Cartwright, D. Achieving Change in People: Some Applications of Group Dynamics Theory, *Human Relations,* 4, 1951, 381-392. See Chapter 5 of this book for a more complete discussion and relevant references.

14. Lewin, K. *Field Theory in Social Science.* New York: Harper, 1951. See Chapter 7 of this book for a more complete discussion and review.

15. Lippitt, R., *et al, op. cit.*

16. Blake, R. R. & Mouton, J. S. The Managerial Grid as a Framework for Inducing Change in Industrial Organizations, *op. cit.;* For an excellent collection of behavioral science work and review in this area, see Bennis, W. G., Benne, K. D. & Chin, R. *The Planning of Change: Readings in the Applied Behavioral Sciences.* New York: Holt, Rinehart & Winston, 1961.

17. Lippitt, R., *et al, op. cit.;* Bennis, W. G., *op. cit.,* 1963.

18. Rogers, C. R. *Client-Centered Therapy.* Boston: Houghton Mifflin, 1951; Bradford, L. P., et al. *Explorations in Human Relations Training.* Washington, D.C.: National Training Laboratories, National Education Association, 1953; Shepard, H. A. An Action Research Model. In *An Action Research Program for Organizational Improvement.* (In Esso Standard Oil Company.) Ann Arbor: Braun & Brumfield, 1960; Argyris, C. *Interpersonal Competence and Organizational Effectiveness.* Homewood, Ill.: Dorsey-Irwin, 1962; Leavitt, H. J. The Manager of Tomorrow. *Training Directors Journal,* 17, (9), 1963, 37-47.

19. Fenichel, O. *The Psychoanalytic Theory of Neurosis.* New York: Norton, 1945; Fromm-Reichmann, F. *Principles of Intensive Psychotherapy.* Chicago: University of Chicago, 1950; Rogers, C. R., *op. cit.;* Redl, F. & Wineman, D. *Controls from Within.* Glencoe, Ill.: Free Press, 1952; Argyris, C., *op. cit.* See *Management Development* under Chapters 3 through 7 of this book for relevant discussions and references.

20. Lewin, K. Behavior and Development as a Function of the Total Situation. In L. Carmichael (Ed.), *Manual of Child Psychology.* New York: Wiley, 1946; Lewin, K., *op. cit.;* Lewin, K. Frontiers in Social Science. In D. Cartwright (Ed.), *Group Dynamics.* New York: Harper, 1951.

21. Lewin, K., *op. cit.,* 1946; Cartwright, D., *op. cit.*

22. Haire, M. Role Perceptions in Labor-Management Relations: An Experimental Approach. *Industrial Labor Relations Review,* 8, 1955, 204-216; Blake, R. R. & Mouton, J. S. The Intergroup Dynamics of Win-Lose Conflict and Problem-Solving Collaboration in Union-Management Relations. In M. Sherif (Ed.), *Intergroup Relations and Leadership.* New York: Wiley, 1962, 94-140; Blake, R. R. & Mouton,

J. S. Intergroup Therapy. *International Journal of Social Psychiatry,* 8, (3), 1962, pp 196-198. Blake, R. R., Shepard, H. A. & Mouton, J. S. *Managing Intergroup Conflicts in Industry.* Houston: Gulf Publishing Company, 1964.

23. Newcomb, T. M. Stabilities Underlying Changes in Interpersonal Attraction. *Journal of Abnormal & Social Psychology,* 66, (4), 1963, 376-386; Roethlisberger, F. J. Twenty Years of Management Development. *Training Directors Journal,* 17, (9), 1963, 4-14.

24. Mahoney, T. A. *Building the Executive Team.* Englewood Cliffs, N.J.; Prentice-Hall, 1961; Shaw, M. Changing Concepts in Management Development. *Training Directors Journal,* 17, (9), 1963, 15-24.

25. Thelen, H. *The Dynamics of Groups at Work.* Chicago: University of Chicago, 1954. See Chs. 5 and 7 of this book.

26. See Ch. 7, this book. Review the work in Bennis, W. G., *et al,* 1961, *op. cit.,* and Blake, R. R., *et al, Intergroup Relations, op. cit.*

27. Chapter 7. Also see Herzberg, F., Mausner, B. & Snyderman, B., B. *The Motivation to Work.* New York: Wiley, 1959.

28. Marrow, A. J. *Making Management Human.* New York: McGraw-Hill, 1957

29. Argyris, C. *Personality and Organization.* New York: Harper, 1957. Also, see Chs. 3 and 5, this book.

30. See Bennis, W. G., *op. cit.,* 1963, for a discussion of the work of others in this area. Other relevant studies in the area of interpersonal phenomena include, Jacques, E. *The Changing Culture of a Factory.* London: Tavistock, 1951; Sofer, C. *The Organization from Within.* London: Tavistock, 1961; Walker, C. *Modern Technology and Civilization.* New York: McGraw-Hill, 1962. Also, see Shepard, H. & Blake, R. R. Changing Behavior through Cognitive Change. *Human Organization,* 21, Summer, 1962, 88-96.

31. Blake, R. R. & Mouton, J. S. A 9,9 Approach for Increasing Organizational Productivity. In W. G. Bennis (Ed.), *Organization Change.* New York: Wiley, 1963, (to appear).

32. Lippitt, R., *et al, op. cit.*

33. One-week Seminars, for all levels of management, are open to the public. These public sessions enable participants to explore Managerial Grid concepts in depth in order to assess their application back in the organization.

Scientific Methods, Inc., Box 195, Austin, Texas, conducts Managerial Grid Seminars for the upper levels of management in the United States and Canada, Great Britain, Australia, Japan, and other countries in Europe and the Middle East.

34. Bennis, W. G., *op. cit.,* 1963.

35. Lewin, K., *op. cit.,* 1951.

36. Newcomb, T. M., *op. cit.*

37. Prior to the formal beginning of Phase 1, all organization members complete prework in the form of answering a number of training instruments of a quantitative nature. Where possible, these data are stored in a computer and, therefore, are readily available for use during the various phases of the organization development activity. In addition, during the month prior to attending any Seminar,

each participant prepares himself through study of training materials and completing an additional set of instruments. Altogether, approximately 20 hours of prework are completed prior to the Seminar.

The educational model pictured here presumes that all organization members are congregated in one physical location. Other arrangements are possible in a dispersed organization.

38. Blake, R. R. & Mouton, J. S. A 9,9 Approach for Increasing Organizational Productivity, *op. cit.;* Blake, R. R. & Mouton, J. S. *Group Dynamics—Key to Decision Making.* Houston: Gulf Pub. Co., 1961.

39. Bennis, W. G., *op. cit.,* 1963.

40. Blake, R. R., Mouton, J. S. & Blansfield, M. G. How Executive Team Training Can Help You and Your Organization. *ASTD Journal,* 16, 1962.

41. Read, W. H. Upward Communication in Industrial Hierarchies. *Human Relations,* 15, (1), 3-15; Blake, R. R., *et al, op. cit.,* 1962; Blake, R. R. & Mouton, J. S. Headquarters-Field Team Training for Organizational Improvement, *op. cit.*

42. Likert, R. *New Patterns of Management.* New York: McGraw-Hill, 1961.

43. Blake, R. R. & Mouton, J. S. Improving Organizational Problem Solving Through Increasing the Flow and Utilization of New Ideas., *op. cit.,* (10), 38-54.

44. Likert, R., *op. cit.*

45. Blake, R. R., *et al, Intergroup Relations, op. cit.*

46. Blake, R. R. & Mouton, J. S. Reactions to Intergroup Competition Under Win-Lose Conditions. *Management Science,* 7, 1961; Blake, R. R. & Mouton, J. S. Union-Management Relations: From Conflict to Collaboration. *Personnel,* 38, 1961; Blake, R. R. & Mouton, J. S. The Intergroup Dynamics of Win-Lose Conflict and Problem-Solving Collaboration in Union-Management Relations, *op. cit.;* Blake, R. R., *et al, Intergroup Relations, op. cit.*

47. Blake, R. R. & Mouton, J. S. Headquarters-Field Team Training for Organizational Improvement., *op. cit.;* Blansfield, M. G., *et al, op. cit.*

48. See preceeding references.

49. Sherif, M. & Sherif, C. *An Outline of Social Psychology.* (Rev. Ed.) New York: Harper, 1956.

50. Blake, R. R., *et al, Intergroup Relations, op. cit.*

51. Blansfield, M. G., *et al, op. cit.*

52. Bennis, W. G., *op. cit.,* 1963

53. Blake, R. R., *et al, Designing the Managerial Operations of a Subsidiary Organization., op. cit.*

54. Blake, R. R. & Mouton, J. S. The Managerial Grid as a Framework for Inducing Change in Industrial Organizations., *op. cit.;* Bennis, W. G., *op. cit.,* 1963

55. Fleishman, E. A., Harris, E. J. & Burtt, H. E. *Leadership and Supervision in Industry. An Evaluation of a Supervisor Training Program.* Columbus, Ohio: Ohio State University Bureau of Educational Research, 1955.

56. The organization improvement program described by Blansfield has replicated several aspects of the design originally applied here. Generally, comparable results described by him increase the likelihood that interpretations provided here are essentially correct. See Blansfield, M. G. Depth Analysis of Organizational Life. *California Management Review*, 5, 1962, 29-36.

CHAPTER THIRTEEN

Organization Development and Performance

"Catalytic is a good word to describe it . . . things started rolling and the momentum has been maintained ever since" . . . "a chain reaction was set off with a thousand unexpected results; an organizational log jam was broken . . . we began doing things everyone knew we should have been doing all along . . . once the tempo shifted . . . you could feel it everywhere, and our efforts came to point in a single direction." "The way to say it is that we stopped being at cross purposes . . . we had been complacent, but no one is complacent anymore . . . everyone is awake and moving since the organization *development project* began . . . this was no tune-up job, it was an organization overhaul."

These quotations picture reactions of organization members to a large scale experiment in organization development conducted in an industrial plant of 2400.

This effort in organization development is in its fifth year, but the point of diminishing returns has yet to be reached. Because of its open-ended nature, an interim evaluation of results obtained seems appropriate at this time.

The strategies employed are essentially the sequences of phases depicted in the previous section.[1] Once the approach to problem-solving and production-improvement had been learned, the goal was to insure its continuous application until it became a stable way of organization life. These latter stages are continuing.

RESULTS

Changes are described in several sections. First is a discussion of changes in indices of performance of the organization, such as P/(L), manning, and organization structure. Following is an analysis of changes in intergroup relations. Included are headquarters-plant, union-management, staff-line, and other relations. Next are changes in the character and uses of team action. Then, results that are best pictured as changes in individuals are evaluated. A summary and interpretation are presented in the final section.

To aid objectivity, changes described have been assessed in comparison with those occurring in other plants carrying out similar manufacturing activities where no deliberate improvement effort was underway during the period observations were made. These latter organizations provide baseline information. As such, they are useful for drawing comparisons.

ORGANIZATION-WIDE CHANGES

Profit Improvement: P/(L)

During the five-year period, plant P/(L), has undergone significant improvement. The shift is from a profit position where the plant was operating at a serious deficit to one that is now returning a substantial profit. The shift is due to a multitude of considerations. Contributing factors are equipment modernization, reduced raw material costs, improved finished product price structure, leaner manning, etc.

The organization development effort is linked to some of these factors. *Without it, a number of decisions that led to profit improvement actions almost certainly would not have been made.*

Judgments are difficult to make as to the degree each of these factors contributed to profit improvement. The organization excellence effort has influenced a variety of operating decisions by facing up to difficult matters. Persons in positions permitting evaluation of contributions attributable to the various factors involved, estimate that the organization development effort accounts for approximately 30 per cent of the gain. Their judgments are of considerable interest as this estimate is on the basis of comparison with P/(L) improvement in other plants where deliberate organization excellence efforts were not a consideration.

Many of the same factors affecting profit were present to influence P/(L) in comparison plants. However, absent in the comparison plants were the kinds of actions subject to local managerial control that led to the advantages realized by the experimental plant due to the organization development project. Since these judgments were made, an organization development effort has been introduced in one of the controlled plants. In this organization development project, where more objective post assessments of effects have been made, the profit improvement figure is higher than 30 per cent. Based on the best evidence available, then, a 30 per cent profit improvement due to organization development appears to be a conservative estimate. This means, for example, that on a base of a $10 million profit, an organization development effort would contribute something in the neighborhood of three million dollars.

Profit Awareness

Important underlying changes in attitudes that are related to profitability should be mentioned.

There is greater awareness, and acceptance, throughout the organization of the importance of achieving a more favorable competitive position. There is, for example, better recognition that plant health is related to efficiency through advanced equipment technology, sound manning practices, and the effective use of people. As another example, one basis for judging organization effectiveness involves performance comparisons with other plants whose products seek to penetrate the same market area. Such performance comparisons are now used far more extensively than formerly, and serve to aid the organization through a continuous comparison and self study to identify ways in which further operational improvement can be brought about.

Beyond these, there is greater understanding and acceptance of what is called the chain store concept. By this is meant that plant economic health, long term, is, and should be, judged by *local plant performance as against overall corporate year-end results*. Another way of saying it is that, even though corporate level profit performance may be at an acceptable level as a return on investment, it does not mean that a local quasi-independent unit which is losing money will be kept open. Each store has to make its own way.

Personnel

As far as employment is concerned, the general industry trend within which this plant operates is in a downward direction. Over the entire industry, fewer persons are employed today than a decade ago.

The number employed in the plant which is engaged in the organization development project has decreased at a faster rate than for the industry as a whole and at a faster rate than in comparison plants. This is true for both burden and wage personnel.

The question is, "Why?" Perhaps the major influence has been an increase in conviction that achieving and retaining competitive leanness is essential for continued plant health. This has come about through greater confidence that such changes can be made—that fewer people can, by working differently, contribute as much or more than was formerly produced by larger numbers.

Significant in this personnel decrease has been greater readiness to release high potential performers for advancement beyond the plant into corporate positions. A secondary result has been more rapid advancement of personnel within the plant to fill vacancies created by people moving up. At managerial levels there have been reductions through separation, based on merit rather than on seniority. Finally, the recruiting rate for technical personnel has been reduced to a point considered adequate for long-term needs. The new recruitment rate replaces one that for a long time was considered excessive but was never challenged. None of these changes are observed in control plants.

The decision to work toward leaner burden manning has been quite well accepted through the plant as legitimate and proper. The manner in which decisions were made as to how leaner manning should be accomplished is rather widely criticized. The criticism is mainly with respect to hidden aspects. As one person said, "They (the top management group) lost confidence that we are adult. They made their manning decisions under wraps. Rather than consulting and explaining the problems and getting needed help on solutions, they went all the way, and announced a total package. The manning decisions were sound; *the way they were implemented was not.*"

Organizational Structure

Through personnel changes, and a reexamination of how to work with fewer personnel, a more or less continuous revision and modernization of organization structure has occurred. Many facets are involved in redesigning organization structure. Several that appear to be related to the excellence effort are conspicuous.

Greater Planning Flexibility. The present organization structure is designed to promote greater emphasis on long term planning at the top; better intermediate operational level planning in the middle; and increased delegation, with improved local planning of work, at the organization's base.

These are important. One result is that the top management has the time and freedom to break away from operation details. This was not true prior to the excellence effort. This availability of time at the top has permitted increased attention on critical issues of growth and development. As someone said, "The inclination is to let headquarters worry about these matters, while you take care of operations. Alternatively you say to yourself, 'New product development, that's R&D's job. When they think it up, we'll use it." Maybe it should work that way. Sometimes it does. But not enough. In the final analysis—unless the breaks just fall your way—the plant does best when it assumes increased responsibility for solving its own growth and development problems. Then, you get a better hearing from headquarters. Also, you can get a better hearing from R&D. How? Coming up with our own proposals and projects has increased the likelihood both groups will look at your ideas. It helps us understand our own problems of growth and to solve some of them locally. It helps headquarters and R&D to see local growth problems, not from their perspective alone, but from a plant insider's point of view as well."

With the top expending more effort on planning, growth, and development, the middle level of the organization has accepted increased delegation involving planning and execution of plant operations. Along with this increase in responsibility for operations at the middle, lower levels have found increased freedom for planning and execution of local operations, etc.

From these changes in the use of organization structure have come a more mature organization. Its character might be pictured as more planful, deliberate and self-assured. There is less fire-fighting at the top and less apathy at the bottom. "Management-at-all-levels" is a phrase which is widely used to picture the resulting changes in approach.

Management Development. Another feature of the organization structure has to do with its deliberate use to promote management development. The question asked is, "How can organization structure be more effective to promote the growth and development of people?" As a result, Assistants to . . . Junior Boards, rotation assignments, and so on have been created in various companies.

The changes from the past are, in part, ones of degree. "Assistant . . ." (not "Assistant to . . ."), rotational assignments, etc., were in use prior to the development effort to contribute to management development. Continued and increased use of these procedures has occurred with only minor influence from the organization improvement effort.

But changes have taken place that are more than ones of degree. For example, while organization structure has been simplified, it also has been shifted away from the horizontal ideal pattern to a somewhat more vertical shape. This shift has promoted increased line delegation and greater opportunity for growth. These are invaluable aids to management development.

Along with increased emphasis on management development, there also has come greater effort toward improving the effectiveness of training of wage personnel. Without going into the details involved in this approach, which are available elsewhere,[2] the general strategy is that of designing training situations where lower levels of management participate simultaneously with wage personnel in learning new operational and supervisory skills. This has led to the concept of job team training, an approach which has aided a number of wage people, who were seen as untrainable, to acquire necessary operating skills. At the same time, skills of front-line supervision have been increased.

Understanding How to Use the Organization Structure to Promote Work. "In the old days, problems of coordination of effort," said one person, "were seen to be due to people shirking their responsibilities. That frequently called for a performance review to get a person back on the track or for a revision of his job description to be sure his assignment was clear. These possibilities are not ignored now, of course. But we look deeper. We ask ourselves if the structure itself is right for promoting effective work, or whether it blocks coordination of effort, etc. Organization structure is no longer thought of as fixed or permanent. It ought to be changed and shifted to keep it functional with changing requirements, and at times that's pretty frequent. It's an endless process of change and adaptation."

The deeper lying change implied in this quotation typifies a different attitude toward organization structure. The change is away from trying to force people to fit the structure when weaknesses in its operation become evident, toward trying to fit organization structure to the needs and capabilities of individuals to communicate effectively to correlate problem solving and productive effort. A specific example here is in avoiding win-lose competitiveness between operating units—such as operations and the mechanical services group—through designing an organization structure which promotes the easier flow and exchange of information, without causing individuals who cooperate across group lines to feel disloyal to their own organization units. Other examples include: designing a structure to get the full potential for organization performance from long-range planning for growth and development; making deliberate use of organization structure for management development; shifting the structure to meet changing conditions rather than trying to impose an ideal logical order; and seeking indices of organization health.

INTERGROUP RELATIONS

Any complex organization faces a variety of situations when two or more groups coordinate their efforts. However, organization improvement in the experimental plant has been striking through increased cooperation between groups where past relationships have involved invidious comparison and competitiveness. The direction of shift has been from win-lose toward relationships of mutual respect and problem solving.

Headquarters-Plant Relations

A change can be seen in the plant's relationship with its headquarters organization as influences flow more effectively in both directions now. The key factor is that plant personnel seem increasingly more able and ready to examine problems, not only from an inplant point of view, but also from a headquarters perspective. Another factor is that plant management is more ready to identify and to reveal its real problems of operation for headquarters examination, understanding, and assistance. Formerly, for example, plant management would dry run and program any headquarters review of its operations far in advance and in great detail. Whatever was to be presented was thoroughly reviewed. It was screened for impact to present a positive image. This has largely been replaced by a more realistic assessment of problems and possibilities, both from a corporate and plant point of view.

One result of the development effort in head-quarters-plant relations is increased mutual consultation between these two levels. As a headquarters representative recently said, "In developing corporate policy, we consult this plant more now than formerly. This gives better acceptance—less resistance—to new policies now than we used to get. A lot of it may be due to better policies, but if so, the improvement in policy quality is from greater refinement through pretesting its adequacy as the basis of plant guidance."

Comments can be heard, however, that put this relationship in a more negative light. The point made is that "Local management has abdicated to headquarters—the focus of influence has shifted. Plant management used to stand up to headquarters. Now they are pawns." Of significance here, however, is that such attitudes are absent in higher organization echelons where people have direct access to knowledge regarding the character of mutual consultation. Nonetheless, such feelings define an unresolved problem of communication within the plant hierarchy itself.

Thus, relations between the plant and headquarters have improved. As with certain other areas where more or less adequate relations already existed, however, the improvement associated with the excellence effort is one of degree.

Union-Management

Relations between the several independent unions and plant management had been in a state of chronic warfare for years. Several union presidents had resigned, only to be replaced each time by new and more militant union leadership. There had been violence. Many regarded finding a solution for this problem of mutual distrust and antagonism second in priority for solution only to improving plant P/(L).

At first slow and tortuous, yet clear, improvement in

union-management relationships was evident, and then, after a certification election, dramatic improvement resulted. One of the union presidents said, prior to the development effort, "Those S.O.B's (management) can't be trusted as far as you can throw them. You need two sets of eyes—front and back—if you don't want to get run over or stabbed in the back. And what do they look through?... green eyeballs with dollar signs tattooed on their lenses."

Today, this same union president says, "Time is here again for bargaining. We think we can get together and wrap it up in a month or six weeks. We understand them reasonably well. They do us. It takes a bit of pushing to move them off dead center, but at least they've got their ear plugs out."

This change is clearly the result of the organization development effort. From both sides, a major change in approach can be seen. The goal is to avoid bargaining, day-by-day problem solving and grievance handling from fixed, final positions that result in win-lose deadlocks. The mutually shared goal of both union and management is to define problems and diagnose causes as the basis for developing alternative possibilities. More detailed descriptions of how these changes were brought about are available elsewhere.[3]

As in other intergroup relationships, here, too, there is increased readiness to look at problems from the other group's point of view. This has reduced volatility on the part of the union and has increased self-restraint on the part of management. Another change is that management respects union officers as elected leaders. Simultaneously, there is increased understanding by the union of itself as a democratic-based institution.

There is another consideration which is of particular significance in evaluating this and other results in the union-management area. Due to plant efforts to become more competitive, there have been a larger number of controversial issues to be resolved than might be expected ordinarily. As someone has said, "We've faced and solved more problems with the union in these four years than in the ten years previous to the development project."

By no means, however, have all aspects of the union-management situation been solved or cleared up. Areas of tension remain over work issues between the unions and specific components of the management organization. In addition, there is more than an average number of interpersonal conflicts between union members and lower levels of management. Beyond this, there are ideologically rooted points of difference. They represent deeply-lying sources of contention for which immediate solutions are not evident. However, these issues no longer generate the heat and acrimony they once did.

Granted the complexity of union-management relations, the impression is wide-spread that much progress has been made toward correcting this chronically disturbed relationship. Perhaps one indication is that more eligible members of the organization currently have union membership than previously. This could well be a vote of confidence that the voice of the unions is heard now better than previously. The same kind of movement away from win-lose positions has not occurred in comparison plants.

Management-Wage Earner Relations

An extremely difficult judgment to make is whether wage personnel—as contrasted with union leadership—feel more identified with the plant and its problems now than previously. The general conclusion is that less direct change has taken place at this level. The development effort has touched wage people, but the contact is indirect. Such aspects as manning decisions, shifts in organization structure, and equipment modernization all have affected bargainable people in one way or another. Wage personnel have been affected to the degree that these changes are related to the development effort, but the influence is indirect. One general conclusion is that bargainable people continue to need a strong union to act in their behalf. Another way of saying it is that the integration of people into the organization through more effective supervision has not as yet been as fully realized as it might have been. Even here, however, new trends can be seen. One is that Managerial Grid training is to be made available to wage personnel in the effort to achieve a more effective integration of people into production.

Changes in Other Intergroup Relationships

A number of other intergroup situations also can be commented upon. They too reveal changes in the quality of interaction. For example, plant relationships between line and staff seem improved. The personnel department, for example, is exerting less direct decision-making influence on the organization. At the same time, its efforts as a consultative and educational agency have increased. Overall influence is up, but the way influence is exerted has visibly changed.

As another example, the business service department, particularly that part concerned with record keeping, is less autonomous and independent today than four years ago. The business service department has reviewed with relevant segments of the line organization the records it maintains and the studies it routinely makes. As a result, a number of record systems which no longer serve useful purposes have been eliminated. This section of the business service department has become a tighter unit and functionally more interdependent with the line units for which it provides record keeping services.

There also are improvements between components within the line organization at the interdivisional level such as between operations units and mechanical services. This has been achieved in two ways. Partly it is through changes between parallel departments in organization structure—divisions that had unnecessary independence have been brought under a single roof. Partly it is from a better working through of causes of tensions, and corrections of sources of poor coordination between parallel departments.

Somewhat comparable are improvements between plant management and the sales organization and plant management and R&D. In the former case, joint committees serve to define how better coordination and pooling of effort might be achieved. In the latter case, reciprocal personnel rotation is used. For example, R&D personnel spend as much as a year in the line organization learning its policies and problems first hand. Similar rotation of line personnel into R&D aids them to become more aware of how R&D might contribute to production. As one R&D member said, "I learned more in one year on the line about the kind of research that needs doing and the way to involve line personnel for them to use it, than I could have in any other way."

By comparison, a line manager, after a period in R&D pointed out, "I used to think R&D was a pretty plush country club. But when you get to know them they seem as much concerned to get mileage out of the company research dollar as we are to get it out of the operations dollar. I think we forget that effective use of the research dollar takes more intelligent supervision than is required the other way around."

Technical-Practical

One of the areas where improvement in relationships was expected, but where it is not very evident, is in cleavages between technically trained personnel and supervisors who are up from the ranks. Early in the development project, this point of intergroup tension was identified. Steps that might be taken to alleviate the cleavage were explored in a tentative way. However, little more was done, and the issue still exists in essentially the same form.

Summary

From a general standpoint, three observations regarding intergroup relations are clear. One is that, without training, there is little awareness among members of management of intergroup problems as problems. As a result, the general tendency is for management to fall into the win-lose trap, seeking to force its will through the exercise of power and authority. Alternatively, the conventional management attitude is to regard such problems as inevitable and to live with them rather than taking a constructive attitude toward solving them. The second generalization is that, when intergroup issues are focused on, from a behavioral science standpoint, as problems of win-lose competitiveness which need to be tackled as such, the change from competition to cooperation seems not too difficult to achieve.

However, a third conclusion also needs to be placed in perspective. It is that problem solving is more easily accomplished when the units involved with intergroup friction are organized in a psychological sense. Management and union, for example, represent two contending units in an organized intergroup relationship. Each has its own more or less clearly defined goals which sometimes are shared in common and sometimes are in opposition.

When the units in an intergroup conflict are easily identified and when the goals towards which they strive are relatively clear, conditions which permit a deliberate approach to problem solving are present. Bringing about improvement in intergroup relationships seems more difficult, however, when one or both sides lack (1) formal organization or (2) explicit goals. For example, relationships between management and wage people (as distinguished from management and union) are essentially informal and unorganized as are relations between technically trained management and those up from the ranks. In neither of these latter cases is there a formal organization nor are there clearly formulated goals through which relationship problems can be defined and identified for resolution and correction.

Based on these considerations, the conclusion is that intergroup problems that have an organized, psychological character are far more easily subject to improvement than are intergroup relationships of an unorganized, sociological character.

TEAM ACTION

One key concentration point in an organization development effort is the natural work group—people who share responsibilities for a given area of organization performance. In contrast with comparison plants, a number of striking differences are apparent in team action in work groups which have engaged in the organization excellence effort. Not all are plant wide. While there are many indications of improvement in the common shouldering of responsibility, in a few instances there is little or no indication of impact from the organizational improvement effort.

One-to-One, One-to-All

A major change comes about from learning how to mobilize team effort, as contrasted with a more conventional approach which seeks to promote individual endeavor.

The key here is in discovering that the whole is more and different than the sum of its parts. Another way of saying it is that the work team as a unit, potentially contains far more organization strength in the direction of problem solving and productivity than is available simply by adding the number of individuals.

As one manager said, "Before, I gave my major thought to each individual subordinate. I saw each as unique and distinct, needing to be managed in his own way. Meetings? There was little or no reason for them. As I saw it, meetings were a waste because they (subordinates) shared little or nothing in common to be dealt with through concerted action. It was only after I recognized that they shared me as their common problem that I was able to see how team action might contribute to organization performance. For example, one of the big difficulties they pointed out was that I rarely had enough time to deal adequately with any one of them *because there was so much I had to repeat to each of them singly.*"

"As a result we began having meetings, but first only for information exchange. Later, it became clear that there were many other matters that could be worked on and solved more effectively by subordinates-in-concert than by subordinates-in-isolation. Included are such routine things as housekeeping, safety, absenteeism, and quality control. These improvements led to other things, too, such as creative approaches to old problems."

Changing Character of Team Action

Others who already were utilizing team action in varying degrees, reported ways their modes of operation have been affected by the excellence effort. A consequence early in the excellence effort was to cause meetings to become more frequent, and longer. Discussions tended to bog down, to get off track or to deal with trivia. As skill in team action improved, however, the fear that things "had gone to pot" began to disappear. Based on a spot sampling of the daily calendars of managers, five years ago in comparison with now, currently there are fewer meetings than before the improvement effort. They are shorter, and they deal more with matters of mutual concern.

One manager said, "After we fought through our responsibilities and got better understanding of our individual as well as overall responsibilities, we found less need to touch base with one another. My people now are *more* independent than they used to be. They have more latitude to manage under their own responsibilities. We have fewer meetings."

The work content of meetings also has changed. It has shifted from agendas that concentrate more or less exclusively on operations, to content that touches a wider range of concerns.

Shifts in topics dealt with are different at different levels in the organization. An indication of the shifting character of meetings can be seen in the following. "Within any three-month interval, I try to see that we discuss major issues of the organization as a whole, as well as operations detail. For example, in one meeting, we'll discuss and review union relations. Another is given to critiquing organization structure. For instance, we debate whether we have too many, too few, or the right number of levels. In a third, we'll talk about market place developments. Because we are at a lower level in the organization, we don't have enough information to do all this ourselves. When we need help we get an outsider in to give us the picture. Why do all this? That's a good question. There is no direct need. You couldn't prove we work better because of it. But there are technical people in my unit as well as practical men. I see these discussions as one way of helping a man get an education by extending his outlook so that he sees the big picture. The practical man gets a better appreciation of what the company is like, and the technical man is pushed to think—like about union relations—of problems of the organization he doesn't have to live with every day."

The conspicuous change here is in a wider number of topics discussed now than previously. This is not a uniform reaction to the organization excellence effort. Neither is it exceptional. Indeed, many would agree that, (1) more topics are dealt with, (2) in greater depth, and (3) with more openness now than before the change project was initiated.

It is difficult to generalize about decision making at the team action level. This is so because of the great variety of problems under consideration, and because of the range of approaches to decisions employed by different managers. A judgment may be ventured, however, that two kinds of changes have taken place. One is that fewer unilateral decisions affecting subordinates are made and then announced "out of the blue." The other is that more pretesting of the impact of a given decision is now undertaken. Even where unilateral, one-man decisions need to be made, there is a greater tendency to preview the solution before announcing it and to condition people for what is coming.

The conclusion can be stated in a positive way. It is that *greater effort is made to insure understanding of problems and to get solutions that result in agreement, at present, than prior to the development effort.*

Greater recognition exists today of the importance of follow-up through critiquing operations and special projects. Overall, there is increased respect for how an activity can be squeezed to get more learning out of it by conducting a review either after it has been completed or when progress has reached some intermediate point. The quality of such critiques, of course, runs the full scale. One man said, "I keep detailed notes on the project. When the time is ripe, I let people know what they did wrong." At the opposite extreme, another mentioned, "One of the best ways to keep work moving without close supervision is to get a good performance critique going every once in awhile. Then people educate one another. The need to watch people every minute becomes less."

Summary

The improvement activity has increased awareness of and skill in the use of team action. An impression is that some managers have changed only a little in this direction. They remain quite rigid and formal, and continue to maintain considerable distance between themselves and those they supervise. Others have found fascination in their quickened awareness of problems of team action. They have shifted their base of management away from exclusive reliance on one-alone and one-to-one direction toward the one-to-all. One-to-all action does not replace the need for one-alone or one-to-one action. Rather, the goal is to find the best mixture so that the fullest advantages of using each can be achieved.

Of particular significance are dramatic changes in the manner in which the organization's top management operates. While the trend is in line with the more general picture, the degree of change is far greater.

INTERPERSONAL RELATIONS

A substantial number of interpersonal tensions and blockages have been cleared up. Included are some famous feuds that had existed for as long as a decade. Much energy that formerly went into the preservation of mutual hostility has been diverted into more constructive problem-solving endeavors.

This result is so routine in organization development work, however, that no further comment is needed. The important point is that channels of communication previously unavailable for organization problem solving have been opened.

Individual Action

A number of conclusions are best described as changes in individuals when considered separately from team action or interpersonal relations.

Output

Throughout the organization, it is widely agreed that people are working differently now than formerly. This is attributed partly to the readjustment of rolls over the years. There are fewer people to do the same and even an increased amount of work. Often reported is the remark, "It's not so much we're working harder; it's we're working better."

These changes are caused by many factors, of which the organization development effort is only one. But the following kind of remark which is related to the effort is heard, though more often at high and middle levels than at the bottom of the organization: "We know more of what's going on so we have a bigger stake. You can invest yourself more when you're in the know than when you're just a cog."

Creativity

Also produced by many factors is the widespread feeling that creativity of individuals has moved up a notch or two. Part of this is directly from the organization development effort, as suggested by the following: "I deliberately search out alternative ways of handling a problem before settling on any one. The result is more solutions that look creative. I don't think they are. It's just better use of plain common sense."

Another speaks of heightened creativity and says, "I get the people together. We try to list and write down all the problems we don't know how to solve. We put the list out for everyone to take a crack at. We've gotten some of the damnedest creativity you ever saw and it comes in the strangest ways. One is that we often come up with solutions, *sometimes even before the problem is clearly defined.* Another is that frequently we've been embarrassed by people telling us that what we think the problem is, is not the problem at all. And, in a number of cases, this approach has generated genuine creativity, in the sense of finding new and good solutions for old, chronic problems."

The third example is of more disciplined creativity. In a few locations, bona fide, but bootleg, benchwork research, is going on to fill a product development gap produced by operations people who "only worry about equipment" and R&D people who "can't afford to put money in on small problems."

Reward System

Along with the greater expansion of effort and creativity is a developing awareness of the relative inadequacy of the reward system. Some effort has been applied to shift it away from salary administration which is heavily saturated with longevity-seniority and across-the-board cost of living adjustments to a system which acknowledges individual competence through merit treatment. Progress towards this has been made through a new system of merit evaluation, but the problem remains to be solved as to how to do this in a most effective manner.

Satisfaction—Security

Another conclusion contains what appears, on the surface, to be a contradiction. On the one side, satisfaction in work appears to have increased. On the other, job security has decreased. The general trend of change has resulted in people being more involved in work, having more influence on organizational life, in being more responsible, and in having more autonomy. These changes all have increased satisfaction with work. The shrinkage of the organization, in terms of number of personnel, has decreased the security people have that their jobs "will always be around." This decrease in security is more prevalent (1) in middle and lower levels of the organization, and (2) among average, mediocre and inferior performers. In general, the change pointed to here is away from an organization where security was more or less insured for those who lived in accordance with organization tradition toward an organization where security and satisfaction are based on problem solving and output.

SUMMARY

This presentation is a sketch of results from a large scale experiment toward achieving organization excellence. Currently in its fifth year, the effort is still continuing.

The strategy of change is based upon the six-phase approach to organization development.

There can be little doubt but that the operation towards achieving organization excellence has left a deep imprint on the organization. Grant, for example, that the 30 per cent profit improvement thus far achieved would not have come about had the change project not been attempted. In itself, this result is of major significance. Evidence from comparable work going on elsewhere suggests that this figure indeed may be a conservative estimate. Based on this result alone, the potential from organization improvement effort is seen to be great. But, there are many changes that cannot be assessed directly in dollar-and-cents terms.

Although many difficulties confront an evaluation of such an effort, conclusions drawn are that the organization development effort has:

1. Contributed to organization profitability.

2. Hastened the improvement of intergroup relations between the plant and the headquarters organization to which it reports, and between management and the unions with which it bargains. The effort also has facilitated organization work between different management groups.

3. Strengthened awareness of and made more effective the utilization of team action in various ways.

4. Aided the reduction of interpersonal frictions and increased the degree of interpersonal understanding among individuals whose work requires coordination of effort.

5. Contributed toward increased individual effort and creativity and toward heightened personal satisfaction in work. It also has increased the job insecurity of individual members of the organization.

These 5 points are at best an approximation. The next decade should provide a more precise basis for evaluating the kinds of changes described here and the most effective ways for bringing them about. Even at this stage of progress, however, it would seem that the renovation of organization traditions and past practices and the improvement in interpersonal and intergroup relationships possible from behavioral science approaches to organization excellence is likely to make a substantial imprint on American industrial life.

The important conclusion to be drawn is that many problems of organizations are not subject to correction just by direct supervision or through management development focused on individuals-in-isolation.

However, by supplementing supervision with educational methods which focus the attention of organization members on the organization itself, the culture of an entire organization can be brought to a higher level of performance effectiveness.

References

[1] The earlier version of the Managerial Grid, referred to as the Power Spectrum, served as the integrating framework of concepts for this project. Blake, R. R. & Mouton, J. S., *Group Dynamics— Key to Decision Making*. Houston: Gulf Publishing Co., 1961.

[2] Bidwell, A. C., Farrell, J. J., & Blake, R. R. Team Training—A New Strategy for Industry. *ASTD Journal*, 15, 1961.

[3] Blake, R. R., & Mouton, J. S., The Intergroup Dynamics of Win-Lose Conflict and Problem-Solving Collaboration in Union-Management Relations. In M. Sherif (Ed.) *Intergroup Relations and Leadership* New York, Wiley, 1962, pp 94-140.

CHAPTER FOURTEEN

Trends and
Practices of Management

The history of arrangements among men for producing things and services is a long one. It reaches into the unrecorded past and already has moved through endless evolutionary phases and changes. For many reasons, it can be predicted that it will continue to do so.

New kinds of materials are unceasingly available. Products and services demanded in a complex of modern living are in constant transition, as are machinery and tools. The same is true for the development of new methods, processes and procedures for accomplishing work. Automatic data processing with its seemingly unending uses in selecting, evaluating, and controlling materials and actions, for weighting alternatives, for pointing up possibilities, etc., also carries implications for the future which are but dimly visible. In addition, the evolution of our economic system is making it practical for larger numbers of people to acquire a wider range of products and a broader range of services than was true only a short time ago. Finally, the wants and appetites of men for new products and services seem insatiable. All of these considerations lead to the view that the products and services possible from work to be done in the future are difficult to picture. There is no end in sight or even an indication of a plateau to this evolution.

EVOLUTIONARY TRENDS

Changes in managerial and supervisory relations among those who perform within organizations are also in evolution, as they have been since times long gone and forgotten. From an historical point of view, change seems to be away from the raw 9,1 control of master-slave, knight-serf, foreign master-native, arrangements. It also seems to be away from the Protestant ethic of hard work, self-control, and rejecting attitudes that pictured the enterprising entrepreneur of decades past. Furthermore, the 9,1 entrepreneural spirit seems less able to exert itself against the rules and regulations of legislation in the temper of the times. However, what remains of 9,1 is considerable. Much of it is to be found in the muted 9,1 approach, as described in Chapter 3. Competitive economic pressures being what they are, particularly from recessions, etc., substantial managerial actions continue to be of the muted 9,1 sort which gets production or else, even as the older 9,1 did. However, in spite of the increased number of managers operating today, the total of 9,1 currently practiced probably is less now than formerly, although much of it still remains.

If this conclusion is even only partly so, then a critical question becomes, "Toward what kind of managerial relationships is the management of work—as contrasted with the products and services from work—likely to move and why?" A related question is, "Can thoughtful men exercise deliberate influence over the direction of development rather than being carried unwittingly into next phases, unable to shape the currents of culture that guide their action?"

In addition to those factors mentioned above that tend to preserve or reinforce 9,1, there are forces shifting managerial practices away from 9,1 into all of the other possible directions.

Toward 1,1

Some factors are driving evolution in the 1,1 direction, such as machines and assembly techniques that completely control decision-making and eliminate the thinking part of work, for example, leaving men idle, watching, and monitoring, but neither thinking nor acting with emotion relative to work. However, this may be only a transitional period. Complex machines and the simplification of routines which eliminate the opportunity to think, also are eliminating the need to work—at least on the same problem. A result is that men at all levels of organizations are being released from work that machines can do better. Beyond that, complex developments such as the revolution in technology, tools, and materials, etc., introduce new problems and possibilities that require more thought, effort, and challenge than ever. Barring international holocaust or severe depression, the possibility of evolution—except here and there—trending massively in the 1,1 direction seems remote and quite far away.

Toward 1,9

A welfare-oriented society developed to its extreme, making as it does few or no demands and providing 1,9 convenience, comfort, and social togetherness while asking little or no effort in return, seems neither so widespread nor so appealing as to constitute a major trend. As long as anti-trust laws prevail and profit motivation carries genuine meaning, the 1,9 style is likely to be impractical if companies are to develop and retain a competitive edge and to stay in business. Yet, certain utilities and near monopolies seem to be drifting in this direction (as well as toward 5,5). Competition is no threat or effort carries little or no reward, and congeniality (or as in 5,5 conformity and status) becomes the most characteristic feature. But even these possibilities of evolution tend to be arrested by self-correcting counterforces of competition in the market place.

Toward 5,5

Many pressures are promoting trends of evolution in the direction of 5,5. Indeed, 5,5 appears to be the most widely practiced organization theory of today, at least in large public-owned corporations. Forces which culminate in a 5,5 adjustment are powerful and they may be increasing. As companies grow in size and as more reliance is placed on bureaucratic arrangements for providing supervision according to systems, guidelines, and handbooks which insure conformity and uniformity over large organizations, 5,5 seems more evident today than even 50 or even 30 years ago. Furthermore, the institutionalization of rewards according to a mechanical progression rather than on merit and contribution, tends to reinforce conformity and adherence to the status quo.

Another emphasis toward 5,5 comes from adopting as natural, the concepts and procedures of politics for use in managerial situations. Compromise and emphasis on the majority rule (as contrasted with genuine understanding and agreement), used as political mechanisms, have far different and less desirable consequences when adapted as the rule for problem-solving and decision-making in managerial situations. In a similar manner, the 5,5 bargaining tactics of compromise, so prevalent and perhaps appropriate in union-management relations where autonomous groups of relatively equal power relate to one another, seem to fall short when they become the model for relations between individuals and groups within the management organization itself. But the transfer of such strategies from politics and from union-management relations to manager-manager relations seems to be taking place without too much thought for consequences.

Union-management agreements in themselves tend to reinforce 5,5 problem-solving, because many give security and consideration in exchange for *some* managerial flexibility without actually solving the real problems associated with production or security. As a result, solutions to problems of people and production come to have an intermediate quality which is a way of life to which people accommodate with a 5,5 mental attitude, thus producing unwitting transference into other walks of managerial life.

Finally, the 5,5 style, even though lacking in excellence, is more or less "acceptable." From the performance side, it does get some of the job done even though imperfectly.

From the people side, it does result, if not in genuine personal gratification and reward, at least in individuals acquiring many of the symbols of status, and in a more or less acceptable state of affairs. The approach of 5,5, as it embraces the concepts of expediency and empiricism, is bound to produce mediocrity and averageness. In a sense, then, 5,5 does represent conformity and adjustment. Through the emergence of the large public corporations and the disappearance of the entrepreneur, the period ahead may well turn out to be one where adjustment is accepted as enough. 5,5 may become the new status quo, the new point of equilibrium among men in organizations, the established way.

Toward 9,9

Other pressures, however, are exerting influences against 1,1 as the state of abandonment, 1,9 as the state of care and comfort, or 5,5 as the condition of accommodation and adjustment among managers within organizations. They point more toward the 9,9 direction.

Education, constantly on the march, provides new insight and skill, introduces new possibilities, and excites new appetites for something better than what now exists.

Political democracy itself leads people to want and to exert a voice in those matters that affect them. Cultural concepts of excellence leave people uneasy with conditions that fail to measure up to what they know is attainable. Modern concepts in the areas of health and advanced education place high value on doing things in the "best" way. Another value is away from status, based on 9,1 power with deference as the basis for relationship, and toward the 9,9 use of hierarchy stemming from accomplishment and merit. This tends to lead to relations which are open, communicative, and problem solving, rather than closed, suspicious and problem generating. Perhaps as important as any factor in establishing 9,9 as an evolutionary trend is the emergence of education within industry through organization development work of the kind pictured in Chapters 12 and 13. This work, coupled as it is with a growing body of behavioral science knowledge, is exerting a definite pull in the direction of 9,9 as a dominant style.

And so the search goes on unceasingly for better ways to manage than anything known in the past.

Already, the direction and evolution that eventually will prevail seems somewhat clear though attitudes about 9,9 vary. The 9,1 attitude is pessimistic. 5,5 sees it as impractical, 1,9 as idealistic, and 1,1 as impossible. As was pointed out in Chapter 2, the actual managerial style is a function of many considerations. While there are numerous factors in any concrete circumstance which may point toward the use of some style other than 9,9, the general picture seems to be one where, to the degree operating requirements permit, 9,9 is the more mature managerial style.

Those who have studied the 9,9 style themselves and who have experimented with 9,9 as an attainable possibility, or who come by it naturally, know what they want. They want the self-respect that comes from respect for others in the context of work, and they want the meaningfulness of relationships from productivity and creativity that only mutual respect around common purpose can sustain.

If the trend of evolution toward 9,9 mentioned above is sound, the great challenge is whether 9,9 can be facilitated so that it can be applied on anything like a mass scale. Beyond that, the critical question is, "Is literal production, not just *concern for,* greater in amount and quality, etc? Furthermore, if it is, what are the consequences for people? Do they, in fact, find more reward and gratification from work contributed under 9,9 circumstances?"

Innumerable individuals, as well as results from the several experiments in organization development mentioned in the preface and again in Chapters 12 and 13, and other evidence, suggest affirmative answers to these questions. In each of the organization-wide experiments, with no one involving fewer than 600 managerial personnel, it is suggested that with the teaching techniques now at hand, mass scale learning that can aid the study and practical use of more effective managerial styles is now possible. Furthermore, evidence at hand is that literal production has been increased significantly and that greater personal reward from work is the result.

Fifty years more will be needed to provide a full and definitive answer to these questions.

Managerial styles based on 9,1 direction with compliance, or 5,5 conformity with compromise, or on 1,9 security and comfort through convenience, or on 1,1 acquiescence and complacency, or the "clever" but corrupt relationships produced by facades or by debilitating paternalism, are, at best, second best. Actually they are quite unacceptable, long-term. In comparison with performance contributed under 9,9 with its condition of candid communication based on conviction and commitment which results in creativity, other bases for work relationships seem to fall short. Social evolution seems to move in directions that add meaning to mental effort and social experience. 9,9 defines a trend leading to maturity and relationships among men toward which production organizations seem to be evolving. Achievement of 9,9 may be the key to strengthening the capacity of men to master their own fates.

Then, a thinking society—which is also thoughtful— will have been achieved.

Author Index

A

Adorno, T. W., 54
Allen, L. A., 16, 137, 139, 140
Anderson, E. A., 55
Anderson, H. H., 53, 82, 83, 140, 141, 188, 189, 190, 191
Appley, L. A., 16, 82, 83, 107, 285
Arensberg, C. M., 82
Argyris, C., 16, 45, 49, 50, 51, 53, 54, 56, 83, 106, 107, 108, 181, 188, 189, 190, 224, 286, 287
Asch, S. E., 83, 138, 184
Atkinson, J. W., 50, 55, 246
Axelrod, H., 81

B

Back, K., 139
Bailey, J. C., 107, 181
Baldwin, A. L., 55, 191
Bales, R. F., 16, 17, 48, 49, 183, 185, 190
Ballachey, E. L., 185
Bandfield, E. C., 191
Barker, R. G., 53, 55, 106, 108, 185,
Barnard, C. I., 49, 138, 188
Barnes, L. B., 107, 181, 185
Bass, B. M., 54, 81, 83, 138, 183, 184, 185, 186, 189, 191, 246
Bavelas, A., 16, 52, 186
Beach, D. S., 137
Behringer, R. D., 189
Bellows, R., 51, 140, 184
Bendix, R., 52, 83, 140
Benne, K. D., 16, 53, 184, 188, 189, 286
Bennis, W. G., 53, 184, 188, 189, 190, 285, 286, 287, 288
Bensman, J., 108
Berg, I. A., 81, 83, 138, 184
Berger, M., 183
Berkowitz, L., 182
Bidwell, A. C., 189, 311
Bishop, B. M., 55
Blake, R. R., 16, 52, 53, 81, 107, 140, 183, 184, 187, 188, 189, 190, 191, 246, 285, 286, 287, 288, 289, 311
Blansfield, M. G., 56, 189, 285, 288, 289
Blau, P. M., 84, 105, 107, 137, 138
Blum, F. H., 108
Borgatta, E. F., 17, 49, 183, 190

Boulding, K. E., 52, 53, 82
Bowers, D. G., 84, 190
Bradford, L. P., 183, 184, 187, 191, 211, 224, 286
Bradley, P., 84
Brech, E. F. L., 140
Brehm, J., 138
Broom, L., 56, 107
Brown, M., 50
Buber, M., 108
Burtt, H. E., 16, 288
Business Week, 188
Butler, J., 137, 181, 184, 185
Byrne, D., 286

C

Campbell, D. T., 182
Carmichael, L., 181
Carnegie, D., 193, 197, 198, 199, 210, 211
Cartwright, D., 16, 51, 52, 53, 54, 83, 107, 181, 183, 184, 185, 186, 286
Cervin, V., 81
Chadwick, I., 81
Child, I. L., 55, 84
Chin, R., 53, 184, 188, 286
Christensen, C. R., 50, 139
Clark, J. V., 107, 181, 191
Clark, R. A., 50, 246
Cleeton, G. U., 80
Cleveland, S. E., 190
Coates, C. H., 246
Coch, L., 182, 183, 185
Cohen, A. R., 186
Cole, D., 83, 139
Collins, O., 105
Corsini, R. J., 183
Couch, A. S., 190
Coules, J., 188
Crutchfield, R., 140

D

Dalton, M., 105, 139
Danielson L. E., 140
David, G., 107
Davis, K., 53, 56, 136, 137, 138, 139, 182
Davis, R. C., 49, 50, 136
de Charms, R., 81
Dembo, T., 55, 106
De Montollin, G., 189
Deutsch, M., 52, 53, 181, 184, 187, 190

319

Subject Index

To avoid confusion with grid numbers, all page numbers in this index *are in italics*.